PLAYS ON WORDS

ALSO BY MARVIN COHEN

The Self-Devoted Friend (1967) Rapp & Carroll (UK) and New Directions (USA); *Expanded 50th-Anniversary Edition* (2017) Tough Poets Press

Dialogues (1967) Turret Books

The Monday Rhetoric of the Love Club and Other Parables (1973) Rapp & Whiting (UK) and New Directions (USA)

Baseball the Beautiful: Decoding the Diamond (1974) Links Books; Second, expanded edition as *Baseball as Metaphysics* (2017) Tough Poets Press

Fables at Life's Expense (1975) Latitude Press

Others, Including Morstive Sternbump (1976) Bobbs-Merrill; *Expanded 40th-Anniversary Edition* (2016) Tough Poets Press

The Inconvenience of Living (1977) Urizen Books

How the Snake Emerged from the Bamboo Pole but Man Emerged from Both (1978) Oasis Books / Earthgrip Press

Aesthetics in Life and Art, Existence in Function and Essence and Whatever Else is Important Too (1982) Gull Books

How to Outthink a Wall: An Anthology (2016) Verbivoracious Press

Five Fictions (2018) Tough Poets Press

Inside the World: As Al Lehman (2018) Sagging Meniscus Press

Women, and Tom Gervasi (2018) Sagging Meniscus Press

Run Out of Prose (2018) Sagging Meniscus Press

Sadness Corrected: New Poems & Dialogues (2019) Sagging Meniscus Press

Life's Tumultuous Party: Reduced to its Essential Partycycles (2020) Sagging Meniscus Press

PLAYS ON WORDS
Marvin Cohen

* * * * * * *

Compiled and edited by Colin Myers and Rick Schober

Tough Poets Press
Arlington, Massachusetts

Copyright © 2020 by Marvin Cohen.

All rights reserved, including the right to reproduce this book or portions thereof in any form. Written permission is required for live performances of any sort. This includes readings, cuttings, scenes, and excerpts.

The Don Juan and the Non-Don Juan
Copyright © 1980 by Marvin Cohen and James Milton.
Adapted for the stage by James Milton from the (then unpublished) novels *Inside the World: As Al Lehman* and *Women, and Tom Gervasi*.
First perfomed at the Finborough Theatre, London, UK, 1981 and with staged readings at the Public Theater, N.Y.U. and Los Angeles' Groundlings Theater.

Reasonable Resignation
Copyright © 1981 by Marvin Cohen.
First performed in a longer version as *Necessary Ends* written in collaboration with James Milton, as a workshop production at The Public Theater, N.Y.U., 1981. *Necessary Ends* published in *Plays from the New York Shakespeare Festival*, 1986.

Anti-Nuclear Love
Copyright © 1982 by Marvin Cohen.

Phonies
Copyright © 1982 by Marvin Cohen.

Spritualistically Predestined Judy, Yes, But Which One?
Copyright © 1982 by Marvin Cohen.

Topsy-Turvy
Copyright © 1985 by Marvin Cohen and Thomas Riccio.
First stage reading at the Cleveland Playhouse, 1986.

A Complaint as a Theatre Goer
Copyright © 1978 by Marvin Cohen.
From *Saint Louis Literary Supplement*,
Vol. 2, No. 1, January–February 1978.

Cover design by Rick Schober.

ISBN 978-0-578-68906-7

This edition published in 2020 by:

Tough Poets Press
Arlington, Massachusetts 02476
U.S.A.

www.toughpoets.com

For beloved Candace Watt

CONTENTS

Author's Preface 9

How He/She Dramatizes His/Her Life 11

The Don Juan and the Non-Don Juan 13
    (with James Milton)

Reasonable Resignation 57

Phonies 89

Spritualistically Predestined Judy, Yes, But Which One? 111

Anti-Nuclear Love 149

Topsy-Turvy 171
    (with Thomas Riccio)

A Complaint as a Theatre Goer 283

About the Author 285

Acknowledgments 287

AUTHOR'S PREFACE

Mini history in increments went by between the forty or so years ago, when I wrote this oddly assorted group of plays, and the ferocious *NOW* of this preface. I'm a different person.

More or less in between were squeezed in the women's rights movement, the gay rights movement, the sexual revolution, the computer revolution, and various attempts at political revolution.

There was also evolution.

I'm a virtual stranger to the "plays on words" of this volume. Re-reading them is a mainly unrelational experience.

Who was I?

From Brooklyn, I was always poor, and always 3/4 deaf. I'm lucky still to be alive.

I'm still a promiscuously prolific writer, with recent fiction and poetry books published. But I've had no fame.

Forty or so years ago, Richard Dreyfuss, Wallace Shawn, and one of the Carradines read one of these plays in public ("The Don Juan and the Non-Don Juan"), although in three separate performances, in three separate theaters, and on three separate dates. There was also a London performance with none of these actors in it, and a German translation radio performance.

"Topsy-Turvy" was performed at the Cleveland Playhouse (in Cleveland). The other plays were done as staged readings in non-theater-professional amateur atmospheres.

But I feel unknown, and realistically am, for which I apologize.

Marvin Cohen
N.Y.C., April 2020

HOW HE/SHE DRAMATIZES HIS/HER LIFE

(Title character speaks first:)

I love the dramatic.
Oh. What role do you play?
The major one.
And the minor characters?
My foils.
Any environment?
Stage scenery, backdrop, props.
And the action?
It moves the plot.
Tragic? Or comic?
Stay till the end. See.

THE DON JUAN AND THE NON-DON JUAN

Characters:

>Tom Gervasi & Al Lehman (played by same actor)
>Narrator I & Narrator II (more or less in role of well-dressed
>   Devils, unless stated otherwise)
>Woman I
>Woman II
>Woman III
>Other characters: see Production Notes following the play

SONG

(Sung by one or both Narrators as Devils)

>>Don Juan's gift some men have got
>>They're red-hot
>>Others, not.
>>
>>Love in women's hearts they plant
>>Make them pant
>>Others can't.
>>
>>From non-Don Juan the ladies fled
>>Won't be led
>>To his bed.
>>
>>But to Don Juan they'd run pell-mell
>>'Til he fell
>>With a yell
>>Into hell.

PROLOGUE—HELL

Tom Gervasi: Pardon me.

Narrator I (as Devil I): Oh, I'm sorry, but . . .

Narrator II (as Devil II): It's far too late for that.

Tom Gervasi: You see, I'm lost.

Devil I: Precisely.

Devil II: Absolutely.

Tom Gervasi: But don't know where the hell I am.

Devil I: *(Laughing)* Ha ha ha.

Devil II: Yes, very good.

Tom Gervasi: Damn it, will you answer me!

Devil I: My, my, there's no need to damn it.

Devil II: No, not at all. Besides . . .

Devil I: It's *we* . . .

Devil II: And here, "we" refers to all of us . . .

(Lights reveal the Three Women)

Devil I: Who want some answers.

Tom Gervasi: Oh. Oh, yes, I think I'm beginning to see.

Devil I: Good. Shall we proceed?

Tom Gervasi: Please. I am at your disposal.

Woman I: Have you known love?

Tom Gervasi: Yes. First-hand.

Woman II: Have you known religious faith?

Tom Gervasi: Devoutly, if fleetingly.

Woman III: Have you known death?

Tom Gervasi: Remotely, if apprehensively.

Woman III: In which direction?

Tom Gervasi: In the way of the future?

Devil I: The future?!

(The Two Devils laugh and snicker)

Woman I: Please. Have you known love?

Tom Gervasi: First-hand, I told you. The most intimate manner.

Woman I: Was it close?

Tom Gervasi: Skin-tight.

Woman I: To mingle?

Tom Gervasi: In overlapping, to interpenetrate, most intricately entwined.

Woman II: Have you had knowledge?

Tom Gervasi: I've known experience.

Woman II: Has knowledge been an experience?

Tom Gervasi: Continuously. Permeatingly. Imponderably.

Woman III: Have you known pain?

Tom Gervasi: It's been experienced.

Woman I: Did love lead to it?

Tom Gervasi: Yes, often and from every direction. For I've died, have I not, or love killed me. And my knowledge is complete.

ACT ONE

SCENE I

Narrator I: All over this big city of ours, the light is waning, as it should be, for it's scheduled soon to be evening. The light has already received a pat-on-the-back for its nice day-display. But it wouldn't want to outstay its welcome, especially with dinner preparations clanking away in kitchens, mixed occasionally with amorous expectations for the ritual festivities ahead. So the light has stolen away. It won't be missed. Appetites dream of the huge evening feast, throats of evening drunkenness, hearts and loins of erotic evening romance, topped off with the chocolate whip cream of immortal love, by whose grand scale lesser values take on their truly trivial aspects. Love is solemn. The sky is black. Artificial light warms interior rooms. The sexes are about to mingle.

NARRATOR II: All around the city, women are setting places at table. For dinner parties, or just for one hoped-for guest. Some of these women are placing plates, eating utensils, napkins, for a guest who'll never arrive; and this is a mathematical certainty in most of their cases. The reason being, that these particular women are all hoping for the same guest. This particular presumed-upon guest can't be ubiquitous this evening, or ever. So in most cases, he'll disappoint, to degrees of varying severity. Tom Gervasi is his name. The man-about-town, who usually doesn't arrive. There's only one of him, for so many women-fussed-over dinners. He's coveted, but he's rare.

NARRATOR I: He's rare, so more coveted. Mainly, he doesn't materialize. He's the stuff of dreams. Feminine fantasies have woven him in. He's a godly myth, the prince who *may* arrive. He *has* arrived—once or twice. And may, magically, again. He's wished for. He's waited upon. In vain, to sighs. His "turning up" is really *not* expected.

NARRATOR II: Yet, he *might*. Thus come fairy elves from the rainbow,

NARRATOR I: unicorns from a celestial pasture,

NARRATOR II: manna from heaven,

NARRATOR I: the windfall in the night,

NARRATOR II: the surprise sweepstake announcement,

NARRATOR I: Buddha's visit,

NARRATOR II: the student Prince, doffing his disguise,

NARRATOR I: the king who roams Baghdad as a beggar.

NARRATOR II: All come to light, at one enchanted stroke.

WOMAN I: It *is* Tom Gervasi! Why, Tom, can that be you?! Oh, what a delightful surprise! This is *most* unexpected! *Do* drop in, make yourself at home. What can I get you to drink, Tom? Are you hungry? By luck, there *are* a few leftovers. Would you like to try potluck? And now that you're here, you mustn't go rushing off again. Take off your shoes, it's more comfortable. Would you like a bath?—there's plenty of hot water. Won't you stay the night? It wouldn't put me out the *least*, I can assure you. Yes, *do* stay! Oh, what fun! The bed is already made. Yes, do stay. Now that you're here. Stay, Tom. Do.

WOMAN II: What a lovely surprise! Why, Tom Gervasi, of all people! What are you doing, around these parts? Haven't seen you in *ages!* Well, you're not going *anywhere* tonight, Tom. It's too late. You're staying right here! Can I refill your drink? Oh, you naughty boy! You caught me unawares. If only I had known! But let's make the most of it. You look tired. Take off your shirt. Oh, don't wait on ceremony. You know me. Just be comfortable. Just us two. We'll shut the world out, won't we? Just us, all night long. Just us.

WOMAN III: What a pleasant surprise! Why, as I live and breathe—Tom Gervasi! I hadn't expected you! Well, now that you're here, I'm *certainly* not put out. I assure you: it's no inconvenience at all. Not the least. Why, it's delightful! It's an unexpected pleasure, I *assure* you. Take off your clothes. I'm only thinking of your comfort. Let's be casual. Let's not *us* be formal, Tom Gervasi! Why, I wouldn't *think* of it, not with you: But I *do* regret, as I hadn't expected you, that I'm not looking my best tonight. Oh, Tom, I just wasn't prepared! *Look* at me. Am I *that* ugly? Am I turning fat? Here, feel me, here. Too fat? Feel here. Am I *still* good-looking, Tom? Can you *still* be attracted to me? Here, feel up here: are my legs turning too soft? Feel me all over, Tom. Am I still attractive, Tom? Can you still like me, just a little bit? Why Tom!—you're such a naughty boy: Take your hands off me! The dinner is almost ready.

You've already eaten? Oh, but you can eat a little more. It won't hurt you. Tom! You're a beast! You're fresh, you take liberties! Oh, Tom! I'm so excited! It's you: It's you!

NARRATOR I: Thus, the seduction scene goes on. Further explicitness is not required here. In *this* case, Tom Gervasi *did* arrive.

NARRATOR II: Ah, but all over the city, woman sigh. He never did arrive. He just never turned up. The women now turn their hopes off. It's too late, now. The social evening is done. Dark hours will intervene. Then, slowly, morning. With its wealth of light. Too bright, too commonplace, for the private hope. The secret dream. Of Tom Gervasi, as himself. Playing his own role. Turning up, in real life.

SCENE II

TOM GERVASI: I'd like to be with all women at the same time. However, time and space won't let me—these spoilsports, these killjoys! So I have to make do.

This woman, I meet her at *this* time and place. Meanwhile, the rest go begging. Next, *that* woman, at *that* time and place. As slow as a mountain's evolution. At this rate, I'll just know a minuscule fraction of great nature's womandom. Sampling here and there, now and then, of the groaning bounteous board of the great female feast! Letting so much go untested! The vast waste, within my greed's micro-capacity, my mini-lust that nibbles where it would gorge!

Maybe I can hire and train armies of me, make a huge male recruitment, mobilize them to my standards, and commission them, as delegates for my rampant lechery! By proxy of my minions, I could seize all desired women, and possess them by representing myself through a million able bodies.

I'd watch from a hilltop, through binoculars, as my well-strategied campaigns are launched to plunder women wholesale; unleashing satyrs to carry out, down to the last sensual detail, my well-wrought plans on many fronts along the broad belt of the map.

I'll be the lauded hero. But all my men will win many maids. They're my army *privates*, for their *private* pleasure. I'm their noble *general*, taking only the *general* pleasure, as their mist-covered overlord.

Well, I knew my limits. Even as Tom Gervasi, I'm the same number of people as the lowest gravedigger, my one only self.

But there's time, for lots of women. One by one, it *could* add up. Months and years; behind, ahead. A dribble here, a drop there. Thus beavers build their dam, birds their nest, ants their molehill. So Rome and Chartres were built. Thus Don Giovanni added to Leporello's catalogue of conquests by nationality. Bit by bit. A drop here, a drop there.

That's all. But it's enough. Enough for plenty of women, anyhow. I proudly plow through them. I rake them up, like autumn leaves. I collect them, like the greatest stamp collector.

Am I acquisitive? Is it acquisition I do? Compiling. Adding, extending. Expanding. Seizing. Hoarding. Enlarging my having. An empire's possessiveness: To "possess" the women?

I *had* this woman, I *had* that woman. Having and holding. Extending my hold. *My* holdings. The monetary-woman financier. The capitalist of extensive holdings. The holdings of the havings. Still acquiring. To hold what I have. Have, and hold. Not to let go. Nor to turn loose. But to clutch. Tight. Tightly climactic. Orgasmic cataclysms, on a simultaneous brea(d)th of release.

I'll die after growing old. Survived by a reputation. Tom Giovanni. Don Gervasi. That ancient legend, with a modern face.

SCENE III

NARRATOR I: People congregating: that's an excitement for Al Lehman. He's just divorced, and in addition has broken up with an interim girlfriend. He's as lonely as a foreigner who can't speak or understand the language of the country he's suddenly and solitarily been exiled to without a single connection there, a stranger's unrelieved gloom among crowds of natives who glow with belonging to each other: from whom that stranger is kept endlessly alien, an outsider forbidden to partake, always ever only apart.

Wherever people congregate, Al Lehman, if he can, shows up: even when uninvited. Depend on it, he's there: a wake, a christening, a wedding, a memorial service, and there he is, adding his "one" to the attendance.

A lecture, a poetry reading, a concert; and the audience may be seen to include him. Even when he's not interested, he's there, as *though* he's interested—which he's not, in most cases. He has a social disease: He mustn't be alone. Even death seems preferable to a horrible evening of solitude. People whisper:

PERSON I: There he is again.

PERSON II: Who is he? He seems out of place, here.

PERSON III: What's he doing here?

PERSON IV: Why is he here? Is he a spy?

PERSON V: A reporter?

PERSON VI: A crazed solitary, desperate for remote companionship, crowding his lonely isolation with people as stage props, background configurations incidental but necessary to his autistic, withdrawn, hermetic sealed-off, doomed, tragic apartness, his exile from his spiritual kind?

NARRATOR I: He's just crashed a party. Gaiety, hilarity, loud chatter, clanking of ice cubes in intoxicating glasses. Music, noise everywhere. The din prevailing.

He approaches a girl, from the side. She does a little leap of surprise, detecting his sudden presence.

AL LEHMAN: I've just been divorced, and lost my interim girlfriend, so you can imagine how lonely I am; no how *can* you imagine it, if you've never experienced it?

But force your compassion upon me. Love me, if only just a little. I implore you, to the begging of my bent knees. Have mercy. I adore you deeply. Have an affair with me, then let's get married. That alone could cure my chronic loneliness. Lend me your pity, your sympathy, your body, your all. I request no less. I want your whole soul.

GIRL: But I don't even *know* you.

AL LEHMAN: I'm Al Lehman.

GIRL: Ah, so *that's* who you are. The notorious Al Lehman? The failing beseecher of any woman's heart? So we've met at last. I've heard so much about you. You're spurned everywhere. The most rejected man-about-town. It's no wonder. Let me add *my* rejection, to all the others. A mere drop, in your aching oceanful of awful romantic agony.

NARRATOR I: Thus it goes. That illustrates what regularly happens to Al Lehman. A routine matter-of-course, at any party.

SCENE IV

AL LEHMAN: What I wanted most was power over people: to get them to do what I want, to have them in my power, to be on top. But I had no power to persuade them to be in my power; so I tried to develop talents, such as physical attractiveness and more money. I failed to develop these means of power: leading to frustration and the need to compensate for all my failings and littleness. I tried personality defects like sadism, but potential victims resisted and I failed. I felt a growing futility, which I tried to arrest, but it grew into helplessness, which put a stop to my power drive. Then, I made helplessness a virtue.

I traded on my helplessness, and people fell into my power by trying to protect, help, care for me. So I had hit on a method toward my original goal, by the process of having failed. Failure had found out a solution—in fact, *was* the solution. This reversed my fall, which had hit the bottom of total abjection. I exploited people's good-natured compassion and generosity toward a downtrodden underdog; and had them in my power. I wouldn't let go. My helplessness was brutally directed. I drew upon it, ruthlessly.

SCENE V

NARRATOR I: Bernice said, with forceful logic:

BERNICE: If a person can grow up and one day become the president or the country, I could grow up and marry Tom Gervasi. Growing up is essential, in both cases.

NARRATOR II: Well, already she was grown up. So she had already earned the right—to be a *candidate*, at least.

NARRATOR I: Now that growing up is out of the way, the necessary next step, of course, would be to take her chances on *meeting* him.

BERNICE: How *does* a girl meet Tom Gervasi? At a party. Yes, but not at *any* party. It's got to be a party where *he's at*. That, of course, narrows the field.

Now for a contact, a connection, in the person of an invited guest to one of the parties where Tom Gervasi will be. Then I can ask to be taken along.

NARRATOR II: She found one! He agreed! It's Saturday night! She has three days to prepare.

NARRATOR I: She saved her bath till three hours before the party, in order *freshly* to be clean. She bought seductive perfume. And decided on a gown that revealed her shapely form to its many nooks and contours.

NARRATOR II: She went to a hair specialist; and in short, was groomed "to kill."

BERNICE: I'll slay him! The most wanted non-criminal male in the non-Oriental world! Mine! *If.*

If *what?* If me no buts. I feel the tug of destiny. It has "Tom Gervasi" written all over it.

NARRATOR I: The night of the party. To give destiny its long-awaited opportunity.

NARRATOR II: But Tom Gervasi is surrounded! So many women were in the competition. Bernice would win—but she must *get* to him, first.

NARRATOR I: Her perfume was wearing off; her hair messed up; her dress all crumpled; her makeup, by now, stale. Worst of all, her optimism was losing its confidence, her confidence was losing its hope, her hope its courage, her courage its pluck, her pluck its tenacity, her tenacity its endurance.

NARRATOR II: The tide was turning against her. Has she already too wilted? Or should she press on, *now*?

BERNICE: He's making ready to leave. He's going over to give a goodbye to one person, another to another. He's saying to the host and hostess goodbye, now.

NARRATOR I: Bernice is sharply observing to see whether he's taking any one woman along *with* him. Many hopeful *possibilities* for such a candidate are exposing their postures of availability to Tom Gervasi as he goes out. They're looking conspicuous: selectable, willing, in a not-too-surprised way, to be asked, abruptly, to "come along," by that voice which opens women's ears to their own dreams.

BERNICE: He's going out *alone—alone!*

NARRATOR II: Bernice rushes alongside. They're out in the street, now. The building, with its enormous party-apartment-rooms crowded with competitors, with noise and clinking drinks, is behind. She's walking step-by-step with him, in the rushing dark.

TOM GERVASI: I guess you know who *I* am. What's *your* name?

BERNICE: Bernice.

TOM GERVASI: That's as nice as any.

BERNICE: Where are you going, Mr. Gervasi? May I go there too?

TOM GERVASI: I'm going to a woman's apartment. No, you may *not* go there too.

BERNICE: Is it on private business, you're going?

TOM GERVASI: This is Saturday night—in fact, past it, it's Sunday morning. It's not an hour to be conducting business, ordinarily. I'm going strictly for pleasure, if you must know.

BERNICE: Why didn't this woman came with you to the party?

TOM GERVASI: I preferred being on my own, at this party.

BERNICE: It had a good result—you met *me*.

TOM GERVASI: That's a bit bold. What are you suggesting?

BERNICE: Break off your middle-of-the-night erotic assignation with this woman you were intending to visit, and switch to me, instead. I'll make the switch prove itself a worthwhile one, for you.

TOM GERVASI: How do you know what it would be like for me if I kept my original appointment?

BERNICE: I *don't* know. But I offer you my body as sumptuous feast, and my fresh new love.

TOM GERVASI: I can't resist. All right. Take me home.

BERNICE: You can phone the woman who's expecting you, from my apartment, to tell her you were unavoidably waylaid and are very sorry.

TOM GERVASI: No, I told her it was possible that I'd never arrive, so that she wouldn't be *definitely* expecting me. So she won't be *too* disappointed. My warning assured that.

BERNICE: I'm glad you "covered" yourself. Let *me*, now, cover you: with a big, warm skin-blanket. It might keep you awake. In fact, you might reach an *extraordinary* wakefulness, when covered by my big, warm skin-blanket. It may cause you to thrust sleep aside, and do temporarily without it.

But tomorrow is a non-working day: good old Sunday. Have a late night, tonight. Will your mother object?

TOM GERVASI: She won't if I don't tell her.

BERNICE: Then don't tell her. Squeeze me. I'm your Bernice.

NARRATOR I: They embraced on the street, before paging a handy taxi. The night was dark, moonless, cloudy. It even started to rain. Bernice lived a long way away. But they got there. Tom paid the fare. Then, up the elevator. Now, in her apartment. A dim light on. The day had turned out well, for Bernice. Or rather, this all-confirming night.

SCENE VI

NARRATOR II: The women whom Al Lehman saw at the party appealed to him, for various reasons:

AL LEHMAN: All of them sexual.

NARRATOR I: He would collect the phone numbers of those he felt so strongly about; so that the party would be the mushrooming nucleus to a scattering of assorted love affairs owing source and origin to this great meeting ground.

NARRATOR II: Years went by. He finally exhausted those phone numbers and himself.

AL LEHMAN: Some of the women had in the first place refused to give me their phone numbers. Others had given me their phone numbers but then turned down my request for a date when I phoned, or put me off and made me phone again, but always with the result that I never ever saw them again.

Other women, recruited from that party via phone numbers, had responded and made appointments; but saw me only once or a few times and then never again.

A few of the women from that party saw me more often; until they too stopped seeing me, eventually.

A few saw me over long stretches of time; until gradually the meetings stopped with them, too.

None were left from the original batch of phone numbers.

There had been nothing sexual with any of them, as it all turned out.

Original motivation; but consequences of a quite different order.

Such intriguing possibilities, at that party: All declined, in time's full stop.

SCENE VII

NARRATOR I: Brigit was a nun who began to have a few theological misgivings: not many, but enough. Doubt coursed through her, as once faith had. This dismissed her from grace, and led her, lonely, to her "self," outside God's umbrella. She's shunned sure salvation. She's reneged on a holy vow. The secular, not the celestial, became her immediate future.

NARRATOR II: Off with the old habit. She donned civilian dress. Got an office job, in a commercial outfit. And, to complete the perverse conversion transition, and enlarge the dangers thereof, she, as ways went, by the grim lot of chance, met, and fell in love with (and she was a virgin intact), Tom Gervasi.

NARRATOR I: Tom Gervasi didn't represent evil, nor embody it, as the Devil's hardworking advocate commissioned to tempt good women to slip and slide down to sin's slush.

NARRATOR II: —No. All he was, was a simple male. With a hedonistic appetite for good hearty fun, on the carnal carnival's happy-go-merry-go-round. He needed partners, and women loved it.

Brigit had become a woman. Despite having been a nun, her organs were all in the same place (or places) as any *fallen* woman's.

NARRATOR I: Also, she was attractive. That pinned her quite up on Tom Gervasi's notice board. She spinned his head around. Who more exotic, than a virgin former nun, as sophistication's arch foil?

TOM GERVASI: Let me initiate you: into the sacred rites of the fertility ceremony. I'll be your High Priest. I'll lead you, to the body's holy temple.

BRIGIT: Stop satirizing religion, you unblemished heathen. I'm not a nun anymore, not because I stopped taking religion seriously, but because I *did* take it seriously. I'm God's. But not as a nun. As a woman; so test me. *Confirm* me in my womanhood. Bring out the full woman in me. With lust-covered love, and base bodilyness.

TOM GERVASI: Sounds fine with *me*, Brigit. Come visit my apartment. Test my bed's bounce. And *my counter*-bounce. *You'll* be bouncing, too.

BRIGIT: *I* have an apartment, and a bed. Come *there*, with me.

TOM GERVASI: Yes, but why?

BRIGIT: Is your bed old?

TOM GERVASI: Yes.

BRIGIT: Then *other* women have been on it. But *my* bed is *new*. As new, to the "game," as *I* am. Let *two* virginities fall, by your one stroke.

TOM GERVASI: What an order! Suddenly, I feel impotent. For years, I've been seeing experienced women, none but non-virgins. I fear I'll fail. Why, it's momentous: So sacred! Not just frivolous fun. Not just an easy, automatic, fornicating lark. I'm treading in the garden of de-flowering: holy ground.

BRIGIT: Does it cow you? Unman you, quite?

TOM GERVASI: My powers are fled. I cower.

BRIGIT: With *your* reputation!?

TOM GERVASI: What has *reputation* to do with *us?* It's just you and I, Brigit. And heaven, for a witness.

BRIGIT: Why, Tom: *You're* the serious one!

TOM GERVASI: I'm solemn. Impotent, too.

BRIGIT: It remains to be proved. We'll put it to the test.

TOM GERVASI: To the *testicle*. Off we go. To your bedroom: clad in stillness.

NARRATOR II: He was right: he couldn't do it. Her nun's preserved virginity overdaunted his manly resolve.

TOM GERVASI: Do you *still* love me?

BRIGIT: Yes, but I love God more.

TOM GERVASI: God's omnipotent; I'm only impotent.

BRIGIT: *Now* you are; later maybe no.

TOM GERVASI: I'm humiliated. I've disappointed you?

BRIGIT: Just on the physical surface. My *soul*, though, has been deeply penetrated.

TOM GERVASI: Yes, by mine. I have a soul in love with you. Shall you not *remain* virgin, in the puritanical convention of another generation, till we, Brigit, wed?

BRIGIT: But I'm *already* married: to God.

TOM GERVASI: Oh, that's on a different plane. Remain constant to Him, on *that* plane; devote *this* plane's fidelity, please, to *me*.

BRIGIT: I take the vow, as I once did. *Not* as I once did. I failed the *nun's* vow; my faith wavered. But *this* vow I'll keep: in conjugal holiness.

SCENE VIII

NARRATOR I: "Clara Convinces Al Lehman, A Bit Roughly, that the Passion he's Conceived for her would do him no Good, since she Cares not a Whit—"

NARRATOR II: *(Interrupting)* Title sums up, so it's best placed after what it sums up, which has to go first.

NARRATOR I: Al Lehman was trying to improve his appearance, to make a better impression on Clara, to whom he took a shining fancy, to which she responded with total indifference.

NARRATOR II: Good.

CLARA: Nothing you do would make the slightest difference to me. Alter yourself, change yourself, it'll do you no good, you'll go through all that trouble for nothing, for its own sake, for it won't affect me the slightest, you simply don't appeal to me, you're just not my type, I can't help it, I just wasn't made to take to you, you can dance on your head all day long and it won't get a rise out of me. Sorry to have to put it so bluntly. I'm kind enough to hate to see you go through all your vain efforts, for my sake. I'm sorry to see you waste yourself. Better try somewhere else. Some other girl may respond.

AL LEHMAN: Some *other* girl!? I only crave *you!*

CLARA: Don't be mulish. Give up, I'm a lost cause for you. Better results could be obtained elsewhere.

AL LEHMAN: Can *you* become someone else, Clara? Then I'd woo the someone else that you'd become. It wouldn't be *you* anymore, but at least it would be *derived* from you. That way, I could maintain my passion, seeing that you're the source for the someone else. Isn't that a grand solution?

CLARA: Theoretically, it may be. But I'll remain me. I *can't* become another girl.

AL LEHMAN: You can't?—or you *don't want* to?

CLARA: Both. So give me up. Accept total rejection, from me, unqualified, unconditional. Weep a little, then get over me.

AL LEHMAN: Goodbye, Clara. I see, now, that this must be the end.

CLARA: How very intelligent of you, Al. Or perceptive. Or both.

AL LEHMAN: Don't make fun of me, please.

CLARA: A little fun, at your expense? It's really quite harmless. You cut a ridiculous figure. You've wooed me in vain. Only now, your failure has dawned upon you—at my urging. You're a silly ass.

AL LEHMAN: It's unkind of you, to humiliate me.

CLARA: I can't spare your pride and vanity: they took the risk, in my cause, and have become compromised. Go repair your pride and vanity with a girl who'll love you—one, furthermore, whom *you'll* love. How much better that will be, in all respects, for all concerned, than your dismal failure with *me!*

AL LEHMAN: Your point, Clara, is well made. I abandon all hope, for you. Farewell, lost love.

CLARA: Goodbye, you fool.

NARRATOR I: The summing-up title:

"Clara Convinces Al Lehman, a Bit Roughly, that the Passion he's

Conceived for her would do him no Good, since she Cares not a Whit for him, and Nothing he does can make the Slightest Difference in Altering her Confirmed, Absolute, Total, and Complete Indifference to him. So, since he can't Influence her, she Influences him. His Pride Reels, under the Blow. Time, though, will See him through, to his Eventual Recovery. Ah, Clara: Goodbye."

NARRATOR II: Good.

SCENE IX

NARRATOR I: Valerie easily sensed how close Tom Gervasi was to the end of his love for her, and thought how she could recharge it, rekindle it, and restore it to its flaring peak of their earlier courtship rapture.

NARRATOR II: She'd better hurry. It was dwindling rapidly, and soon there wouldn't be enough to revive. She had to inject a shot of plasm serum, or something, into the bare remaining vein of that meager love.

NARRATOR I: But the love was draining away.

VALERIE: Tom! Tom! Recover yourself!

TOM GERVASI: What on earth from?

VALERIE: The lassitude and languishing, the near-expiring, of your love formerly for me.

TOM GERVASI: Oh, I'm too lazy. Let it run itself out.

VALERIE: *Please* don't practice inertia on what means such a great deal to me.

TOM GERVASI: Sorry, Valerie. I'm overwhelmed by indifference for you. While we where speaking, my love had a croak or stroke and stopped breathing. How parallel to an entire person's mortality, itself!

VALERIE: Oh Tom, *you're* dead to *me*.

TOM GERVASI: No, *you're* dead to *me*.

VALERIE: But this is too, too sad!

TOM GERVASI: But Valerie, that's what happened. It's done. My love no more than a corpse, can be revived. Thus, for us, it's goodbye.

VALERIE: Tom! Tom! It *can't* be!

TOM GERVASI: It *is*. It all too definitely *is*. It's dead. But *you're* not; *I'm* not: only the *love* is dead.

VALERIE: *Your* love is; but not *mine*.

TOM GERVASI: Then yours might just as well follow suit. It does no good anymore, since *mine* is extinguished. *Your* love for *me* is folly, obsolete, once mine for you has died.

VALERIE: But Tom, how can I stop?

TOM GERVASI: I'll be gone. Your love will starve, for I was its nourishment. From that starvation, it'll die.

VALERIE: Will my dead love and your dead love meet in a dead love's heaven?

TOM GERVASI: Heaven is for dead *people;* not for dead loves.

VALERIE: Oh Tom, I can't bear it! Hug me, Tom. Hold me. Don't let me go.

TOM GERVASI: But Valerie, my heart just isn't in it any more.

VALERIE: Oh Tom, my life is ruined.

TOM GERVASI: Sorry that it had to turn out this way, Valerie. What a grand beginning our love had! It knelt in the stars of romance. Little did we foresee...

VALERIE: Tom, Tom, stop! My heart is breaking, as you're saying that!

TOM GERVASI: Sorry to torture you. But *I* feel *fine*—if that's any consolation to you.

VALERIE: Tom, for *my* sake—*please* be miserable.

TOM GERVASI: I'd have to love you in order to be miserable. As I don't, I'm not.

VALERIE: Oh, you're so heartless!

TOM GERVASI: Let's not prolong this. There's no good in our lingering.

It only makes things worse.

VALERIE: Is it, then, goodbye, Tom?

TOM GERVASI: It finally is. But our love lived a long, brave life. We'll mourn its passing. But *we* must survive. We must survive our own love's death. Valerie, I'm moved to tears. Our love was brave, and led a long, noble life. Long live our love, in the hereafter. But this is earth, not heaven. Earth is time's field. Our love has been shuffled off it. We'll remain, but separately. Our final kiss. Goodbye.

VALERIE: Tom! Don't leave! . . . Oh, he's left. He's gone. Here I am—Valerie. That's my name. It stands by itself, now. Friends had coupled it with Tom's. The "Tom" half has been ripped away. There's only me, left. To finish my days. To live them out. To see them down. To follow, fast. Alone. To go the way of Tom's love for me. To dwindle out. To decline, past reviving. In grosser imitation, of Tom's love's demise, its draining away.

That's what's left. That's what I face, and follow. In frenzied replica. In hollow mockery.

SCENE X

NARRATOR II: Love and "Making Love": Two things, sometimes related, sometimes not, in varied human undertakings.

JANET: I loved Al Lehman, giving him the opportunity to make love to me, which he was far from slow to do. Gradually, though, he loved me too. The more he began loving me, the less and less became my love for him, until the point was reached where he felt all the love and I felt none. All that while, we had been "making love." At the point when I felt no love for him, and he all for me, I decided to pull out from our union.

AL LEHMAN: Such pain I felt!—all the pain was mine; all the relief was hers. Finally, I got over Janet. I've finally joined her, in our lasting indifference, which is the final state of affairs between us. Janet is "making love" with a new man, now: a man whom she doesn't love, and who doesn't love her. I'm "making love" with a new woman, whom I don't love. She's Judy.

JUDY: I'm growing to love him. Will my love for him influence the growth of some love for me, in him? Time will tell. We "make love," while waiting.

SCENE XI

NARRATOR I: Rose and Iris were positively flowery in garlanding Tom Gervasi in festoons and wreaths and bulging bouquets of love and adoration.

TOM GERVASI: I wish they'd stop. I prefer Lila to them. She'd be a Lilac, except that she "lies" in "lack" of the final letter. Lila is about fifteen percent prettier than Rose, and ten percent prettier than Iris. But why measure those intangibles? Love is not percentages and statistics; love is a feeling, pure and simple. I could economize by dropping Rose and Iris, and limiting my amorous life to Lila. But then Lila would get possessive. As it is, since each of the three knows I'm going with two others in addition to her, they're more in awe of my privacy, take nothing for granted, and endeavor always to please. I retain the advantage over each girlfriend by having two others. But this is also tiring! I'm succumbing to sexual exhaustion, to worn-out genitals, to heavy fatigue in the groin. I'm sagging down badly in the erotic division. Oh, for a long holiday from the arduous life of keeping three women at bay by tempering their love for me with the discipline of maintaining them in a suspenseful limbo of rivalry. And how their love comes pouring in!— with restraint. As though it stops short, at the window pane. While I sit inside, quite dry.

NARRATOR II: All alone, Lila was thinking:

LILA: Tom Gervasi prefers me to either Rose or Iris. Yet he continues to see them just about as often as that fickle brute sees me. I want to clutch him *always*. I remember as a little girl I had a doll; other girls wanted to play with my doll, but I didn't want to share it with them.

Well, Tom Gervasi is that doll today. I want him for my very own. But Rose and Iris take equal lumps of his time, while I pine at home. Oh Tom Gervasi, please stop regarding it necessary to have two other girlfriends. By the time it's time to be with me again, these hussies, those vixens have drained you of your precious sperm, pumped your old well dry, and you arrive with nothing left for me, while I've been waiting so eagerly, with nervous patience and tense ardour. I feel like exploding. *Please*, dear Tom . . . oh, I'm talking to myself again. He's out of hearing. I'm alone in my apartment. He's out with Rose or Iris. Oh, Tom Gervasi: *Please* tire of them; but of me, never. Monogamy is a decent human invention. It's civilized practice. Try it. I'll make it work, for you.

NARRATOR II: Lila's meditation became fervent prayer, convulsive sob. Tom Gervasi is her religion.

NARRATOR I: So is he, as well, for Rose and Iris. Here's Rose in solitary reverie:

ROSE: Tom Gervasi, you like Iris as well as me, and Lila better than both, while still falling short of *loving* her. I'm desperate for you. But I brood, in pessimism. You'll *never* love me, I'm afraid. Oh, that horrid word—never!

NARRATOR I: And Iris, alone, cogitates:

IRIS: Tom Gervasi, you care for Rose and me a bit, and for Lila somewhat more. That's all you give us, a little trickle; by comparison to which we bombard you with three lifetimes of immortal love. Oh foul ratio! If only both my rivals could drop dead! But that's an evil wish. But only that way, could I ever get you for myself. For all my own.

NARRATOR II: Tom Gervasi is squeezed of sex; he's gone dry. He sees a doctor, who examines him somberly with some dead-looking instruments in the private parts where male love flowers. The verdict is indeed dismal!

NARRATOR I (as DOCTOR): Tom Gervasi, I have a sad diagnosis to report. You've become impotent, and will remain so for about five years, during which span of time your sexual activity will not even exceed that of a gelded eunuch with a high little-girl's voice, called a castrato for lovely madrigals. But this is no music lesson, I'm afraid. You're a neuter now, Tom Gervasi. For five years. Here's my bill. Pay soon. Goodbye.

NARRATOR II: When Tom Gervasi left the doctor's office, he felt strangely relieved, even exuberant. He raised a wild song of exhilaration:

TOM GERVASI: Halleluyah! Thank you, God. Now Rose, Iris, and Lila will recede somewhat, and keep their arms and legs off my own body. My body is my own! However, they'll continue to go on loving me. It won't discourage them. Their love for me is fatal. Platonically, I'll go on seeing all three. Even sleep with them, one at a time. But *chastely* sleep. Ah, a long rest. From riots, of the flesh.

NARRATOR I: Lila accepted this condition, as also did Rose and Iris, in their three-pronged, doggèd, unqualified love, on an unconditional basis, for their temporarily monk-like Tom Gervasi. He feels so rested! So quiet! His lusty waters are stilled. He falls back, and dreams of love. Not *from* him, but for.

NARRATOR II: He has Lila's preferred love, reinforced by Rose's, by Iris's. It bombards him. In soft feathers. In light rain. In weak sunshine. In mild, easy-to-take doses.

NARRATOR I: He sleeps on a soft, downy bed of soft, cloudy love. It's trained on him, with filter. He's regulated it. Like the lighting manager for a theater play, who has light filter down from three nice directions onto a stage basking in it. Nice rays of love. From sweet Lila. From somewhat lesser Rose and Iris. It lights him up, softly. He gleams, with soft highlights. In muted terms. Golden Rembrandt, yellow Vermeer. Subdued. But lit.

ACT TWO

SCENE I

NARRATOR I: "Drunkenness and Afterward."

NARRATOR II (as MURRAY): You're drunk enough to be too lazy to do what you're drunk enough to want to do,

NARRATOR I: observed a friend, Murray, to Al Lehman: who exactly fit that uncomplimentary description, even down to certain hazy details, which, though vivid to Murray, were lost on Al Lehman in his present condition. He gamely tried to make coherent sense in conversation:

AL LEHMAN: What's that, Murray? Drunkenness makes me want to do what I'm too drunk to have the energy for doing?

MURRAY: You twisted it, Al. But you've grasped the drift, in some slant.

AL LEHMAN: Good. Sober me up, will you? Where's the party? It's not going on anymore.

MURRAY: It's over. The guests have gone home. All but you. You're in no fit condition to go home. So I'm putting you up here for the night, in my guest-room. Just sleep it off, and you'll be recovered by the morning.

AL LEHMAN: That's kind of you. Say, Murray, what did I want to do in drunken craving that I was too drunk to carry out?

MURRAY: To fight someone and to fornicate with someone else. They both dismissed you, from your feeble overtures.

AL LEHMAN: How disgraceful! Did I look foolish?

MURRAY: Enough to be laughed at.

AL LEHMAN: What else did I ineffectually muddle at, in stupor?

MURRAY: You tried to explain something to an intellectual, but merely babbled. You also tried to eat, but spilled the food. You began things, went through motions, but couldn't carry them through. You were left hanging, from your own projects, snuffed out in the drowse of inertia.

AL LEHMAN: Was I uncoordinated, incoherent, fumbling, disjointed, not of a piece?

MURRAY: All those, in classic drunken syndrome.

AL LEHMAN: I'm disgusted. I repent.

MURRAY: No-one cared. You lost a little pride and vanity. But people made allowances for the drunken circumstance. Your credit is still good, on past character performance.

AL LEHMAN: Which I proceeded to degrade.

MURRAY: But not destroy. Go easy on drink, next party: You'll redeem yourself.

AL LEHMAN: Thanks for your description and encouragement. You're a good friend, Murray. You're good to me. Now, I'll fall asleep.

MURRAY: Your drunkenness is wearing off. You're making sense. You still have enough drunkenness left, to achieve good success in going to sleep. Use it.

AL LEHMAN: Thanks, Murray. Good sleep to *you*, too.

MURRAY: But not yet.

AL LEHMAN: Why? What's first?

MURRAY: Margaret is in my bed. You weren't *really* the only remaining guest. She'll honor me by staying, too: But more actively.

MARGARET: *(Offstage) Murray!*

AL LEHMAN: With you?! But I was trying to seduce her all night!

MARGARET: *Murray!*

MURRAY: You might have, but were too drunk. Your failure became, then, my opportunity.

MARGARET: *Murray!!*

NARRATOR I: Murray closed the door behind him, bouncing off to some pleasure. Al Lehman brooded jealously. It slightly soiled his recent gratitude.

AL LEHMAN: Well, if I can't have her, at least she'll make *Murray* happy, who now extends the party to an exclusive amorous conclusion, in that private party of completely two.

NARRATOR I: Al Lehman was asleep. In another room, Murray and Margaret were hardly that. They were doing what Margaret might be doing now, instead, with Al Lehman, in her or his apartment, had only he not lost out by losing his hold, dropping contact, in alcoholic blur, which can barely support just one solitude, despite such terrible overtures to the contrary, such violent intentions, such frenzied behavior. Alone. In transitional oblivion. Toward a restored social will, in good sober force. Tomorrow.

SCENE II

NARRATOR I: May and June are not only months, but women's names.

NARRATOR II: They're not only women's names, but in these two cases they actually *are* the women. The women being, of course, May and June.

NARRATOR I: By coincidence, though they've never met, they both love the same man. Through him, within him, they meet. He's their spiritual go-between: Tom Gervasi.

NARRATOR II: May says:

MAY: If I ever meet that June, she'll be taught to learn that May takes precedence, that I come first, in the love and life of Tom Gervasi. I'll enforce that lesson with nails and teeth, fists and feet, and a boiling tongue. She'll never forget it. She'll retire, in defeat, from the calendar of events. Then the coast will be clear, for Tom Gervasi and me to romp through the dear year freely in each other's arms, with June out of the way. Then I'll marry Tom Gervasi, with June retired from the fray.

NARRATOR I: June, however, is of the opposite way of thinking:

JUNE: May is only the prelude, the building up, the laying groundwork for June's triumphant entrance. She's preliminary, I'm climactic, in the spring calendar. Thus nature has it. And so it is, between us. June will *bury* May, will supplant it altogether, in Tom Gervasi's heart of spring. June's a wedding month. That augurs well. With May out of the way, having expended herself, having drained Tom Gervasi of a few wild oats in his seedy season, *I'll* take him over, altar-bent, to the bridal suite. Garlanded by nature, at her prime.

NARRATOR II: They demand a showdown. From two sides, they force their lover-in-common to bring them together. They'll clash, settle, resolve, this stormy issue. Tom Gervasi is their link, their broker.

NARRATOR I: He's their point, their angle, their circle.

NARRATOR II: He's their fulcrum, lever, pivot, or see-saw.

NARRATOR I: He's the odd one, whereas they're even.

NARRATOR II: At the meeting, both turn against him.

NARRATOR I: From combatants, they've become allies.

NARRATOR II: From loving the same man, they've gone to hating him.

NARRATOR I: Jointly!

NARRATOR II: As a pair!

NARRATOR I AND NARRATOR II: Together!

MAY: So you're June. I had imagined you as some ogre, some man-eating monster. But now I've encountered you, I think highly of you. We have an affliction in common: Tom Gervasi. He's been our bane. He played us off, for his erotic delight and romantic vanity, against each other. It perversely stimulated him, like a wicked fetish. Let's gain some measure of revenge. I detest him, now. Don't you?

JUNE: Oh darling May! I agree with every word you said. He's our nemesis, our curse. We were destined to meet, but he kept us apart. He delayed the friendship we were fated for. Well, let's deal harshly with him. His being our mutual adversary will of course cement our new friendship: Having an enemy-in-common is great for making alliances firmer. Let's kiss each other, and beat him up.

NARRATOR I: And that's what they do, in his own apartment. They quite "manhandle" him: They mete out a stern measure of punishment. Their love for him is transferred to each other.

NARRATOR II: Have they become Lesbian lovers?

NARRATOR I: That's a bit immodest. Let's say that they're *platonically* homosexual.

Arm in arm, without so much as a glance back, they leave Tom Gervasi lying there in some daze of stupor, and storm out of his apartment, matching strides, in glee and joy for being liberated from Tom-Gervasi-tyranny.

NARRATOR II: Tom Gervasi staggers up.

TOM GERVASI: Two losses, in one night. Both my girlfriends. But what a blissful gain *they* made! They have a double find, I have a double loss. Well, I've done it all for *them*. Why be selfish? I made them happy. It was my *duty* to. As their lovers, both.

SCENE III

NARRATOR II: Every time Harriet wriggled past him, in the office, she distracted Al Lehman from his desk-work. He was being closely monitored, on the job. The new company policy was to reduce the staff in the economic cut-back, in order financially to survive. Half the employees would have to be let go. Al Lehman's job was in dire jeopardy. He resolved to work at an extraordinary pace, to get mounds of work done at high calibers of excellence, so as to create an impression of overwhelming competence on the vice-presidential executives who were hawkishly noseying about to detect flaws and performance failures to justify the firings they, like hangmen, had been given the solemn office of executing.

NARRATOR I (as EXECUTIVE): Hence our rank, "executives."

AL LEHMAN: I'm fighting to retain my job. I arrive early, remain late, bent down in devout concentration on my sacred desk papers.

NARRATOR II: For all his determination, he found himself distracted by Harriet, wriggling by. She was a shapely secretary whose job was secure. She could type rapidly and accurately on her streamlined machine bolted upright on her desk. To look at, she was gorgeous. Al Lehman cast looks upon her. These looks could be fatal. They sapped his concentration on work. He had, by main effort of force and will, to plunge himself back in business matters. But then she'd wriggle by again: His grasp on work would weaken. She was slowly costing him his job. Vice-presidential executives in charge of discharge, noticed his slackening attention. They smiled, detecting Harriet's body for the cause. Finally, Al Lehman was given his notice:

EXECUTIVE: Despite the long hours you've put in every day, your efficiency production output has fallen below required standards. You're fired as of next Monday. The *firm* has to be *firm* with you. You're finished.

AL LEHMAN: Harriet, why did you wriggle past me all the time like that? See what it's done? Why did you walk enticingly by *my* desk, at the peak at my concentration? Couldn't you have been more inconspicuous, and chosen other routes that less diverted my attention? My wife Marge, with whom I'm on near-divorce terms, will hold my firing against me, to her advantage, in our incessant "power" struggle of incompatible wills. My son Gregory—how can I afford, when the time comes years hence, to put him through college? My life is ruined: due to you.

HARRIET: Don't be too harsh with me, Al Lehman. I *had* to do it.

AL LEHMAN: "*Had to,*" Harriet?! You "had to" get me fired, by your seductive weakening of my concentration during key office hours? Is that a confession? But why?!

HARRIET: I had to, because your direct rival for retention of identical posts which the management had decided to reduce to one, is Bob, whom I love. My chances of marrying him would be lost were he to lose that job. Thus, I sabotaged you, his sole rival, by lowering your work performance efficiency production output results quota by swaying my lovely body in the way of your lust-lost eyes. It worked, perfectly. You're fired, Bob's job is safe and secure, and he and I will soon marry. I'm grateful to your weakness—which is for sex—for the fulfillment of my love in the happy promise of domestic bliss. We want to invite you to our wedding. Without your optical seductibility, our romance would have died an ugly commercial death. Now, Bob is blooming, thanks to you. Hie future gleams with glorious promise. It was either you or us. Sorry.

NARRATOR I (no longer EXECUTIVE): What could Al Lehman say? He was speechless. She had brought him down, with low tactics: aiming at his signal weakness below the belt. All, though, is fair, in love, and business—which is the peacetime equivalent of war.

NARRATOR II: Friday came: Al's last day at that firm, forever. He exchanged farewells with all his former colleagues. Some of them would soon lose *their* jobs, as well. Throughout the offices, tears could be spotted.

NARRATOR I: Bob was out sick that day. Harriet looked luscious, in a see-through dress that added to poor Al Lehman's already overwrought torments.

HARRIET: You can make love to me, if you wish, after work, today. Bob need never now. It's my recompense, or reparation, for what I've done to you. You can take your frustrating disappointment out on my gripping body. I owe it to you. I brought you low.

AL LEHMAN: You did, Harriet. I'll take you up, on your ethically ambivalent offer.

NARRATOR I: It was a squalid affair. Al couldn't "do" it. He was impotent. Here was his chance for some slight consolation, all condensed in anguished brevity. He failed.

Harriet teased him:

HARRIET: You're fired; you bungled *this* job, too. Your impotence is of course situational. You're too miserable to perform. It's enabled me to remain faithful to my dear Bob. He has both me, and your job. Both of which, *you'd* like, wouldn't you?

NARRATOR I: She dressed and left, while Al Lehman sobbed. His life had sunk very low. He had, in fact, touched the murky bottom of his depths of misfortune. He was undressed, in a dingy bed. Without job, soon without wife. Harriet was gone. Now, he felt lust. Too late.

SCENE IV

NARRATOR II: Mary didn't appeal to Tom Gervasi anymore. But he wasn't callous. He had to break it to her softly, so as not to upset her. He wanted to ease her out, with minimum pain. Even to contrive such a way of putting it, as—paradoxically—to make her glad, relieved, happy, unburdened, to be losing him. He needed a diplomatic touch, for that, or a greasy sales executive's palaver, or an oily merchant's tongue, adroit in hypocrisy's witchcraft, the insincere poet's stylish wind of rhetoric.

NARRATOR I: Mary was sensitive, and she loved him. He had to exercise much care in handling how poor Mary gets the news: which, if bluntly stated, would be:

NARRATOR II: "You don't interest me anymore. It's all over between us. Don't bother to appeal. My mind is settled, and that's it."

TOM GERVASI: Mary, I have something to say.

MARY: Tom Gervasi, how glad I am of that! I love your melodic voice, and your way of putting words together. I love *everything* of you. I love you to pure heaven. I love you beyond life itself. I love you beyond *love* itself. You *are* love, yet you transcend it, and are much greater. What have you to say, Tom Gervasi?

TOM GERVASI: It'll make you very happy.

MARY: Of *course* it will: because *you're* saying it. *You* bring all my happiness to me. Now, what's your latest bit?

TOM GERVASI: Mary, let me put it this way. I'm going to freeze, arrest, ossify, make permanent, our love: to eternalize it. We'll not see each other any more. Our knowing each other will stop at its highest, absolute state. The stars, sun, and moon will claim it. It's already at its immortal zenith. Let's not tamper with it *any more*. Let's abandon it, just as it is. Kiss me our last kiss, dear Mary. Then, let's surrender our love, to its infinity.

MARY: That's a lousy idea, Tom Gervasi. I definitely turn it down. So you've tired of me, oh? You don't love me any more, is that it? Well, it's not acceptable to *me!* We remain together, always! I'll *never* let you go!

You gave me a lot of hocum, using sacred words like "infinite," "eternal," "heaven," "immortal," "pure," "absolute," and all that baloney! Well, *stop* that drivel. You're *mine!* I won't let you go!

TOM GERVASI: Mary, you're being too possessive.

MARY: Not *too* possessive. I *do* possess you. You *are* my possession. And I'm not about to relinquish it. You're stuck. You can't unload me, in a million years. I'll shadow you every inch of your motion; you'll go nowhere without my already anticipating it and being there already, waiting. I'll stalk you, I'll dog you, I'll echo your least cough or sneeze. I'm there with you. You're bound, head and foot, to me. You remain, as my prisoner, in involuntary servitude. I *own* you, Tom Gervasi.

TOM GERVASI: But . . .

MARY: If you've stopped loving me, then suffer instead of enjoy my presence. My presence goes on, like it or not, as an *omni*presence that binds us continually. Every crevice of your hour I'll fill with ubiquity. I'll make you *re*love me. I'll force my love-sustaining upon your love-insufficiency, and do a takeover of your mind and heart. You're my prisoner of love. Emergency regulations are in effect. Bow down in every respect. Hand in your will: it's invalid, as of now, as defunct as the dodo.

TOM GERVASI: But . . .

MARY: Don't speak. This is Mary talking to you. Mary is telling you to take your clothing off. Now, "make love" to me. Now. Good. I approve of your obedience. I'm a *benevolent* despot. I'll reward you, Tom Gervasi. With more love. Love, unending. Love, upon its absolute.

Undying. Eternal. Infinite. Immortal. On earth, for heaven. Limitless. Boundless. To hell, and back. *In* hell. As your Mary. Your *always* Mary. Your *only* Mary.

Well, I've had enough "lovemaking," for this physical instance. Withdraw from me. Fall asleep. I'll survey you, under my rapt gaze. And keep you well covered. And looked after. You needn't want. Or will, or hope.

That'll be *my* concern. *I'll* take the trouble. Fall soft. Be my object. Don't object. Be still. Be "dead," in a way. *I'll* take over *our* vitality. Let *me* worry. My passive one. My infant, all asleep.

SCENE V

NARRATOR II: "Al Lehman's Manhood Gets Disvanitied."

NARRATOR I: A girl said "yes":

GIRL: Yes.

NARRATOR I: So Al Lehman set upon her with the full enormity of his beast driven furiously to lust.

NARRATOR II: Yet, when he was finished, he saw that he'd barely made a dent upon her.

NARRATOR I: She rose unperturbed, untumbled, untarnished, unflapped, unruffled.

AL LEHMAN: Is that all the effect I've had upon you?,

NARRATOR I: He asked.

NARRATOR II: To which she replied:

GIRL: Oh, was it you? Sorry, my eyes were closed. I thought my pet kitten was scampering over my lap on its light little toes.

AL LEHMAN: Was that all my manhood did to you!?,

NARRATOR I: Al Lehman, dismayed, cried.

NARRATOR II: She nodded gaily.

GIRL: Men are so vain. My job is to disvanity them. Where better, than at their vulnerable seats of sheer manhood's colossal vanity?

NARRATOR I: Poor Al Lehman wept. The girl was lighthearted. In glee, she danced, with her sly mocking.

NARRATOR II: Al Lehman thought back:

AL LEHMAN: All the women known. Through the last thirty years. Different times, different phases. Different feelings, different women. Now, they're all mixed together, assembled from eighty-five bodies, mingled from eighty-five faces, all flowered into one montage, the composite of separate hours and separate places.

All dumped into my one small cell of imagery. One of me to each of them, and all of me to every one.

I was abundantly faithful. To the whole lot, I stood steadfast in my constancy.

Thirty years gave me a fickle appearance. But I was *true*—one by one.

And the truth spread thin.

SCENE VI

NARRATOR II: "Deborah, her Husband, and Tom Gervasi."

Deborah had heard of Tom Gervasi. It was enough to make her, via mutual contacts, arrange a "casual," "accidental" meeting between them. It was all to appear quite artless. But the mill of gossip churned out endless surmises. The official, well-kept secret was that Tom Gervasi had quite turned her head, by the violent force of his reputation, even before Deborah had ever seen him. She was the joke of the whole social world. Even her husband got wind of it. His pride sank. He brooded on divorce.

Her husband was really a force to be reckoned with! He wore his respectability with the assurance that all the fear, awe, and respect he inspired in others had deeply implanted in his "nature." Deborah had been his highest acquisition. Was he to be made a fool of, now, by this grand little man, Tom Gervasi? His dignity required a prompt settlement of this nasty little disorder; and he made his interception before Tom Gervasi and Deborah would ever meet. It was a social occasion, with Deborah absent.

NARRATOR I (as HUSBAND): Are you Tom Gervasi?

TOM GERVASI: So I am. What of it?

HUSBAND: I'm Deborah's husband.

TOM GERVASI: That doesn't enlighten me. And how is it *my* concern?

HUSBAND: Very much. More than you realize.

TOM GERVASI: Are you accusing me?

HUSBAND: Yes: of inspiring in my wife—the love of my life—an illicit passion for you.

TOM GERVASI: Was it based on my reputation alone?

HUSBAND: Apparently, since she never met you.

TOM GERVASI: On my honor, I'm innocent. I won't exploit her silly infatuation. You look too important, and too menacing. Let's conspire together, sir, to prevent my *ever* meeting Deborah! Together, with our allied strength, we'll ward off a domestic disaster, dishonor, and your brutal revenge upon me. Let's shake, and be partners, in this.

NARRATOR II: They shook hands: the husband and his "rival." It was a pact between gentlemen. It was a sacred bond, between true men. Deborah was in the dark about this. Feeding on her dreams, her Tom-Gervasi-obsession flamed up like a myth. She played "Don Giovanni" on the record player, and was transported into strains of rapture, dizzy flights reminiscent of Madam Bovary's French ecstasies. She and Madam Bovary knew how to dream! The banal world can be shut outside. She'll have her dream, and her Tom Gervasi too.

Her contacts informed her that the elaborately planned, carefully staged, long-last meeting with the fabled Tom Gervasi would not come off:

HOSTESS FRIEND: The occasion itself, as scheduled, will go on; but Tom Gervasi can't attend. He gave me his regret. But something came up. He must go somewhere else, instead.

DEBORAH: Well, can you arrange *another* occasion? At his convenience, of course. I quite want to meet him. Just a whim, on my part. It's nothing serious. I adore, more and more, my majestically important husband; compared to whom—if comparison will so dishonor itself between then—Tom Gervasi is but a pipsqueak, of no consequence whatever. It amuses me to meet him. It's harmless, I assure you.

HUSBAND: Deborah, listen to me, I'm your husband.

DEBORAH: Of course you are. Who else is?

HUSBAND: Rumors have been spreading. About you and Tom Gervasi.

DEBORAH: They're untrue, of course. Why, I assure you, my dear (and I'm not exaggerating), I've never laid eyes on him. I've heard about him—who hasn't? He *does* sound amusing. He could be fun, I think. To see what he's *really* like.

HUSBAND: Deborah, the rumors about you and him are *ugly*. I don't want to sound like Anna Karenina's husband, talking to you, but I must warn you. I can see through your attempts to reassure me. Stop having fun. I'm as serious as death.

DEBORAH: Is it that bad!? Oh dear!

HUSBAND: I must warn you. Tom Gervasi has a dangerous reputation, as a wrecker of households, a notorious cuckolding adulterer. He exerts a subtle radiance on married women, from afar. Rumor has it—

DEBORAH: Oh, confound rumor! I, Deborah, am above suspicion. I stand up, now, to my full height. Jealousy demeans you, dear husband. Stop being like Othello. I have no intention of betraying you, with that sorry excuse for a Casanova legend. Your reputation is safe, when reposed in me.

HUSBAND: You *don't* love him? Rumors said you did.

DEBORAH: Rumors are malicious, spiteful. I love you alone.

HUSBAND: Are you *positive* about that statement?

DEBORAH: You can have it in writing, if you'd like. In black and white.

On legal stationery.

HUSBAND: We're already sufficiently married, by Ordinance of the Church. Don't you *dare* desecrate our vows! Or I'll ruin *you* and bring *him* low!

DEBORAH: My husband, stop this. Consider your high position, and your well-known dignity. Such petty jealousy—which you display so comically and without the least foundation, I assure you—quite crumbles your stature. *Confound* Tom Gervasi! Would that I had *never* heard of him! He's wrecking our lives, our social standing, our good names. I give you permission, dear, to punish him. Get rid of him—of his infernal non-presence. He mustn't come between us. Some of your employees are mobsters, racketeers. Could you assign a few rougher ones to "rub out" that menace? Then, we'd be rid of our nemesis, our curse. It'll save our marriage. Please!

NARRATOR II: The husband was surprised. Deborah had become hysterical. Earlier, her tone was one of banter, light irony, mild sarcasm. Her hysteria worried him. It seemed too genuine not to cause him grave concern. He phoned Tom Gervasi to have a confidential talk. They met in a dim, out-of-the-way bar. Tom Gervasi said:

TOM GERVASI: Well, I've done *my* bit. Deborah had commissioned mutual contacts to arrange a social occasion where I'd—accidentally, casually—encounter her. But I dropped out of it! I told the go-between that I couldn't make it—a pressing engagement had intervened. So you see, I kept *my* end of the bargain. And you—did you have your showdown with Deborah your wife yet?

HUSBAND: I did; and I must tell you what my sweet little wife begged me to do, concerning the matter of what to do about *you*. To rub you out! Via certain henchmen in my field of business. To do you in! She recommended, in fact, your death!

TOM GERVASI: That's really going too far! My death is no light matter, I assure you. It would make a mockery of my rights, the killing of me would! It would be altogether too violent!

HUSBAND: But she's my wife. I have no choice, really. I have a weakness, a fondness, for her moods and whims. If she craves your death, and I have means to do it without drawing suspicion on myself (or her), then why shouldn't it be done?! Sorry, Tom Gervasi!

TOM GERVASI: But you've violated our pact we made before, as gentlemen, in alliance against our common adversary, the woman.

HUSBAND: Well, that's dishonorable of me.

Deborah and I have two little children. They have futures before them. It would be injurious to them socially, should a scandal follow them. "Their mother was a tart, in high circles," it would he said. Your death would prevent that. It would spare the reputation of our whole family. Have *you* a family?

TOM GERVASI: No.

HUSBAND: Then, be sacrificed. The family comes first. The bachelor is taxed extra.

TOM GERVASI: This seems *most* unfair.

HUSBAND: Was life *ever* fair? *Really!* Where's your philosophy, Tom Gervasi?

NARRATOR II: The killing was done, and hushed up. It was unobtrusive.

However, Deborah still loves Tom Gervasi—*however* dead he is. That's what rumor reports. So even in death, Tom Gervasi is casting a malicious influence on a married lady's heart. It's a scandal between two worlds: life and death. The husband is exceedingly embarrassed. He's contemplating suicide. Or at least, divorce.

SCENE VII

NARRATOR I: Al Lehman was aware that his cat Pat, who was old as cats go by the scale of cats' average longevity ratio, was doomed some day to die.

His awareness of his cat Pat's mortality was made more poignant by the fat fact that the cat Pat himself was limited (due to the species he belonged to) to no awareness himself that he would some day die.

So Al Lehman had to be aware for *both* of them, of their double impending deaths.

He looked at his cat Pat.

AL LEHMAN: Poor little thing. It has an Irish name. (Anything Irish is human, except for the vegetable, mineral, and animal kingdoms in Ireland that simply aren't.) Poor little cat Pat.

NARRATOR I: Al Lehman had their deaths down pat. First it would be Pat's turn; then, long years afterward, his own.

NARRATOR II: He knew that his wife Marge, from whom he was estranged and soon to be divorced, knew well enough about her own mortality to exempt Al from having to be aware of it *for* her, as he was for his cat Pat.

NARRATOR I: Their son Gregory, who was residing with Marge, was by now old enough to be more than dimly aware of his own awful impending mortality years and years hence—presumably quite a while after his parents have shuffled off to meet their separate fates.

NARRATOR II: Al's mother and foster-father were closer to that "divine" date, and surely their awareness would he brimming with it.

NARRATOR I: Al's father had no awareness of anything by now, being completely "in the grave," as the saying goes.

NARRATOR II: Al's two brothers and their respective wives—four more separate sets of awareness.

AL LEHMAN: But cat Pat—cute little thing—is sweetly oblivious, the little brute.

NARRATOR I: Al Lehman is tired of cat Pat. This is Saturday. No work at the office today. Al Lehman is home in the apartment. Tonight he has a date with a potentially exciting new girl whom he met at a party last week.

GIRL: He can imagine all he wants about me, since he's had no experience of me beyond talking with me at last week's crowded party on a few scattered occasions near clusters of people. He can dream into how he might imagine me to be. He's to call on me with his car and take me to a restaurant. Tonight will be romantic or erotic maybe. Spiked by mortality's fine flavor, heightened by mortality's acid herb.

NARRATOR II: Cat Pat goes to sleep on a chair, curled up into a fur-ball. Al Lehman goes to sleep on his bed, stretched out. That's his momentary cure for boredom. Tonight is excitement, potentially ahead. A girl he doesn't know, but has hopes for.

NARRATOR I: Romantic, erotic, glorious spice.

NARRATOR II: Heady, enticing.

GIRL: Boredom-killers.

NARRATOR I: Mortality-delayers.

NARRATOR II: Prime distractions,

GIRL: high awareness packed deep.

NARRATOR I: Close human company.

NARRATOR II: Close and tight.

GIRL: Hugs, and ecstasy.

NARRATOR I: He's asleep, in the late afternoon. He'll wake up refreshed. He'll ignore cat Pat, save to feed him,

NARRATOR II: He's all fired up. The date is soon.

NARRATOR I AND NARRATOR II: Who is she?

GIRL: Death's matchless rival, tonight.

SONG

(Sung by one or both NARRATORS as DEVILS)

        So non-Don Juan dreams of his date
        Wakes too late
        That's his fate.

AL LEHMAN: Oh, hell.

SONG (continued)

        And Don Juan still will not behave
        Women crave
        What he gave
        Even in the grave.

EPILOGUE—HELL

TOM GERVASI: Have you known love?

WOMAN I: Yes, first-hand.

TOM GERVASI: Have you known religious faith?

WOMAN II: Devoutly, if reverently.

TOM GERVASI: Have you known death?

WOMAN III: Remotely, if apprehensively.

TOM GERVASI: In which direction?

WOMAN III: In the way of the future.

TOM GERVASI: That's safe. Have you known love?

WOMAN I: First-hand, I told you. The most intimate manner.

TOM GERVASI: Was it close?

WOMAN I: Skin-tight.

TOM GERVASI: To mingle?

WOMAN I: In overlapping, to interpenetrate, most intricately entwined.

TOM GERVASI: Have you had knowledge?

WOMAN III: I've known experience.

TOM GERVASI: Has knowledge been an experience?

WOMAN III: Continuously. Permeatingly. Imponderably.

TOM GERVASI: Have you known pain?

WOMAN II: It's been experienced.

TOM GERVASI: Did love lead to it?

WOMAN II: Yes, often and from every direction.

WOMAN I: For I died, or love killed me.

WOMAN III: And my knowledge was complete.

TOM GERVASI: Complete?

WOMAN II: Truly complete?

WOMAN I: Absolutely, completely complete?

WOMAN III: Well, on second thought ...

(End of play)

PRODUCTION NOTES

[Adapted from Jim Milton's notes on the original production]

Assigned Parts:

Tom Gervasi, Al Lehman played by same actor
Woman I also plays Girl, Valerie, Judy, Rose, May
Woman II also plays Bernice, Clara, Iris, June, Mary, Hostess Friend
Woman III also plays Brigit, Janet, Lila, Harriet, Deborah
Narrator I also plays Doctor, Executive, Deborah's Husband
Narrator II also plays Murray, Bob (non-speaking)
Party scenes fleshed out with Narrators.

Music and Setting:

Music was used as a bridge between scenes and hence between the two title characters. Tom Gervasi was established by themes from Mozart's *Don Giovanni* and Al Lehman by Gershwin's solo piano pieces (*Promenade, Prelude #2, Impromptu*). Sound effects such as thunder and wind for Hell, party sounds, office sounds, etc., were used to create a sense of place and to give the impression that there were more people on the stage than there actually were.

Little in the way of a set was used, or is necessary, though the one piece on the stage was a bed (or the suggestion thereof). The last portion of the Brigit scene, the Valerie scene, the end of the Rose, Iris, and Lila scene, the end of the Harriet scene, and the Mary scene, were all played "between the sheets."

THE DON JUAN IN ALL OF US

[Excerpts from an interview with Stella Saunders, Kensington Post, London, UK, February 20, 1981]

"If we only report what is in the world, that is journalism. Art is imposing on the world some sort of absurdity, a special tone or rhythm."

* * * * * * *

Currently he is in England to publicise his play "Don Juan and the Non-Don Juan"...

"My attitude to the play is that I leave it in the hands of the director, June Abbott. I don't feel possessive or proprietorial. I feel I am a father of a son or daughter who is growing up and the play is in the hands of a lover."

* * * * * * *

"I am unimpressed with the banality of everyday life and want to give it zest and a new angle. I have found surrealism is a way of looking at life differently while imposing your own personality on it. Don Juan has always interested me particularly from the point of view of the power he has over other people.

"This time it's power in an amorous vein. It's a matter of who comes out on top, who submits and who demands. It can be likened to sport—one side demands and the other side tries with all its might to win. Ultimately no-one wants to lose.

"There's a lot at stake and the person who loses can be humiliated and suffer as a result.

"In all of us there is the Don Juan and the Non-Don Juan and these two aspects of our character are to be reconciled."

REASONABLE RESIGNATION

Characters:

BURT: Friend of JASPER, close boyfriend of GEORGIA
GEORGIA: Close girlfriend of BURT
JASPER: Friend of BURT, close boyfriend of GINGER
GINGER: Close girlfriend of JASPER

ACT ONE

SCENE I

(BURT, in pajamas, and GEORGIA, in nightgown, both sitting up in one bed.)

BURT: I'm worried about Jasper.
GEORGIA: But Burt—why?
BURT: He appears to be crazy.
GEORGIA: On what evidence?
BURT: He wants to end death.
GEORGIA: In that event, we're *all* crazy.
BURT: You mistake me. I mean, Jasper thinks he can pull it off!
GEORGIA: Pull *what* off?
BURT: The trick of eliminating death.
GEORGIA: You mean he's *serious!?*
BURT: Yes, he's as serious as . . .
GEORGIA: Death?

BURT: I'm afraid so. He's also mad at me.

GEORGIA: What did you do to him?

BURT: I was skeptical. I doubted he could do it.

GEORGIA: Do what—end death?

BURT: Precisely.

GEORGIA: *(Enthusiastically, hopefully)* But Burt—what if he's right!?

BURT: Right? About what?

GEORGIA: That he *can* end death! Oh, Burt—what that could mean! Just think! *(Takes BURT's hand in hers)* We'd be alive, always!

BURT: *(Skeptically)* How lovely, Georgia. It's just *too* romantic—to be true.

GEORGIA: *(Hurt)* Burt! Don't you love me?!

BURT: Of course!

GEORGIA: Forever?

BURT: Naturally.

GEORGIA: *Not* so naturally. Jasper must succeed, first.

BURT: Succeed? At what?

GEORGIA: *(Loudly)* At ending death. Otherwise, how could our love be immortal?

BURT: You have a point there. Rather, *two* points. Or rather, *three*.

GEORGIA: Three? *What* three?

BURT: There's *you.*

GEORGIA: *(Counting on her fingers)* That's one.

BURT: There's *me.*

GEORGIA: *(Counting on her fingers)* That's two.

BURT: There's our *love:* undying.

GEORGIA: *(Hugging BURT impulsively)* Oh Burt! Let's pray!

BURT: But why? Are we religious?

GEORGIA: *(Excited)* For Jasper to liberate us!

BURT: What from?

GEORGIA: Death!—Naturally.

BURT: *Not* so naturally.

GEORGIA: Why? How?

BURT: Because ending Death is unnatural—so far. It just hasn't been done.

GEORGIA: You mean, being done makes it natural?

BURT: Of course.

GEORGIA: How will he go about it?

BURT: Artificially.

GEORGIA: Oh. But will it work?

BURT: I doubt it; that's why Jasper accused me of unfriendly disloyalty: I was skeptical.

GEORGIA: Of what?

BURT: His pulling it off.

GEORGIA: *What* off?

BURT: That business of ending Death.

GEORGIA: But Burt!

BURT: Yes?

GEORGIA: How can he do it?

BURT: Do what?

GEORGIA: End death. He's certainly no scientist!

BURT: That's what *I* told him. That he's crazy.

GEORGIA: *(Disappointed)* You mean he can't do it?

BURT: Be realistic: how *can* he?

GEORGIA: *(Weeping)* Goodbye, love.

BURT: *(Clutching her closely)* But not yet!

GEORGIA: *(Weeping)* But *one* day. *(Sobs violently)*

BURT: Calm yourself. It's Jasper's fault.

GEORGIA: For what?

BURT: For falsely getting your hopes up. You accepted—or were resigned to—our death before. Now, you're all upset.

GEORGIA: *(Still crying, but not so violently)* Burt, how did Jasper hatch his scheme?

BURT: What scheme?

GEORGIA: The one to end death?

BURT: It's no scheme—it's a dream.

GEORGIA: *(Disappointed)* No plan? Only a wish?

BURT: *(Sadly)* Only so. The merest dream.

GEORGIA: He's crazy, then?

BURT: Not only that, but wrathful. He expelled us from inclusion in his immortality-for-all feast: You and I to be the sole exceptions to an otherwise democratically unexclusive eternal-life gift for every human universally alive enough to be a perpetually grateful recipient of Jasper's landmark endowment that's an amendment on the Creation's constitution and a staggeringly major biological mutation, a vital revolution to liven up man's long evolution.

GEORGIA: But Burt—in such largesse, why are *we alone* to be dreadfully cursed as exceptions?

BURT: To punish me, for it was my sin to doubt.

GEORGIA: Doubt what?

BURT: That he could do it.

GEORGIA: Do what?

BURT: End—finally for ever—Death.

GEORGIA: But that's cruel—he's your friend!

BURT: No longer. I'm guilty of a high crime: actively sabotaging his proposed abolishment of Death, by virtue of treacherous skepticism, in not lending my moral support. *(Ironically)* But if his invention works out in spite of my "sabotage," then his revenge shall take effect: to deprive you, me, our love—all three—of the everlasting bounty of that impossible invention's humane worldwide munificence in miraculous salvation of all souls physically entire, save ours.

GEORGIA: So we'd be out in the cold?

BURT: Such is Jasper's threat—or rather pronouncement. *(Apprehensively looks at her)* Georgia—*please* don't credit it!

GEORGIA: *(With a glazed look of determined faith)* Jasper passes your understanding. You did wrong, withholding your support. At such great cost!

BURT: At *no* cost, since he won't do it.

GEORGIA: He *can* end Death!

BURT: *(Paternally, protectively, tenderly)* Nonsense. You're as bad as he, you poor deluded darling. It's strictly impossible.

GEORGIA: *(Poignant, tragic)* But what if it's not!? Our love leaps high with life's blessing. To lose those irreplaceable prizes of love and lives —*(Accusingly)* merely because you doubt! *(Desperately pleading)* Burt, Burt, retract that doubt! Go back to Jasper, and beg his forgiveness! For all our eternal sakes!

BURT: Georgia—you're no more sane or rational than poor Jasper! Surely you can't believe—

GEORGIA: I *can*—if there's an outside chance that belief, by magic, can help pull it off—

BURT: Pull off *what*?

GEORGIA: To our everlasting glory, Death's end!

BURT: Please recover yourself! You disgrace us, by placing belief in—

GEORGIA: *(Fervently)* But he *could* do it! Impossible or not, he *could* do it!

BURT: *(Defiantly)* Are you on *his* side—or *mine?*

GEORGIA: How can I tell? Yours is reason's side—cold stoical resignation, with Death waiting surely at the end. *His (Glowingly, fervently, in a leap of piety)* is magic's side, that defies reason by leaping past scientific barriers of realism: the reward for such belief is *(Ecstatically)* Eternity! *(Suddenly switching to worldly suavity)* That appeal surely is not without a certain undeniable charm?

BURT: Hedging, you want your cake and yet must eat it. Are you on *his* side, or *mine?*

GEORGIA: I'll be a judge at high stakes. Fairly I'll give you a hearing, and decide. Bring before me the discussion you had with Jasper. Set back alive that scene, re-enact its dialogue, as I sit in judgment, choosing between an eternal soul—*(Wistfully ecstatic)* if possible!—or *(Sternly, bravely)* the damnation of cold reason's consoling resignation.

(Curtain, darkness. Then, after pause, Scene II)

SCENE II

(Some time shortly before Scene I. JASPER and BURT, sitting in living room of former's apartment. JASPER looks innocent, unworldly. BURT seems more self-possessed and prepared with "all the answers," low-keyed, often cynical, tastefully negative)

JASPER: The world is in dreadful shape. What's it coming to?

BURT: Who knows? But once it gets to where it's coming to, it won't stop *there*—that's no resting place; it'll plunge right on: right into another generation. You and I, meanwhile, by that time, will be dead.

JASPER: That's what I really hate about life—*mortality!*

BURT: Your hating it is a good sign—shows your values are in the right place: you love life.

JASPER: Of *course* I love it; it's *me*, isn't it?

BURT: Life isn't only you; it's the whole world, without which, there would be *no you*.

JASPER: Well, that puts me in my place. *(Pause)* But I have a surprise for you.

BURT: *(Urbanely)* What on earth can it be? Please, spare me any further suspense. Life is tricky enough, without the upset of unnecessary palpitations. Don't tease me. What's on your sleeve—or up your mind? Spill it!

JASPER: Don't get so excited! I'm referring to this mortality business. I intend to outdo Death, at his own game, cut him off, and purge life of its own worst enemy, which lurks hidden within and resists all subtle onslaughts to free human life of its secret undoer.

BURT: Secret?! Death is out in the open. By now, it's hardly a secret. Otherwise, why all those long faces you see in the streets and on the buses? They've all caught on, about this death business.

JASPER: Death has been in business so long, it must by now have outlived its original purpose—whatever that might have been.

BURT: *(Making JASPER's last phrase into a query and answering it)* To unclutter the stage and unblock the sun, and clean the halls, and clear the decks, for the free access of newborn generations that come to inherit the works that get passed on to them by those who conveniently leave the stage tidy for the next lot to use.

JASPER: That's all very well for the newborn; but drastically unfair for the ones who must "go": the ones who get old reluctantly, having learned to esteem, love, value life. They became so fond of life, learned in time to hold it so dear—*then* must they relinquish it?

BURT: They wouldn't have held it so dear, if life were immortal. Mortality conferred the exquisite preciousness on rare, fleeting, passing moments.

JASPER: Oh, not so fleeting. Sometimes life lags and flags so slow, as dull monotony endures to tedious boredom. Even *with* our mortal awareness.

> (*They both yawn—illustrating* JASPER'S *last point—stretch, get up, move about, do something or other, before sitting down again*)

BURT: *(Changing the tone)* But Jasper—what's your surprise about?

JASPER: I'm coming to that.

BURT: Get to it in a hurry. I'm mortal, you know.

JASPER: You're so mortal, Burt, that of necessity you've learned the valuable lesson of patience.

BURT: But you're making me unlearn it. Stop stalling. Just what's your point?

JASPER: It's about mortality. The gloomy thought of impending doom.

BURT: Well, so what?

JASPER: What! It's not trivial!

BURT: No, but it's hopeless. We're all resigned.

JASPER: *I'm* not!

BURT: No? You're crazy.

> (*Pause*)

JASPER: Burt, have you been listening?

BURT: I was. But not now.

JASPER: I told you my practical surprise. It was so incredible, you didn't credit it. Now, I demand that you recall it.

BURT: I was dreaming.

JASPER: Undream it, then.

BURT: I thought I heard you say that you intend to outdo Death, at his own game, cut him off, and purge life of its own worst enemy. But my ears didn't register what my mind heard. The nonsense invalidated itself.

JASPER: Take me seriously, now. Come under my spell.

BURT: I'd have to be under your spell, to take you seriously. *(Pause)* You mean you're going to take action? Not to be passively helpless about decay's progress toward death? You'll *do* something about it!?

JASPER: *(Enunciating with deliberateness)* Finally, hear my determination: to terminate our termination.

BURT: You're only making sound-music. It's sound—but unsound.

(Pause)

JASPER: Burt, are we not fellow mortals together?

BURT: Of course, friend. We're both doomed.

JASPER: Such a double state, I wish to reform.

BURT: A crackpot notion! I fail completely—

JASPER: *(Sharply)* Then listen!

BURT: *(Brought to)* Yes?

JASPER: *(Sternly)* And answer!

BURT: *(Subjugated)* Yes?

JASPER: Are you aware of the deadly nature of the adversary I'm planning to rid us of?

BURT: Yes, but what on earth can you do about it? I fail to see *that*.

JASPER: First, what *is* it I'll try to erase? What *is* this undesirable hitch, or fatal clause, in our existence?

BURT: You know I know what it is.

JASPER: Start from scratch: What *is* life's true bane?

BURT: Its nature eludes me. It's too stark to face.

JASPER: *(Urging)* Come—what is it?

BURT: It's... the fly in humanity's ointment. The rotten apple in mankind's contentedness barrel. The black lining on an otherwise spotless horizon. Our ancient, and still-going-strong, nemesis: Death, the dread of which has given rise to religion, metaphysics, the occult, magic, superstition, astral speculation, tragedy, drama, art, philosophy, music, literature, romance, and idealism. Death: the eternal worm slowly trickling through the core of our pathetic, body-based egos... *(Suddenly defiantly)* Well, what about Death? This subject, since time immemorial, has already been thoroughly covered, picked through, and worn out by discussion, fretful worry, and intermittent anxiety. What can you add, to that primal unknown curse that plagues what otherwise is our crown blessing: consciousness?

(Curtain, darkness. Then, after pause, Scene III)

SCENE III

(Setting and positions of BURT and JASPER are identical to such at end of Scene II. Time resumes immediately from where left off, at end of BURT's speech)

JASPER: Burt, promise me not to laugh or mock. Otherwise, I refuse to divulge my desperate plan.

BURT: I promise. But *what* desperate plan?

JASPER: I don't intend idly to stand by like all our other doomed sheep, to watch Death gradually unfold its malice with decomposing cells, physical decay, bodily rot, working insidiously from within like a Trojan Horse of classical treachery or deception.

BURT: *(With arch cynicism)* So *you* are to be history's very first circumventer, forestaller, arrester, outwitter, and ultimate undoer of our prolific devastator, Death?

JASPER: I confess to that purpose.

BURT: With what means, at hand?

JASPER: My goal will find its instrument, my aim its tool, my crusade its revelation.

BURT: That sounds evasive. *(Pedantically explanatory)* Yours is no desire, with its achievement-possibility; rather, it's a *wishful dream*, with no achievement-means.

JASPER: I'll attain what I set out to do. As this feat is to be unprecedented, which I intend to pull off, you lack a base from which to view my unique enterprise with any understanding or confidence in what you'd term my "audacity." My vision will blaze its own true path, and find its best efficient way, with the tested effectiveness of results, a proven method to its objective. Lacking, friend, your faith—which I *might* need—I'll light my own progress in a steady blaze in self-enlightenment. *I* don't doubt. Death won't withstand the heat of my applied inspiration: I'll snuff out, forever, that evil, dark fate to which collectively our race has submitted in the meekest ignorance of our resignation.

BURT: That's what I'd call a "speech." Your words have that truly hollow ring of the braggart infatuated with the wild promise of his emptiness.

JASPER: Wait. Give me time.

BURT: You'll need more than time. Not even an eternity would avail your efforts to tame a realistic impossibility to the persistent fever of a wish.

JASPER: *(Darkly)* We'll see.

BURT: Stubborn? Clamming up? The man of action, the man of few words? You don't impress, in that new switch of roles.

JASPER: I'll withstand your barrage of relentless sarcasm. You show no faith in me, in shallow mockery. I pronounce you now—my *former* friend.

(They glare at each other. Pause)

BURT: I pity you. You'll recover.

JASPER: You're low. Put *blind* trust in the awful rightness of my true pursuit.

BURT: Your tone is dangerously fanatic. You show the erratic, debased perversion of a strained religious faith.

JASPER: *(Simply)* I'll win.

(Pause. One or both get up, do something, before resuming sitting)

BURT: Let's assume that you do succeed in taking Death on and managing a triumph. Let's only assume that.

JASPER: Such is but fair, to assume that which I'll bring about to *be*. It will reach the endeavor stage, before rising to a deed done, carried off, bearing the proof and demonstration of a reality new to the amazed world.

BURT: Will you selfishly save yourself alone?—Or is your salvation to extend its miraculous mercy, its joyous reprieve, to *all* of us scattered and thronged on our human planet?

JASPER: I'd be a narrow, petty little bastard to stop at myself, when my discovery could spread its blessing in universal application to all fellow kindred creatures of our biological genre.

BURT: Let me skeptically persist in asking: What's your method? Alchemy? Black witchcraft? Mumbo jumbo? Astrological revelation? Revealed truth, by divine visitation? The hocus pocus of science assassinated by the misuse of logic to the twisted demonology of ideas all at sea, estranged from the network mainland of our connectiveness? *(Brief pause)* In short, by what methodology will you arrive at your outlandish scheme, by what working plan, to put into effect the supreme urging of your brainpower, converting wish to will, and will to deed?

JASPER: You doubt me?

BURT: I do.

JASPER: *(With finality)* Then you deserve no answer.

> *(Somewhat prolonged pause. One or both could meanwhile do something or other)*

BURT: That's clever. You revert to silence, which is supposed to screen a profound, unfathomable, brooding depth that gravely plots the demise of no less a thing than Death. *(Brief pause)* Mysticism is your laboratory, and fantasy your workshop. Idleness shows through your pretensions. You're a holy fake.

JASPER: I forgive you. You know not what you say. But you're too ignorant not to say it.

BURT: Hypocrisy swears by false magic.

JASPER: Accuse me. I'm unharmed.

BURT: You've "wished" yourself into a trap of magic.

JASPER: What *seems* magic now, will be commonplace later.

BURT: Your pompous fraudulence conceals perhaps a deranged disorder of your soul.

JASPER: That would justify the contempt and condescension and privileged piety of your pity.

BURT: My pity, I assure you, is founded greatly on a firm fact. You claim to want to do what can't be done. We've reached, finally, an unarguable point. Reality refuses to budge.

> *(Pause. They remain sitting, glaring at each other)*

JASPER: Since you're taking an objective stance, I insist on asking: Why *can't* I do what I propose? Answer me, now, precisely.

BURT: Why can't you do what you propose?

JASPER: Precisely. Why—on this old earth teeming with possibilities —may I not?

BURT: You *may* not, because you *can* not.

JASPER: Don't quibble. Why not?

BURT: Why not?

JASPER: Yes. Don't say it's impossible. Why not?

BURT: *(Flatly)* It's never been done.

(A short, glaring pause)

JASPER: *(With emphasis) Other* things were done for the first time. Why not this?

(With JASPER *momentarily in ascendancy: curtain, darkness)*

ACT TWO

SCENE I

(Setting and positions of BURT *and* JASPER *are identical to such just before Intermission at end of Act I. Time resumes immediately from where left off, with* JASPER *momentarily in ascendancy and* BURT *forced to assume defensive.)*

BURT: I'm forced to play a cynical, negative role. I know you, Jasper. You're smart in some things, but dumb in science. To dust Death off the human map without resorting to magic of a supernatural kind, you'd have to be up on biology, anatomy, physics, chemistry, organic molecular structure, medicine, right up to the borderline of mystery itself, on the frontier of unprecedented discovery.

JASPER: *(Admitting)* I *am* scientifically ignorant, that's true.

BURT: True? Not merely true! It's a handicap, considering what you propose to do.

JASPER: Handicaps *can* be overcome. They're not all insurmountable.

BURT: *(With heated emphasis)* But in *this* case, your optimism would be the very height of certifiable folly! You've hatched an unworkable scheme. It's unutterably implausible.

JASPER: How do *you* know? Are you an expert?

BURT: *I'm* not. But others are, or were. There've been plenty. Genius has been in no short supply: Population and time, on our rotund global sphere charged with history, have abundantly seen to that. Great minds have abounded. They've tackled many problems, conquered health barriers, extended medical frontiers, plowed into the thickets of mystery on pioneering tractors that cultivated wilderness into hygienic sophistication and refined our primitive fear. Longevity has inched ahead; yet Death itself, with its borders mildly retracted, slightly retrenched, remains ever grimly, immovably, monstrously, mythically, in an ironbound control over the fragile, swaying destiny of each proud mortal.

JASPER: But Burt—that was before *I* was reckoned on.

BURT: Are you, then, of Christlike proportion, to historically create a new tide on our astronomical surface, ridding our sensitive skins of the Death-pestilence?

JASPER: I'm a major figure. My advent is nigh. I've arrived.

BURT: And with you—the era of the immortals? Immortality filtered down to all democratic levels in the triumph of permanent life on a continuous human scale?

JASPER: *(Darkly)* We'll see. *(Resumes undarkly without pause)* Since your lifetime will undergo a new time magnitude of colossal grandeur of dimensions, the concept of "hurry" becomes rapidly obsolete. Now, *take* your time. There's no hurry.

BURT: You talk as though you've already achieved, with gloating boasting, that which I continue to doubt you have any knack or talent for doing. Nor does anyone else—before or now or ever—have a hope or clue or capacity for waging even the remotest challenge, the most forlorn defiance, the least audible protest, against Death's august unassailability.

JASPER: Your negative rhetoric embarrasses me. There's time. I'll do it.

BURT: There's time if you do it. Once you've done it, there'll be time for everything—including even doing what you now propose to do. Right now, you're *still* mortal. Time is against you—so long as you haven't yet done what you propose to do. So you have no time to lose. You have a little time, to create timeless amplitude.

JASPER: *(Calmly, offhand, leisurely)* Oh—I have my plan.

BURT: You spoke, before, of a plan soaked in desperation. Now, you've changed your tune, and are calm.

JASPER: Calmly confident.

BURT: *(Exasperatedly)* But—based on what!?

JASPER: *(Unperturbed; loftily)* Never mind. That's *my* affair.

BURT: Mine too—if you spare me from Death. And *Georgia's*—my dear love. And the *love itself*, of Georgia and me. It most definitely concerns us. She and I, and the love between us, all three, would benefit hugely, should success crown the casual effortlessness of your proud boast and claim of easing us all from under the sharp strain of Death's stalking shadow.

JASPER: You two—or three—are guaranteed not to be overlooked: no-one will. Least of all you and Georgia. Nor *Ginger*, my *own* love. *(Pause. Visionarily)* It'll be like a secular Last Judgment, with results of paradisical enormity on literally a global scale; and lovers will dally forever.

> *(Pause, while both contemplate, from contrasting viewpoints, the euphorically all-sweeping vision JASPER has evoked)*

BURT: I'm thrilled, and much obliged. How I'd dearly love to be in your debt—to join all other no-longer-mortals in a rejoicing, jubilant cry of endless gratitude. Alas, I fear that being obligated to you will not be my great fortune—nor my Georgia's, nor your Ginger's, nor anyone's—due to your not coming through on your vaunted promise.

JASPER: The promise I make, I vow to keep. Whatever extraordinary or divine means this entails, I'll make it my uncanny business—if I haven't already done so—to find; then to put to work. Then *(Gesturing with Godlike grandeur)*—Behold!

BURT: *(Disdainful, scornful, contemptuous)* Fake magnanimity! I don't buy it!

JASPER: I give you my supreme Word! To the old Creation I affix an amendment, augmenting, appendix—a royal addition, a crucial editorial revision, a drastic radical alteration.

BURT: So only you say. Your claim is idle, your vow inane.

JASPER: *(Crossed, threatening)* Beware my thundering wrath!

BURT: That's a *pagan* gesture. Nor does a *Saviour's* posture suit you; all your poses fail to impress or convince. They're upheld by the flimsiest pretense at authority. Truth's jury confers a negative verdict.

JASPER: But I appeal to you as a friend!

BURT: A pathetic appeal. Falsehood shouldn't falsely be condoned by *loyalty's* compulsory strain. Friendship should have free access to contrary truths and not be forced, under duress and conflict, to ignoble concessions in binding conformity to blackmail trials of ultimatum on a narrow point of debate.

JASPER: Not narrow, but vast and broad, is my new gospel that reforms habitual acquiescence to Death in a grand scientific triumph of Faith.

BURT: You don't inspire a Saviour's confidence. Your aspiration—ostensibly lofty—is left empty of practical implementation. You're a world-saver by the bombast of vapor, lacking the device of workable means.

JASPER: *(Warning)* Guard against being negative!

BURT: *(Pointedly ignoring that warning)* Not even specialists and experts of renowned caliber, in spite of all their humanitarian zeal and inspired benevolence on a high philanthropic order, have been able to retard cellular decay and arrest decomposition's steady rot. *You, (Contemptuously)* armed with ignorance—what can you possibly do that hasn't already been tried, in vain, millions of morbid times in mankind's losing warfare against the slow, ticking time-bomb in the mortal confines of each protester? Lacking science—which is itself finite, even to technical specialists—your only hope has to be somewhat in the nature of the unnatural—a miracle.

JASPER: *(Rhetorically)* You're advocating a miracle? Nothing short of one would do?

BURT: Nothing short, nothing less.

JASPER: *(Loftily)* Would a miracle—that specific one precise and proper in heroic measurement to my noble cause—vanquish your skepticism?

BURT: In fairness, yes.

JASPER: *(Apocalyptically)* Then—soon Behold.

BURT: Show me the result. Till then, I offer you doubt.

(Curtain, darkness. Then, after pause, Scene II)

SCENE II

(Setting and positions of BURT and JASPER are identical to such at end of Scene I. Time resumes immediately from where left off, at end of BURT's statement)

JASPER: I won't exclude you—nor your own darling Georgia with whom you wage a deathless love—from my universal cure. But as a friend, you should be *supporting* me. Your doubt shows the trait of treachery. Spare me any counter-lecture on friends' freedom to pursue opposite truths without taint of disloyalty nor constraint of the liberty to form an opinion at odds with a friend's sworn ideology. In defying what's sacred to me, you deny all of me—you're unfriendly.

BURT: Your stupidity harms my sense of fair play; and injures my character.

JASPER: Stupidity? *Who's* offensive!?

BURT: Either apologize, or show cause how you'll make practical, for the first time, that ancient myth of eternal life.

JASPER: *(In mounting wrath) You* apologize. Or I'll exclude you and your Georgia from the Eternity feast to which everyone else is warmly only too welcome. *(Threatening)* I'll withdraw my invitation that you and Georgia join in. You dare prevent me from achieving my mission by withholding your moral support? That's sabotage—traitor! You'd ruin my blueprint—however vague—for liberating the human race from Death's ancient tyranny and ever-undiminished plague. With the authority entrusted in me—from sources I prefer at this time not to divulge—I pronounce, on you and Georgia—Death!

BURT: You'd murder us?

JASPER: No: you'd live out your "normal" lifetime—without entitlement to my New Dispensation.

BURT: Your insane delusions border on the frenzy and mayhem of a pseudo-semblance of mock violence.

JASPER: *(Amused, undaunted, superior)* What a quaint accusation! Let me remind you, my former friend, that the material deaths of you and Georgia will be automatically fatal to the spiritual *Love* that binds you two together in an enduring blaze of passion.

BURT: That's unkind of you, Skunk. Whereas, the love between you and your Ginger will partake of your joint personal immortalities?

JASPER: Quite! *Our* love survives, in glorious plenitude, outlasting the obsolete datedness of mere former mechanical time. The love of *you* two becomes a tragic martyr to *your* spiteful, stubborn, retrograde unwillingness to co-operate with, believe in, or encourage my plan which—though hardly sketched in and not worked out just yet—remains in grand potential the most humane strategy ever devised to prolong indefinitely each marvelous illustration of the human condition on the level of the intimately personal from the gut roots of each person's living the secret public adventure of his own social private delicious serious game of a living self. To those living selves, I contribute—by projected intention—perpetuation without end. *(Contemptuously)* And you?—what are *you* currently working on? Forgive me—I mean *against?* For that's all you're capable of: to be *against*. *(Brutally, savagely, rancorously)* May my great scheme survive your horrid little opposition, and greatly prevail: your death-loving venom notwithstanding!

> *(They stare antagonistically at each other, partly squaring off in sparring battle stances, miming the exploratory foreplay of fisticuffs, pretending boldness with serious play. Suspense and tension that a fight may actually break out. Then each backs off, habitually resuming their long-drawn-out bout of words)*

BURT: You have strange ideas. You theorize without foundation, then accuse me of disloyalty in friendship just because I honestly proclaim my misgivings as to just how tenable your life-perpetuation proposition sincerely seems to me. As of now, your craziness has impaired our friendship. I will now leave you. *(Begins to leave. Firmly, solemnly, in grim warning)* Alone, perhaps, you'll reconsider just what's in your power and what's not. Over ultimate death, we're granted no control. This, realistically, is the assessment even science—normally given to optimism—has taken its stand on. Science withholds its co-operation, on behalf of reality, which it represents. Your only chance, in your desperate strife, remaining, is unscientifically fabulous—a miracle. *(Continues walking away, as JASPER remains standing still)* I leave you the solitude to seek one. Unassisted by divinity, your chances look wretched. Well, good luck: Luck is the commodity you stand currently—lacking, after all, skill—in the gravest need of. You're dealing in life-or-death intangibles—and are groping to make tangibles from them. *(Slight pause)* Do you grope in the dark? *(Savagely)* No, you boast with idleness. Deep in your heart, you *know* that your undertaking is too hopeless to undertake. That spares your idleness from the compromise of even the slightest work. Work is to as much avail as idleness is. We live in a world from which miracles are barred. Nor is there any other world for miracles to be found. Sorry to be so level-headed. No theory, conjured by a mind, can oppose reality's sadly negative policy that excludes the impossible from a foothold on the soil of existence. Death will not be swayed. The potent "magic" of your wish, however passionately felt, is only an unseen mental thought. Its manifestation *would* be Death's end. But that thought's *actual* manifestation is—simply put—your temporary leaving of your senses; or rather, your senses' leaving of you. Sensibly, I do too. Good-bye. *(Exits on a firm; final stride)*

JASPER: *(Alone now; standing, shifting about, restless, resolute, determined, offended, smarting)* He'll rue that speech: he'll eat it. May my venture succeed. On it hangs so much. First, let the means of attainment give my scheme an articulate method, to make happen that "miracle" Burt rudely referred to. Going on the moon was once a miracle. Now, it's only history.

(Curtain, darkness. Then, after pause, Scene III)

SCENE III

(BURT, in pajamas, and GEORGIA, in nightgown, both sitting up in one bed as before: Setting identical to that of beginning of play, Act One, Scene I)

BURT: There: that's what took place between us. I'm able to include in my thorough report his final soliloquy, having eavesdropped on it after walking out to conclude our dialogue. Scientific curiosity, and concern for a deranged old friend, justify my sneaky snooping: which also helps to round out this report I file, to completely inform you; as I abide, I hope, your verdict kind to me.

GEORGIA: His insanity has replaced your friendship. He should be looked after. I'm worried.

BURT: *(Charitably)* He's not dangerous—to himself or to anyone else. He's removed himself, for awhile, from the modest, moderate bounds of human mental sharing and communication. Alone, he grapples in the grip of a grandiose idea—his back turned on the collective commonplace shallow sanity of his fellow men. He's in the strenuous toils of an uncompromising idea. Let him wrestle with what has taken full possession of his deranged senses. He'll lose, and then—bowed, subdued, humble, modest, he'll return to us his friends and partake of our plain and simple aspirations; the bounty of our doomed and mortal kind.

GEORGIA: Oh Burt—what a sublime, supreme, noble, glorious goal Jasper is consumed by. It's too anguishing—it's wrenchingly poignant—to think that he must fail; as also must the rest of us who lacked the high folly to hope with his absurdity. *(Pause. In dreamlike quavering)* For *you* to live forever—*me*—*us*—our *love*—is such a happy idea that by the same rate it's so sad that it can't come true. *(Pause: Recalling, as though coming to her senses)* But Jasper had condemned us to unique deaths: to punish your unfriendly disloyalty, should his salvation-for-everyone scheme succeed in the face of your disbelief. *(Sternly)* Infidelity and treachery deserve no less, than the death penalty. Why should *my* innocent life share your awful fate? I terminate, then, my alliance with your coldly reasoning, irreverently rational cause; and switch to *him:* however fanatical or futile his storming the fortress, of secular logic, that guards the dark secret of Death's final word over human life.

BURT: *(Incredulous, in the first stab of misery)* Be plain—is it him or me?—are you sure?

GEORGIA: *(As if making pronouncement)* Let your grief flow.

BURT: But Georgia!—we're in love—remember?!

GEORGIA: Our love is only doomed, if I remain with you. It's finite: we're condemned to death, without mercy, by our Lord Jasper. He's my *salvation*—you're my *damnation*. I transfer affection, convert to the winning side. I'm now *Jasper's* devotee!

BURT: *(Agonized)* Darling! I've lost you!

GEORGIA: *(Reverting back to her bond with BURT)* Never! Darling! *(They hug and embrace in rapt devotion and desperate pangs of unquenchable longing, spilling over from the deep and pure well of love)* I'll *never* leave you!

BURT: *(As they break apart from their embrace)* And you renounce Jasper?

GEORGIA: *(In conflict; reverting back to her new longing to believe in JASPER's lofty aim)* Ah, the greatness of Jasper's vision!

BURT: *(Trying to reason)* But, really!

GEORGIA: Oh, that sad word: "if"!

BURT: "If" what?

GEORGIA: If desire could have been converted to deed, he'd have done the greatest thing and been the greatest man, by token of how greatly we all would have benefitted by the great gift of the great change—*(Breaks into sobs; wretchedly clinging to BURT, hugging him despairingly)* Oh, pardon my hysteria. To think of what *could* be. To think how it *cannot* be. What I gain in a burst of hope, I lose immediately in a plunge and dive from what I dared to soar in hope of. *(Repentantly)* It was weakly vulnerable of me to be tempted by that hope—it snared my soul's dearest dream: that you and I and our love—all three of us—could be forever a romantic trio, in the prime and glory . . . *(Breaks down again, in sobs)* Oh, I *hate* mortality. *(Tormented by conflict; wavering between BURT and JASPER)* My soul goes out to Jasper. *(Suddenly apprehensively, as though struck by an awful thought)* Quick, let's save him! He could be dead by now, in his heroically foolhardy daring to tamper with Death's hold over life. Death could punish his meddling—by doling out a deal of itself that spells a finish to all of Jasper's life!

BURT: You're like Jasper—out of control. You and he rave wildly, in stark demons of imaginings. Let me caution you—as in vain I cautioned him—to level down your passionate peaks from that heady atmosphere where fulfillment frantically follows and tumbles in an agonized reeling intent to keep up with the spiral of inflated dreams, the balloon voyage from which fulfillment must bail out and plunge—parachuteless—to its absolute wreckage on the plains of hard sense.

GEORGIA: *(In final decision, resolution, and conviction)* Burt—our love is dead!

BURT: *(Alarmed)* No!—not that!

GEORGIA: *Jasper* shares my soul—you *never* can.

BURT: True, I *did* caution you to beware of similarity in romantic hysteria to his passionate derangement—

GEORGIA: *(In the process of getting out of bed)* Burt, he and I dare to dream. We brave the risk. We share great yearnings—loftily remote from the dreary banalities of your levelheadedness. My soul's true partner is Jasper. By describing your fateful discussion with him, you brought home the crucial differences—as I see them—between his great but flawed soul, and your impeccably realistic one cowardly bound by narrow duty to the surface safety of what's sensible and secure. *(Completes getting out of bed)*

BURT: *(Frozen in shock and disbelief, remains sitting up in bed as before, his horror turning to indignation)* Georgia, you're abandoning me, for a crazed soul whose ravings I took at length exacting trouble, on your demand, to relate to you. I set before you—in this very bed you've just quitted—my discussion, sparing no recall in that total debate, with a man stupid enough to question the unquestionable, confusing fantasy wish for practical desire, pushing past magic's illegal boundary with a serious actual hope to which no mortal, given the charter of our limitations and the off-limits nature of Death's unknowability, is entitled . . .

GEORGIA: *(Cutting in; hysterically babbling)* You're a strict stickler to danger's restrictions. But brave Jasper sets his heart, against whatever odds, beyond conventional prohibitions that threaten to banish him from society's timid respect to penalize his high-minded defiance of tame conformity's complacent code that serves reactionary realism's rigid doctrine of scared obedience to the numb pagan idol of Death.

BURT: *(In an urgent rush of common sense)* You're sentimentalizing courage. Jasper's pursuit of his "noble goal" is a rhetorical exercise in the art of complete idleness! Nor does he risk Death's wrath; since Death is not a deity or a person, but just Jasper's own future ceasing to be himself, the stopping of action in a body turned inert. *(Gets out of bed on the opposite side from which GEORGIA had got out and is now standing. They continue their argument standing on opposite sides of bed)* Our love was developed over a long time, in organic stress and trial. Now, in a wayward perversion and superstitious dread of Death, you toss aside our sacred love, and betray it, abandon me, to share the faith of Jasper's folly, in your protective dash of maternal pity for so vulnerably insane a self-proclaimed Saviour of scientific ineptitude.

GEORGIA: I follow my heart!

BURT: To the heartless betrayal of our long-developed love! But your cruelty sentimentalizes itself into irresponsibility, with staggering self-justification. You join Jasper's flight into Godliness, two fears of Death sublimated in a holy marriage of your spirits.

GEORGIA: He's the better man, Burt. By far. He looks far. You accept the mean near.

BURT: My dialogue with Jasper, on your request, was faithfully represented to you. You were my love when I began. My rendition is finished, and so is your love for me.

GEORGIA: *He* came to life—at your expense. Your reason paled to brittleness, while my heart went out to his soul that flowed free from the man-made manacles of petty reason that shackles itself to the miserable confines of reality in a voluntary laying down of liberty's priceless gift.

BURT: But Jasper isn't free—he's possessed! He's chained! He's deluded!

GEORGIA: He fights Death. Cravenly, you accept it.

BURT: He's *against* Death, but how can he fight it? It's unopposable. Cellular decay, deterioration, decomposition, stop at no theory, at no ideal, at no hope, in anyone's idle or resisting brain. Jasper's thoughts hardly delay Death's quite impersonal process in each specifically personal victim! Death is oblivious, in its innocent operations, to any such menace as Jasper; and is not the least deterred in its business of breaking down cellular vitality in all aging organisms.

GEORGIA: *(In finality and loathing)* Burt, you're a physical materialist. I hate to think that a body belonging to such a mind ever made love to mine. I'll purge your body from mine, in the violated shrine of my memory, by alliance with noble Jasper!

BURT: You forgot: he already loves and is loved—with Ginger.

GEORGIA: I'll easily relieve her of him. She's practical, realistic—*(Contemptibly)* like *you! I* merit him. As I've awakened from you, so will Jasper from Ginger, converting truly to me, in a match suitable to our shared yearning for eternal life in a love no less enduring.

BURT: *(Anguished)* No! Say you're joking: Put out this sudden nightmare, and let sensible light illumine our resumed sanity!

(Curtain, darkness. Then, after pause, Scene IV)

SCENE IV

(Setting is identical to that of previous scene just ended. BURT, in pajamas, and GEORGIA, in nightgown, are standing just as before, at opposite sides of bed)

BURT: *(Tense, anxious)* Having reversed your reversal, revised your revision, do you return to your senses, and to me?

GEORGIA: I "saw" you side by side with my new idol, when you recounted that fatal talk you had with him. Whether effectually or not, at least his *attitude* resists Death. His immortal vision, on behalf of us all, shames your shortsightedness. He's an aspiring God; while you're a clay longing to rejoin itself in the alumni reunion from nature's far-flung campus of dust.

BURT: *(With bitter sarcasm)* You and Jasper were made for each other, in a heaven of your own joint creating. Such an immortal union—shouldn't you hasten to inform Jasper? It will divert him from his idle, harmless pining for eternal life; or rather, add to that the extra incentive of an immortal love. Go and tell him the doubling of his endless horizons.

GEORGIA: The sarcasm *he* suffered from you, *I* now do.

BURT: Another bond in common!

GEORGIA: What your cynicism negates, his-and-my great and boundless faith shall restore—and more!

BURT: More and more, you're his. To my loss, I see how already joined you are, to him whose conversation with me—not knowing at what cost—I recounted to you. When you'd heard me out, you deliberated, wavered—but, drenched pale in Death's fear, you called *me* the coward, and superstitiously playing it safe *just in case* Jasper should possess the magic he claims, cravenly slunk over to him.

GEORGIA: I chose him *nobly* as, with clear rainbow sight, I would choose Infinity over the finite.

BURT: Murky, muddy sight! Fear-drenched!

GEORGIA: *His* sights dared an out-gazing duel—whatever the despair—with that grim antagonist, Death. Death was *his* antagonist; and *he* was *yours*. How could nobility but choose, when you set the comparison before me, and talked yourself out of my heart and him into it? For he faces Tragedy tragically: You've come peacefully to terms with it, with passivity I find unheroic.

BURT: He's a fighter? How does he fight Death?

GEORGIA: By mental opposition.

BURT: That's a losing battle.

GEORGIA: Better than no battle at all. Pacificism and acceptance earn you no hero's laurels.

BURT: Before you broke our love apart, I described my struggles to reason with a man long past reasoning. I failed to convince him that he'd gone too far in false thinking. Faithfully, I took pains to place before you an unequal argument on separate and unjoinable planes. For all my elaborate pains, you heaped on me the pain of losing you to one whose loss of reason won him the ache of your maternal sympathy, since his vain longing could only bring suffering. Idly he questions Death; you invent the danger that thereby he *courts* Death, whose malign revenge thrills you with romantic dread. You warm to his imagined boldness, and join the outrage of his delusion: outrage to rationality, and to me. I must stoically accept mortality; this to you seems cowardice. Mortality circumscribes our limits. It's excessive to expect to exceed what we can only heed, despite the cravings of a limitless will for a paradise of our own making—not making: devising; mental conjuring: the vain fop and folly of our hope.

GEORGIA: *(Blandly, with indisputable finality)* You're unsuitable to my new vision, which Jasper has inspired and awakened. I linger overlong with you; Jasper's wasted time with *his* wrong love, Ginger. As I unload you, Jasper will unload Ginger. Discordant unions need correcting. My match with Jasper needs confirming. I'll locate or phone him, to work it all out.

BURT: So Georgia—we're done?

GEORGIA: Goodbye, you defective man. I leave you to the lonely solace of your reason. Our love is now a warm corpse. In breath and beat of heart, our love has gone still. From this burial, a new love leaps for me: for Jasper, and his noble crusade to wage war in a holy match against Death, a mortal combat with me racing to be his ally or nurse or lieutenant or assistant, ministering to his distress or to his glory, in his unarmed fight to the very finish.

BURT: "Unarmed" is right. He'll prove a pushover for Death. *You'll* topple, alongside: the foolish warrior, and his silly bride.

> (GEORGIA, *having exchanged nightgown for street clothes, now exits.* BURT *is left standing there, sharply outlined in the shock of sudden loneliness, unloved. Curtain, darkness. Then, after pause, Scene V)*

SCENE V

> (JASPER *in pajamas, and* GINGER, *in nightgown, both sitting up in one bed, resembling the* BURT-GEORGIA *settings)*

JASPER: Ginger, Burt thinks I'm crazy.
GINGER: On what basis?
JASPER: That I want to end death.
GINGER: In that case—we're *all* crazy.
JASPER: But I'm serious.
GINGER: About what?
JASPER: Ending death: I want to find a way to do it.
GINGER: Then, Jasper, Burt is right.
JASPER: On what count?
GINGER: Indeed, he's right.
JASPER: How?
GINGER: You're crazy! Get out of my bed.
JASPER: But Ginger—don't you love me?
GINGER: Not if you're crazy.
JASPER: I'm *not* crazy. But I'm annoyed to be thought so by you. Our love was patiently built up over years. Now an issue has come on which

to sever our bond by driving home a basic incompatibility. You and I agree on only one thing: to part. To that extent, our love harmoniously ends. *(Had been getting out of bed. Puts outdoor clothes on and stomps out)*

GINGER: *(Remains alone sitting up in bed, pleased to be rid of the man she's so disenchanted with)* I'm a realist. It's unreasonable to try to end Death. What was I doing, loving him all this time? It was crazy of me. But I kicked him out, and am happily rational now. Next man, I'll know better.

> *(She gets out of bed, puttering about. Exchanges nightgown for day clothes. After a while, phone rings)*

GINGER: Hello? Oh, it's Burt. Jasper was telling me you thought he was crazy. I asked him why, and when he told me why, *I* also accused him of craziness, and the altercation proved fatal to our love. We broke up, he walked out, we're through. You and I, Burt, are realists: passively resigned, fortified by stoical reasoning, to Death's ultimate, future, inevitably impending, conclusively unconquerable eventuality. *(Listens silently on phone, with a gradually appearing smile)* Your Georgia sympathized with Jasper, so she and you ended your love and broke up? She's going to exchange you for Jasper in her new-fledged heart? Earlier, she would have had to fight me to take Jasper away. But as I've kicked him out, I've left him free to be plucked up easily by her. They deserve each other, it's a fitting match of irrationals. *(Listens silently on phone, her smile increasingly gleeful)* All that's left, dear old Burt, now that *we're* each newly rid of respective mates suddenly discovered to be defective of reason, is for us, now that we've both unlumbered ourselves—or been unlumbered—of loves abruptly grown incompatible, to . . . Oh Burt! I finally realize! It should *always* have been you! We . . .

> *(Listens silently, in enraptured bliss. She turns her face—*

still listening—to the audience, and makes the ecstatic pucker of a tangible, imagined kiss. Her face glows, beams, in the exquisite delirium of new love's fiery, ascending dawn.)

(Curtain, darkness. Then, after pause, Scene VI)

SCENE VI

(Much time seems to have gone by. JASPER *in pajamas, and* GEORGIA, *in nightgown, sitting up in one bed, resembling previous* GEORGIA-BURT *and* JASPER-GINGER *scenes. However, this short, final scene gradually gets darker and darker—without getting too dark—until final, abrupt, total blackness in which play is to suddenly end)*

GEORGIA: When will it be? It should be before we're too old.

JASPER: It'll come! It'll come!

GEORGIA: Hurry! We're getting old!

JASPER: Death's end comes of its own accord. By voluntary will, I'm powerless to hasten it.

GEORGIA: Our love mustn't go the dwindling way of our flesh. Spare us! *Meet* this Death, and slay him!

JASPER: *(Irritated, admonishing)* For that, grant me peace. Across great Darkness, encountering terrors that belong only to the Unknown, double-mounted on one slow steed of Love, we travel in quest of timelessness. Suspend your breath. Stop your heart. We're not in this bedroom. We're lost directionless, and hand in our senses, abandon them . . .

GEORGIA: *(Alarmed)* It should be the *other* way: brighter! more vivid!

JASPER: *(In comparison with* GEORGIA: *gravely, slowly, wonderingly, discoveringly)* Hush up your interference! Ordinary expectations don't apply here. Stop preparing. Abandon habitual logic. We're in a worldlessness. It's beginning to envelop us. No more mental "moaning," now. We're coming into word-lessness.

GEORGIA: *(Half-shrieking)* I'll quit! I back out! Is there no will left?!

JASPER: *(Slow tempo, gravely)* Are we there? My final feeling is only familiar fear.

GEORGIA: Have you won? Or lost?

JASPER: It's *"we"*—in *either* case.

GEORGIA: *(Ordering)* Define our state!

JASPER: No definitions ease this complete change. It's beyond our figuring out. We're converted into sound-lessness. What *we* are . . . is only what we *were*. *(Pause)* Something we've never been without, is stopping: It's what we knew as . . . "Now."

GEORGIA: Am I deceived? You fraud or saint! Am I unforgiving—or grateful? I insist I be told! This loyalty I invested . . . What returns on our faith? *(Slight pause)* How did we come out?

(Total blackness, with total stillness: Play ends)

PHONIES

Characters:

MEL: Friend of ROGER
ROGER: Friend of MEL
HENRIETTA: Friend of ALICE
ALICE: Friend of HENRIETTA

ACT ONE

SCENE I

(ROGER *and* MEL *are standing up, indoors or outdoors somewhere, but in very dim light*)

ROGER: I'm the completely modern man, in every respect.

MEL: Then you've left your sense of tradition behind—if you ever did have it.

ROGER: Tradition is behind the times.

MEL: Is that any excuse for ignoring it?

ROGER: I've traditionally ignored it.

MEL: Then what's going on *now?*

(*On cue with the word "now?," stage is suddenly bathed in light, to visibly make the preceding lines a preamble, while the following lines introduce the main theme*)

ROGER: I'm determined to become a real writer.

MEL: What will you write?

ROGER: Not a thing. *(Taking a "pose")* I'm going to *be* a writer.

MEL: How can you assume the *identity* of a writer, without earning it by working at words and piling up an output of written pages to show for it?

ROGER: If by that standard is to *honestly* come by the title, the role, the mantle, of "writer"—then I'll bypass that *honest* deserving of the name of "writer," by deviously cutting across the work output requirement and simply *calling* myself a "writer."

MEL: Will you get away with it?

ROGER: It will be my secret, hidden social affectation. People will take me at face value, will take my *word* for it—especially as the *word* is what the writer is all about.

MEL: But then *(With contemptuous disrespect)*—you'd be a phony!

ROGER: But I won't *appear* to be one. In social life, I'll play the role of a *genuine* artist—that is, writer—all the more convincingly: in that directly to *act* like a writer, and to *present* myself as one, will get all my attention: undiverted, undistracted, by the private bother and boredom of *trying to write,* itself. Unimpeded by *trying to write,* I'll be free to concentrate on all the social appearance props, trappings, dress, hairstyle, posture, accent, of a genuine-seeming "writer."

MEL: *(With the patience of superior logic)* I hate to ruin your scheme, but all writers look different and act different from each other: Different accents, different manners, different backgrounds, different eccentricities, even different ways of being *conventional.*

ROGER: But I'll bypass, cut through, all those differences, by becoming the rounded out *consensus* representation that averages out the ideal blending, into the very image of *The* Writer, the true pure type of the *writer himself,* distilled from the odd assortment of miscellaneous types, the mishmash of examples all combining into me, as the living image of what ideally the writer *ought* to look like, act like, talk like, and seem to be.

MEL: *(Morally appalled)* Without writing a single word?!

ROGER: I'm above that. *Being* a writer, I'm absolved from mere craftsmanship. I'm too true-to-type, to fuss with technical stuff.

MEL: *(Suspiciously probing)* Your ulterior motive?

ROGER: *(Letting his hair down, making a clean breast, in confiding tones of a confession)* Look Mel, I'm poor, I've got no good job prospects, I'm not qualified for any proud professional career. I need to marry a rich woman. *Some* rich women go for writer types. That's my ticket, to love and financial security.

MEL: *(Morally relieved)* Finally, your phoniness can be seen in a sympathetic light. Now, there's a sensible *reason* for your phoniness. At last, you've become *authentic*. *(With false humility or modesty, ROGER bows to acknowledge MEL's praise)*

(Blackness, end of Scene)

SCENE II

(HENRIETTA—in cheap clothes, bearing-marks of poverty—and ALICE, seated in living room setting)

HENRIETTA: I'm tired of being poor. I grew up poor in a poor household with poor parents. No wonder I developed a fantasy for rich taste.

ALICE: *(Sympathetically)* I'm not the least bit surprised. How do you propose to compensate?

HENRIETTA: I want to marry a rich man—but not *any* rich man. I go for literary types. I'd like to admire a real writer.

ALICE: But what does marrying a rich man have to do with admiring a real writer?

HENRIETTA: Simple! If a writer is a *real writer*, he's going to be a very rich man!

ALICE: *(Partly disbelieving)* Both?!

HENRIETTA: I'll marry both of them, by marrying the same man.

ALICE: That's old-fashioned monogamy. Also economical.

HENRIETTA: No, not economical, but extravagant. His wealth will easily afford my most extravagant dreams, while his being a real writer will wildly gratify my cultural snobbery.

ALICE: Have your cake while eating it too?

HENRIETTA: Cake is a poor metaphor. Better make it imported Russian caviar, rare lobster soufflé, melted pearls of oyster, and century-old champagne from the fortified vaults of a gentlemen's monastery!

ALICE: You dream: How can you—look at you—*(They both contemplate HENRIETTA's appearance)*—dressed virtually in rags—hope to procure a proposal in marriage from such a paragon mongrel of wealth and literary authenticity?

HENRIETTA: A real writer is, Freudianly-speaking, basically insecure. Even though I'm only a wretched, obscure, ill-paid librarian, I'll pretend to be the wealthy queen of the psychoanalysts!

ALICE: How? Your clothing is too poor for such a disguise.

HENRIETTA: *(Cunning)* Are you my friend?

ALICE: *(Suspicious)* Yes, but why?

HENRIETTA: *(Boldly)* Withdraw your savings account, lend it to me, I'll buy clothes befitting the wealthy queen of the psychoanalysts, by being which I'll lure a marriage proposal by a rich man who's really a real writer!

ALICE: But if he's a real writer, will he really be a rich man?

HENRIETTA: Listen to reason! A real writer gets tons of publicity. The promotion department works overtime in desperation to recoup at least the advance of the tremendous contract the publisher was forced by the real writer's agent to fork out. A whole sales force stocks bookshop shelves with identical copies of the real writer's masterpiece. It's a raging hit. It's but one step from fame to wealth. How's that for power?

ALICE: But do you already love him?

HENRIETTA: Completely! But I'll act cool, and play hard to get. That'll make him wild to win me!

ALICE: *(Won over)* I can see that your intentions are sincere. As your friend, I'll withdraw my bank account so that you can enough resemble the wealthy queen of the psychoanalysts to appeal to the basic Freudian insecurity of a real writer's wealth that derives from the frantic fortunes of fabulous fame—rather than the *inherited* fortune of a settled family income, which makes for such emotional stability and peaceful inner security that there's nothing to be remedied, even by the most persistent psychoanalyst.

HENRIETTA: Thanks. When I marry him, I'll pay you back in triplicate.

ALICE: I find your loyalty generous to a fault.

HENRIETTA: Not to a fault: to *you*—who are faultless in your initial outlay of generosity! *(They embrace, sobbing emotionally, then break apart to dry out their eyes)*

ALICE: *(Suddenly)* But Henrietta—*I* need love, too.

(Pause)

HENRIETTA: *(Conspicuously thinking, to solve the problem; then:)* I have it! The perfect solution!

ALICE: *(Eager)* Really?! Who?!

HENRIETTA: My rich-man real-writer will have a friend—just like *I* have *you* for a friend. Well, you and that friend—

ALICE: That's perfect! Two friendships, two love matches, and two marriages!

HENRIETTA: All from the same four people! And we're two of them!

ALICE: Oh, what divine symmetry! Such a perfect pattern seems too artistic to be real.

HENRIETTA: It's both artistic *and* real.

ALICE: *(Awed)* What an ideal combination—artistic and real!

HENRIETTA: Yet, this is no dream.

ALICE: *(Slowly, in a dream-resembling trance)* No? Prove it!

HENRIETTA: *(In contrast, vigorously practical, taking charge)* Prove it to yourself! The very act of withdrawing your life savings will have a sobering and down-to-earth effect on you. Get your bankbook, darling. *(Consults watch)* We still have time to trot over to your bank, and give them a shock. The shock will wake *you* up, too. How's that, for a dream-cure?

ALICE: *(Blinking—caught between dream and real)* Then—this is real?

HENRIETTA: Yes, leading to love and marriage for us both.

ALICE: *(In a semi-swoon or trance)* But is love ... truly real?

HENRIETTA: *(In contrast, level-headed, tough-minded)* That's what we're about to find out. But first find your bankbook. *(Consults watch)* It's near the closing hour.

ALICE: *(Suddenly curious)* Since the bank is open, why aren't you working in your library?

HENRIETTA: I've just been laid off. What perfect timing! *(They trot off to Alice's bank)*

(Blackness, end of Scene)

SCENE III

(At a party. Setting full of clothed, gesture-frozen dummies sprinkled in clusters as party guests. MEL and ALICE have just met)

MEL: I'm Mel, and I'm the friend of a real writer!

ALICE: *(On her guard; dubious, skeptical)* Are you? That *seems* like impressive credentials, but I warn you—I'm not easily fooled by name-dropping.

MEL: *(Outraged, defensive)* It's true! The real writer actually *is* my friend!

ALICE: *(Still eyeing him suspiciously; suddenly issuing a challenge)* In that case, let me test your truthfulness—what's his name?!

MEL: Roger! *(Pause; tentatively triumphant)* Is that proof enough?

ALICE: *(Giving nothing away)* Perhaps. *(Competitively boastful)* My friend, though she may not be a real writer, is something much more than that!

MEL: *(Competitively, defiantly)* Look who's putting on airs!?

ALICE: You don't believe me? You've just met me, and already I'm a liar?!

MEL: *(Combative)* Convince me to the contrariwise!

ALICE: *(In fury)* Is that a direct challenge?!

MEL: I'm not being coy! I'm not flirting!

ALICE: Not flirting! But why are we suddenly arguing?

(Music and light change come on, appropriate to following development)

MEL: Because impulsively—

ALICE: Waywardly—

MEL: Quite without warning—

ALICE: Unpredictably—

MEL: Spontaneously—

ALICE: Instantaneously—

MEL: Most suddenly—

ALICE AND MEL TOGETHER: But mutually—

ALICE: We love—

MEL: Each other!

(As music reaches peak; they clinch the foregoing in the impassioned ferocity of an embrace, in the middle of the party—peopled by clothed dummies—where they've just met)

(Blackness, end of Scene)

SCENE IV

(A few nights later. MEL and ALICE, holding hands like a dearly devoted, courting couple, sitting close together on her parlor room sofa. Setting looks seedy, down-at-heels)

MEL: *(Looking about)* Your clothes as well as this whole apartment look tatty, seedy, threadworn, in the downward spiral of impoverishment.

ALICE: Thank you for your candid criticism. Though short on compliments, you're long on honesty.

MEL: You orally gave me your employment record, your resumé or curriculum vitae. The wages you've earned have been sufficient over the last few years to enable both you and your apartment to look at least respectable. Where, then, has your money disappeared to?

ALICE: *(Simply)* I loaned my life savings to my friend.

MEL: The friend who you boasted was something much more than *my* friend, even though I dropped the name of my friend as being a real writer? *(ALICE nods)* But *why* is she much more than the real writer that *my* friend is? And if she's that much more, I find it impossible to believe that she needed to borrow your life savings.

ALICE: She only *pretends* to be great. She's really only actually poor. For her to pretend to be great, I had to lend her my life savings.

MEL: How sacrificially loyal of you, what devotion your friendship shows! Specifically, what is she pretending to be?

ALICE: The wealthy queen of the psychoanalysts.

MEL: That's her pose? To what purpose?

ALICE: To lure a real writer who's also a rich man, into courtship and marriage, since a real writer, being basically insecure by way of Freudian orthodoxy, automatically needs both psychoanalysis and love. Falsely glorified as the wealthy queen of the psychoanalysts, my friend hopes to cure, at one stroke, her poverty, her loneliness, and the non-realization of her acute cultural snobbery.

MEL: *(Kissing ALICE)* How clever! I have just the man for her!

ALICE: You mentioned, when we met at the party, quite boastfully that your friend—whom you name-dropped to be Roger—is a real writer; to complete the package deal, is he also necessarily rich?

MEL: *(Warring between wanting to tell the truth to his love, and wanting to lie to loyally protect his friend ROGER's disguise; finally solving the conflict with this equivocation:)* To the extent that he's a real writer, so is he also a rich man.

ALICE: That completes the ideal qualification combination to render him suitably eligible to woo, court, and contract a marital match with Henrietta—who's *my* friend.

MEL: The one you loaned your life savings to, so that she could phonily pose with appropriate clothes as the living incarnation true to the role of the actual genuine article as the wealthy queen of the psychoanalysts?

ALICE: The very one! Her pose would be therapeutic and romantic, not to mention monetary, *bait*, to exploit the vulnerably basic insecurity of a real writer who's a rich man: bait to catch and land him, under fraudulent pretenses, as her prize financial, cultural, and amorous acquisition, to cure her of poverty, snobbery-frustration, and the aching void of inner loneliness.

MEL: How diabolically clever of this scheming Henrietta! *(Protectively:)* Then she'd repay you for the loan of your whole life savings?

ALICE: *(Naively and loyally boasting)* And generously so—in triplicate!

MEL: You're a fool. You'll never see that money again.

ALICE: You mean your friend Roger isn't rich? Is *he* an imposter, too? He's neither a real writer nor a rich man, but only setting himself up as such so as to snare a poor, unsuspecting rich woman?

MEL: Yes, such as *your* friend!

ALICE: *(Accusing)* You've been legally protecting hie pose—and lying to me!

MEL: *(Counter-accusing)* How disloyal of you to *your* friend, to expose *her* pose!

ALICE: I chose to betray her, in truth and fidelity to *you:* love's priority over old friendship.

MEL: *(Guilty)* You've found me out. I *had* intended to protect him. *(More boldly:)* But let me defend Roger, at your Henrietta's expense. *(Defiantly:)* At least he never asked me to lend him *my* life savings, to finance the crass immorality of his subtle deception in counterfeit guise in assuming the entirely bogus identity and crooked posturing as a real writer who doubles simultaneously as a rich man to breathlessly combine, in one peerless role, the successfully ideal with the ideally successful, reconciling the creatively pure and the worldly powerful at the same supreme stroke!

ALICE: By tempting coincidence, your Roger's masterful status pose embraces the actual qualities in a man that my Henrietta, via *her* elaborate disguise and crooked design, looks to hook.

MEL: That coincidence *is* tempting. We must loyally restrain ourselves from maliciously bringing about an introduction, which would be self-defeating—though deservedly so—for them both.

ALICE: We must keep them apart. In trying to fool each other to become rich at each other's expense, the fiasco would leave them even poorer than before, in that they'd squander sorely needed money in attempting to gull and beguile.

MEL: *(Laughing maliciously)* Double duping, double duplicity! It's too pathetic: two dopes in their desperate plight, plotting to plunder and exploit.

ALICE: *(Enjoying the idea)* Too comically hilarious! But remember, as their friends, we must restrain ourselves from the temptation maliciously—*(Giving way:)* oh so deliciously—to introduce them!

MEL: *(Warming to the kill)* Those scheming devils!—it would serve them right!

ALICE: *(More compassionate: Vehemently resisting temptation)* We'll *not* stage their meeting—*no!*

MEL: *(Reluctantly half-agreeing)* We'll protect those two would-be victimizers from the reverse fate of becoming victims!

ALICE: *(Also warming to the kill)* At each other's hands! Oh, what poetic justice!

MEL: *(Giving in to the idea)* What play, to make them mutual prey to their worthless wiles!

ALICE: Is it worth our whiles?

MEL: What fun!

ALICE: *(Viciously)* Let's! *(They embrace, with vicious, wicked grins)*

(Blackness, curtain. End of Act I)

ACT TWO

SCENE I

(ROGER (who's made himself into ideal embodiment of the real writer who's also a rich man) and MEL, seated in MEL's apartment)

ROGER: She's the real one?

MEL: According to her friend, yes.

ROGER: She's likely to go for a real writer who's also a rich man?

MEL: Your phony pose would powerfully appeal to her.

ROGER: But as the wealthy queen of the psychoanalysts—wouldn't her special training and professional experience enable her to see through even my tightly woven disguise?

MEL: I thought of mentioning that very scruple myself to her friend my loved one, namely Alice.

ROGER: *(Suspiciously)* And what did Alice reply?

MEL: That the wealthy queen of the psychoanalysts—namely Henrietta—will lose her critical skepticism and analytical insight in the process of falling madly in love with the man of her dreams, which specify that he be a real writer and also a rich man. Her dreams thus play directly into your cleverly prepared hands. She'll serve you well, by conjugal and financial slavery.

ROGER: *(Ecstatically)* I refuse to believe what incredible luck this is! My thickly laid plot has actually worked!

MEL: *(Suavely)* Not so fast! May I caution you that you haven't as yet even *met* your victim?

ROGER: *(Buoyantly, expansively, optimistically)* A mere formality! You and your love, her friend, being in on my scheme, are setting this up for me. What's your scenario, in arranging this delicately casual, seemingly unrehearsed meeting? As you can see *(Primps himself, posturing and posing)*, I'm dressed for the kill. If she finds "a real writer who's also a rich man" irresistible, then I've won the day, and will be secure for life.

MEL: Here's how my love (her friend) and I propose you go about this. On being introduced, gaze longingly *(Illustrates this in comical exaggerated melodrama)* into Henrietta's eyes, and make this prepared speech: "Henrietta, I'm not only pleased to meet you, but refuse ever to part from you."

ROGER: Isn't that set speech too pat, or rather forwardly premature? I don't want to come on too strong too soon.

MEL: Trust my love, her friend... *(ALICE enters)*... here she comes—hello! *(MEL goes over and hugs ALICE)*

ROGER: *(Eyeing their embrace enviously)* I envy you, Mel. You already possess your Alice, while I haven't even yet met my own dear to be, my intended by destiny and you: Henrietta.

ALICE: *(To ROGER)* So you're the Roger my Mel speaks so loyally of! Your friend has convinced me to help all I can—you being a poor man and not a real writer—to convince my friend Henrietta that in both cases you're stunningly the opposite of what you truly only humbly are. This campaign will win you the following: a rich woman, to cure your poverty forever; and a free psychoanalyst, to cure your basic insecurity that your disguise is supposed to indicate; and—in the bargain—undying love, to cure you of chronic loneliness.

ROGER: *(To ALICE)* Alice, well met! I'm already up to my neck in debt of gratitude for your kind assistance in pulling off my shrewd design.

ALICE: Did Mel rehearse you what to say, once the introduction to Henrietta takes place?

ROGER: *(With difficulty, concentrating on recalling; then:)* Mel said I'm to say: "Henrietta, I'm not only pleased to meet you, but refuse ever to part from you."

ALICE: *(Lightly applauding)* Neatly memorized! That'll win her!

ROGER: But Alice—I already voiced this doubt to Mel: Isn't that set speech too pat, or rather forwardly premature? I don't want to come on too strong too soon.

MEL: *(Scolding ROGER)* And I already told you to trust Alice! She knows the right strategy that'll work on her longstanding friend, Henrietta!

ALICE: *(Severely, to ROGER)* Do as I say! You stand to gain!

ROGER: *(Contrite)* I won't question you further. But when do I meet Henrietta?

ALICE: *(Solemnly)* The fatal evening is all set up. Firmly act the role of a real writer who's also a rich man!

ROGER: *(Earnestly)* I've so taken on that role in full sincerity of absolutely genuine affectation, that my well-studied falseness will seem totally natural!

MEL: *(Warning)* We don't want your *falseness* to be natural, but your *pose* to be natural.

ROGER: Whether it is natural or not, I guarantee it to *seem* natural!

ALICE: Honestly?

ROGER: *(Swearing)* Honestly!

MEL: *(Throwing up his hands in disgust)* All this integrity is killing me! I long for a slice of cynicism!

(Blackness, end of Scene)

SCENE II

(HENRIETTA *(who's made herself into ideal embodiment of the wealthy queen of the psychoanalysts) and* ALICE, *seated in* ALICE's *seedy, poor-looking apartment)*

HENRIETTA: He's the real one?

ALICE: According to his friend, yes.

HENRIETTA: He's likely to go for *(Self-consciously primping herself)* the wealthy queen of the psychoanalysts?

ALICE: Your phony pose would powerfully appeal to him.

HENRIETTA: But as a real writer who's also a rich man—wouldn't his special training and professional experience enable him to see through even my tightly woven disguise?

ALICE: I thought of mentioning that very scruple myself to his friend my loved one, namely Mel.

HENRIETTA: *(Suspiciously)* And what did Mel reply?

ALICE: That the real writer who's also a rich man—namely Roger—will lose his critical skepticism and analytical insight in the process of falling madly in love with the woman of his dreams, which specify that she be the wealthy queen of the psychoanalysts. His dreams thus play directly into your cleverly prepared hands. He'll serve you well, by conjugal and financial slavery.

HENRIETTA: *(Ecstatic)* I refuse to believe what incredible luck this is! My thickly laid plot has actually worked!

ALICE: *(Suavely)* Not so fast! May I caution you that you haven't as yet even *met* your victim?

HENRIETTA: *(Buoyantly, expansively, optimistically)* A mere formality! You and your love, his friend, being in on my scheme, are setting this up for me. What's your scenario, in arranging this delicately casual, seemingly unrehearsed meeting? As you can see *(Primps herself, posturing and posing)*, I'm dressed—thanks to the loan of your life savings—for the kill. If he finds "the wealthy queen of the psychoanalysts" irresistible, then I've won the day, and will be secure for life.

ALICE: Here's how my love (his friend) and I propose you go about this. On being introduced, gaze longingly *(Illustrates this in comical exaggerated melodrama)* into Roger's eyes, and make this prepared speech: "Roger, I'm not only pleased to meet you, but refuse ever to part from you."

HENRIETTA: Isn't that set speech too pat, or rather forwardly premature? I don't want to come on too strong too soon.

ALICE: Trust my love, her friend . . . *(MEL enters)* . . . here he comes—hello! *(ALICE goes over and hugs MEL)*

HENRIETTA: *(Eyeing their embrace enviously)* I envy you, Alice. You already possess your Mel, while I haven't even yet met my own dear to be, my intended by destiny and you: Roger.

MEL: *(To HENRIETTA)* So you're the Henrietta my Alice speaks so loyally of, and loaned her life savings to! Your friend has convinced me to help all I can—you being (aside from the loan of her life savings) a poor woman, an ill-paid librarian recently laid off—to help all I can to convince my friend Roger that you're in stunning, glamorous, opulent contrast to what you truly only humbly are. This campaign will win you the following: a rich man, to cure your poverty forever; and a real writer, to satisfy your cultural snobbery; and—in the bargain—undying love, to cure you of chronic loneliness.

HENRIETTA: *(To MEL)* Mel, well met! I'm already up to my neck in debt of gratitude for your kind assistance in pulling off my shrewd design.

MEL: Did Alice rehearse you what to say, once the introduction to Roger takes place?

HENRIETTA: *(With difficulty, concentrating on recalling; then:)* Alice said I'm to say: "Roger, I'm not only pleased to meet you, but refuse ever to part from you."

MEL: *(Lightly applauding)* Neatly memorized! That'll win him!

HENRIETTA: But Mel—I already voiced this doubt to Alice: Isn't that set speech too pat, or rather forwardly premature? I don't want to come on too strong too soon.

ALICE: *(Scolding HENRIETTA)* And I already told you to trust Mel! He knows the right strategy that'll work on his longstanding friend, Roger!

MEL: *(Severely, to HENRIETTA)* Do as I say! You stand to gain!

HENRIETTA: *(Contrite)* I won't question you further. But when do I meet Roger?

MEL: *(Solemnly)* The fatal evening is all set up. Firmly act the role of the wealthy queen of the psychoanalysts!

HENRIETTA: *(Earnestly)* I've so taken on that role in full sincerity of absolutely genuine affection, that my well-studied falseness will seem totally natural!

ALICE: *(Warning)* We don't want your *falseness* to be natural, but your *pose* to be natural.

HENRIETTA: Whether it *is* natural or not, I guarantee it to *seem* natural!

MEL: Honestly?

HENRIETTA: *(Swearing)* Honestly!

ALICE: *(Throwing up her hands in disgust)* All this integrity is killing me! I long for a slice of cynicism!

(Blackness, end of Scene)

SCENE III

(At a party. Setting full of clothed, gesture-frozen dummies sprinkled in clusters as party-guests. Set is identical to that of Act I, Scene III, in which MEL and ALICE had just met. This time, MEL and ALICE are introducing ROGER and HENRIETTA.)

(ROGER looks every inch the perfect image of a real writer who's also a rich man. HENRIETTA, in her turn, looks every inch the perfect image of the wealthy queen of the psychoanalysts. Their assumed identities are enacted with naturalness and conviction.)

(MEL and ALICE have just made the introductions; then, stealthily disappear into clusters of party-guest dummies while following is recited:)

ROGER: *(Simultaneously with HENRIETTA's words)* Henrietta, I'm not only pleased to meet you, but refuse ever to part from you.

HENRIETTA: *(Simultaneously with ROGER's words)* Roger, I'm not only pleased to meet you, but refuse ever to part from you.

ROGER AND HENRIETTA: *(Simultaneously)* But those are my lines!

(ROGER and HENRIETTA look about for MEL and ALICE, but latter pair have meanwhile disappeared into the

clusters of party-guest dummies)

HENRIETTA: Were you prompted, cued, rehearsed, to recite by rote those lines so pat? Was it a set-up?

ROGER: I might as easily ask you the very same thing.

HENRIETTA: *(Suspicious)* Although you certainly *look* the part, to flawless and faultless perfection—is this a ruse, a con-job? Are you only a poseur?

ROGER: I might as easily ask you the very same thing.

HENRIETTA: You're not what our friends assured me you are?

ROGER: No more than *you're* what they assured me *you* are.

HENRIETTA: Then we're both just as poor as before.

ROGER: But you borrowed your friend's life savings.

HENRIETTA: A mere pittance, compared with what I had hoped, by that capital outlay, to gain by winning the alleged prize of you in a marriage far above my pre-pretense rank.

ROGER: *I'd* expected to raise my fortunes to a magical magnitude by marrying—far above my station—you, were you only what you were promised to be by those now fled.

HENRIETTA: Having intended to dupe each other, we've been, instead, duped by our friends *(Looking about)* who, when now we wish to confront them on their treacherous prank of malice, have, in cowardly deceit, vanished away.

ROGER: *(Depressed)* I'm back, most dismally, where I started from.

HENRIETTA: *(Sadly)* So am I—and I've almost already spent that loan of my friend's life savings, on this *(Indicating her get-up)*, my trumped-up security-allure.

ROGER: Our desperation sadly slumps into despair.

HENRIETTA: Yet, at least, we've met.

ROGER: *(With irony)* But we don't even love each other!

HENRIETTA: Not even *that* consolation. Our friends, who didn't need that consolation, have lucked upon, almost gratuitously, the rare gift of love.

ROGER: And where are *we*?

HENRIETTA: Stuffed into our masks.

ROGER: Retaining counterfeit to our disguises, we're forced now to seek in some other victims what we find so disappointingly absent in each other . . .

HENRIETTA: We know each other all too well . . .

ROGER: Too easily, we see through . . .

HENRIETTA: Despite such gleaming opulence of magnificence, such cunning show, such overwhelming front, such seductive snare of presentation, such glitter impressively propped up to predatory appeal, pumped full of brazen hustle to artificially conceal the monstrous deception of our immorality! The ugly pretense of phony glory! It's wicked of us!

ROGER: Our true selves pant, choked and strangled, under all our overlay.

HENRIETTA: *(Wincing in pain)* This sounds just too dreadful. Shall we reform?

ROGER: *(Decisively)* On what income?

(Darkness, end of Scene)

SCENE IV

(Same party setting as previous Scene, with dummies, etc.)

ALICE: *(Looking)* Look—they're approaching us.

MEL: *(Looking)* We're easy to spot, now that we've come out of hiding from among these dummy-like party guests.

ALICE: *(Looking)* I've noticed something.

MEL: What?

ALICE: They look like they let themselves be fooled by each other.

MEL: Maybe it's an act—to fool *us*.

ALICE: That would be vengeance. But maybe they don't suspect us.

MEL: If we keep our wits alert, we'll find out in three seconds.

> *(ROGER and HENRIETTA, in unified front, come up to MEL and ALICE)*

ALICE: Is this a confrontation?

HENRIETTA: Yes. It didn't work.

MEL: But you looked like you let yourselves be fooled by each other.

ROGER: That was to lull *you*—so you wouldn't run away a second time.

ALICE: Well, it's only harmless. To tickle your phony bones.

HENRIETTA: The fact is—my loan of your life savings has almost run out, and here I am, as poor as before.

ROGER: Me too. I couldn't victimize poor Henrietta—and she's *literally* poor; nor am I *her* choice victim. We each need to pounce on new prey.

MEL: You're both unrepentant—down to your phony bones?

ROGER: We're too poor to afford repentance, just yet. Can you suggest—while we're still in the splendor of our counterfeit outfits and well-practiced in complete identity poses—a more likely couple of victims richly gullible, more fit to fool?

ALICE: *(Severely; morally superior)* We're not normally in the supplying nor procuring racket, to aid and abet immoral get-rich schemes, providing unsuspecting prey to nibble and gorge on such succulent bait and richly laid trap, a cunning con game for those vulnerably lonely in all the innocence of exposed wealth.

HENRIETTA: *(Accusing both ALICE and MEL)* You prim and prissy prigs! Righteous in rectitude, now that, having found that primary good of goods, *Love*—you're above mere money-greed, for which you scorn Roger and me to our hopeless shame!?

ROGER: *(Also accusing both MEL and ALICE)* You found love in each other, by using Henrietta and me as conversation ammunition! We're all tied together, in uneven debts—tangible, intangible, unaccountable . . . You two are joined in love. Separately, apart, Henrietta and I have our greedy ways to make, to return investments on deeply falsified identity guises.

HENRIETTA: *(In increasingly orotund tones of solemn pronouncement and deeply stiff formality)* Let us four now part in three ways. Alice and Mel most fortunately *together*. And Roger to seek *his* fortune, and I *mine*. At an assigned time, we'll take reunion: to settle what our fates will become; and square off uneven debts and recriminations; to rectify two friendships' temporary ruin; and tell tales of predatory money ventures, exploitative fortune seeking, utilizing false identities to wrench security and love from the cold, withheld, frozen odds all randomly chanced in the world's depressed marketplace.

>   *(The MEL-ALICE pair, and ROGER separately, and HENRIETTA separately, bow stiffly and formally to each other, increasingly like automated, mechanized puppets—or like the stiff, surrounding, frozen-gestured dummies which represent the other party-guests. Play ends with still tableau effect of the four actors almost indistinguishable from—having by magical stage effect practically merged with—those surrounding dummies.)*

SPIRITUALISTICALLY PREDESTINED JUDY, YES, BUT WHICH ONE
or Love Naturally Feeds in Its Difficulty

Characters:

    LES
    JUDY
    The same actor or two actors may play all the following, each in turn:
    MAN I
    MAN II
    FORTUNE TELLER
    MALE SURVIVING RELATIVE OF FORTUNE TELLER
    SEANCE PARLOR PROPRIETOR AND PERFORMER
    FORTUNE TELLER'S GHOST
    FORTUNE TELLER II

ACT ONE

SCENE I

(Scene: Somewhere)

MAN I: *(Desperately, nervously eager)* Judy, do you love me?

JUDY: Not enough. Otherwise, you wouldn't have to ask, so pleadingly, the question with the touch of desperate eagerness on the edge of your nervous voice. You've pushed me, and the issue, up against the wall into a corner; and spoiled the equality of our mystery between us, by forcing and driving, and so losing the fascinating distance of your calmness. *(Decisively:)* Having now lost all interest in you romantically, I reject you out of hand, spurn you, and dismiss you.

MAN I: *(Stung)* Ouch, it hurts. *(Posingly pretending:)* Well, I don't care the least. I declare, lest you suppose I bear a hurt and wounded self-esteem, that it's your loss. I wasn't even trying to win our love.

JUDY: Liar!

> *(MAN I, dropping his pretense-pose, leaves, dejected and defeated, head hung low. JUDY is left alone on stage)*

JUDY: *(Solo; facing audience, addressing it frankly and confidingly)* I'm lonely. I must have driven that man away.

Was I committing romantic suicide? No, since I didn't find him sufficiently interesting to have enough patience to stay with him long enough to give him enough of a chance so that I could find out if I really cared enough to develop a fascination in him to balance out intriguingly the love contest between how much he hopes from me and how much I hope from him, at stake in the weighing future.

Now I'm free. The world in my available local environment continues to have a countless unknown number of potentially thrillingly available if not eligible, willing if not suitable, men in it: for me by chance or wicked design to encounter, to meet, to run into, in all sorts of socially exciting situations in a succession of occasions with open possibilities in my personal history of prospects for love in the immediate future.

(Self-consciously preening, assessing and confirming, in looking herself over, her pretty attractiveness:) Wouldn't I make someone a good companion?

(Wiggling self-approvingly:) I'm in no condition, or position, to doubt it.

However, I'm alone. Valuable time is going by; I'm getting older. I don't want the crucial drama of my youth to rush withering away on an aging vine. I want to give opportunities for those who deserve me to be lucky enough to have a chance of winning me. The reward for the most deserving eligible candidate for my affections and devotion will be—my affections and devotion. The tournament is open for the competition—who's suitable to enter the field? I'll expose myself with semi-difficult availability to test the field of entries in the competition for me, and give the most likely a sporting or an outside chance to win me (—against a field of odds that he'll narrow down gallantly in his own puffing favor —) as his own dear and difficultly won prize in the heat and combat of much stiff competition for the prize of dear me. *(Walks off with determined stride toward the open jungle of the civilized social world)*

SCENE II

(Scene: Somewhere social, like a party)

MAN II: Hello. God, you're pretty. You're dressed to kill—to make a conquest. Well, consider me as a prospect for being your slain victim.

JUDY: I have high standards, and you don't meet them.

MAN II: Yes, but I've met *you*.

JUDY: That's only the preliminary stage toward being ultimately—or tentatively—judged as to the suitability of your claim not merely only to meet me, but to win me.

MAN II: Let's spend more time together. Then we'd be able to tell.

JUDY: *(Doubtfully)* Tell what?

MAN II: *(Hopefully)* Whether we're made for each other. Whether we were fated long ago to have destiny take its course in its pushing us in each other's intended paths to make a onesome out of our twosome—or rather, a twosome out of our two onesomenesses. Let's test whether it was in the stars that you and I, together—

JUDY: *(Impatiently interrupting)* Oh, you're already so sentimental! I can't stand you!

MAN II: No? Sorry to let myself go so. I promise to be tougher—

JUDY: *(Interrupting)* Too late! *(With a decisive snap:)* We're finished!

MAN II: Finished? We've hardly begun!

JUDY: It's been long enough for *me! Too* long.

MAN II: God, what high standards you have!

JUDY: Not, I hope, too high for my *ideal! (Contemptuously:)* But in *your* case, hopelessly too high for *you!*

MAN II: You don't have to rub it in!

JUDY: *(Suggestively, mockingly, teasingly)* And I won't allow *you* to rub "it" in.

MAN II: Stop taunting me! I'm *already* defeated.

JUDY: Yes, you're quite annihilated, and dead. Having failed to survive, you thus prove yourself unfit to have won me in the first place.

MAN II: Your logic hardly consoles me.

JUDY: It wasn't meant to, in the least. Now that you're crumbled in a rejected heap, I'll just kick you aside *(They act this out in accompanying mime)*, and leave your defeated presence, abandon your discarded and worthless heap.

MAN II: *(From the floor)* I'm reduced to a pulp, and have been made mince-meat of.

JUDY: I've only treated you according to your desserts.

MAN II: *(Still from the floor)* Desserts! Hell, you've gobbled me up for a *main course.*

JUDY: And spew you out, in loathsome spittle and gristle.

> *(Following exchange picks up immediately from preceding lines into being sung musically, emphasizing rhymes:)*

MAN II: Ugh! Hardly delectable!

JUDY: Nor the least selectable.

MAN II: *(Agreeing)* Quite entirely rejectable.

JUDY: Not even respectable?

MAN II: I'm a mangled vegetable!

JUDY: Oh how execrable!

MAN II: *(Submitting, giving up)* Thus ends the festival.

SCENE III

(Scene: A social setting like a party)

JUDY: *(Alone; looking about for more men to victimize)* Where's my next victim? *(Pause. Introspective reflection:)* Say, why am I always setting out to do my victimizing business all over again? Why have I given myself over to being a victimizer? Should I ought to want such a goal? Or should rather I set my sights on another objective entirely: such as, not victimizing, but the rhapsody and devotion of true love?

(Further pondering:) Am I really going in the right direction? Maybe I ought really to reconsider: to take my bearings, and ponder the right intention.

Am I really on the right track? Or is it the wrong track, leading me to head precisely on a collision course with self-destructive disaster?

Let me do a little self-searching. To clear the air of the rot of rut.

(Scene ends on her determined note)

SCENE IV

(Scene: A FORTUNE-TELLER's modest little front-window-shop)

LES: *(Having been submitting his palm to the* FORTUNE TELLER's *experienced inspection)* Well, what's my future?

FORTUNE TELLER: *(Who, though vaguely Gypsy-looking, also looks neither like a man nor a woman, but both in an amorphous lump)* It's ahead.

LES: *(Sarcastically:)* How illuminating! *(Unsarcastically:)* Be a little more specific, or I won't pay you.

FORTUNE TELLER: *(Threatening)* Then I'll tell the police to arrest you.

LES: *(Conciliatory)* Let's compromise. I'll pay you a little more, providing you tell me what's in store for me.

FORTUNE TELLER: *(Whimsically)* I can tell you what's in store: we're *both* in this store.

LES: *(Ordering impatiently)* Less pun, more prophecy!

FORTUNE TELLER: *(Holding out open palm)* Very well; If you grease *my* palm with more money, I'll further inspect *your* palm.

LES: You strike a hard bargain—and a dirty one to boot, you chiseler! *(Resignedly)* Nevertheless, here . . . *(Hands over more money)*

FORTUNE TELLER: That inspires me toward greater efforts to figure out what's in store for you.

LES: *(Sarcastic)* How noble of you to be thus inspired!

FORTUNE TELLER: Quiet! I'm determining your future. *(Concentrating. Pause)*

LES: *(Finally, after a while)* And what have you come up with?

FORTUNE TELLER: My finding? Very well. Shall I let you have it?

LES: Right between the eyes.

FORTUNE TELLER: Here it is, then: Once you find "Judy," you'll have a very emotional time.

LES: Really? How interesting! *(Pause)* What *kind* of "emotional"?

FORTUNE TELLER: Romantic love.

LES: And how will it turn out?

SPIRITUALISTICALLY PREDESTINED JUDY

FORTUNE TELLER: That's up to the two of you.

LES: *Which* two?

FORTUNE TELLER: You and Judy.

LES: Ah yes ... By the way, since I'm linked with her—who's Judy?

FORTUNE TELLER: Judy?

LES: Yes, Judy.

FORTUNE TELLER: She's the one you're going to meet. You've already paid me to be told that.

LES: Yes—but who is she?

FORTUNE TELLER: *(Enigmatically, but emphatically)* You'll find out, all right.

LES: *(Practical, methodical)* Yes, but in order to find *out*, first I must find *her*. How do I go about that?

FORTUNE TELLER: By meeting her. Then, this will start happening.

LES: *(Canny)* All *what* will start happening?

FORTUNE TELLER: *(Equally canny)* Your romance.

LES: With Judy?

FORTUNE TELLER: Precisely. Now you're in the picture.

LES: *(Reverting back, insistently)* Yes, but how do I meet her?

FORTUNE TELLER: *(Cunning)* You really want to know?

LES: Definitely. How can my future with her be complete without the essential condition being met of, in the first place, my first, of course, meeting her? Frankly, it's necessary.

FORTUNE TELLER: *(Mock-offended)* I'm professional enough to realize that. Give me credit.

LES: I will. First be so thorough as to provide me with this information: What method leads me to meet this Judy, whom, it seems, I'm destined to meet?

FORTUNE TELLER: *(Wily)* Sir, pardon me if I seem mendacious, but I'm not in this business for charity you know.

LES: *(Angrily being dawned upon)* Why, you dirty cheat! You mean I should grease your palm with more money? *(Outraged:)* But that's extortion!

FORTUNE TELLER: *(Blandly)* Precisely! I've already intimated that it's not for charity that I'm in this prophetic business. To *be* a *prophet*, I must *make* a *profit*.

LES: In the process, must I go broke? *(Handing over more money into FORTUNE TELLER's cartoon-like-outstretched palm, then observes what he's about to describe:)* Well, *your* palm was just in evidence, before it closed like a flower or clam on the "more money" I obligingly placed in it. But to tell you the truth, frankly, I'm sick to death of *your* open palm in view all the time, being perused by us. Now it's the turn of *my* open palm to be presented for your experienced inspection and judicious interpretation based on the enlightened precepts of modern science.

FORTUNE TELLER: Oh yes, I'm *strictly* scientific. *Strictly*. *(Inspects LES's open palm)* How you'll meet her?

LES: *(Prompting)* Yes. *Judy*, we're referring to. Right?

FORTUNE TELLER: That's the one. *(Head bent down, peers hard and close into LES's outstretched palm, pouring on it in complete concentration with blazing eyesight till he works himself into a trance)* Yes, Judy is in your future.

LES: We've already determined that. The *present* problem is: how will the meeting be brought about? Should I leave it up to chance? Or, should I plot, strive, scheme, intervene, meddle, with active intentional purpose, to conspire with fate and implement destiny as destiny's active agent?—If after all it's granted that Judy should be my destiny, as you professionally prophesize for a higher price than originally agreed upon in your sharp extortionary practices—Granted that premise, or promise, then doesn't it therefore follow, as the night, the day, or as baby's second step after the same baby's first step, that, were this to be so on the record and impending register of destiny, that then I should, with might and main, do all I possibly or conceivably can to work hard and go after her with intelligent effort, not to shirk, but to help this destiny to form itself, come into being, and actually—in a word—materialize?

(FORTUNE TELLER *has been asleep since beginning of this speech, but* LES *doesn't know it*) Or to put it another way, to materially actualize. But surely you gather my drift. Now, mark what follows. Granted my last point, which I've driven home brimming with implications. Isn't the next step, in bringing this destiny about, precisely, in a word, this: To determine how on earth, in the world, or for that matter *anywhere*, I'm to meet her and she's to meet me, in our simultaneously mutual meeting at one and the same time.

Let me make myself clear, for here's the gist of the point I wish to make. What's at issue here is no less a matter than fate, as interpreted by you from my pregnant palm with acute scientific professionalism that has cost me plenty, but what's free these days? I'll be brief and straight, and not digress. All this is vital to me. For am I not to have an emotional time of romantic love with Judy? Isn't she intended for me—and at the same bolt, I for her? Doesn't it work both ways? I'll dispense with rhetoric, logic, paradox, and poetic license, to got straight to the point. A meeting is in the stars, in the works, fatefully impending, between Judy and me. That being so, then surely—it goes without saying—she and I will find it necessary to meet. Yes, but how? *(Anticipating reply, looks at* FORTUNE TELLER, *only to find that latter, who had worked himself into a trance peering into* LES'S *palm, has been asleep*)

LES: *(Looking away from sleeping* FORTUNE TELLER *to address audience)* For this, I've paid him extra money? Sure he's not in this business for charity—not *his* charity but *my* charity—that's another matter. Yes, he's really giving me the business.

(Curtain. End of Act I. Brief intermission.)

ACT TWO

SCENE I

(Scene: somewhere. Time: daylight)

LES: Are you sure you're Judy?

JUDY: That's my name, isn't it?

LES: I mean the *particular* Judy prophesied for me to meet by the Fortune Teller. Judy is a common name. Thousands of women must own it; even millions, if you count other countries—not that I'm unpatriotic.

JUDY: I wouldn't accuse you of that.

LES: Of course not. *(Pause)* But how can I be sure that *you're* that precise Judy cited by the prophetic Fortune Teller (—at quite a price, I can assure you, as it turned out, for his professional services—) that you're the true and one Judy for whom, by fate and destiny's lot, I'm intended—not to mention vice versa?

JUDY: *(Casually, in comparison with LES's pedantic preciseness)* Well, you'll have to take your chances, I guess. Did that seer who suckered you into an exorbitant fee, whittle the Judy of me down into specific characteristics, the better for you to recognize and identify me as the particular she for whom, in all due destiny and by fate's decree, you're truly intended—not to mention, of course, vice versa, as applied to me in the same approximate relation ratio to you?

LES: No. Other than the Judyness of you in the strictly nominal sense as appertains to your mere name itself, he didn't identify you in the slightest. For all I know, you could very easily be the wrong Judy. In mathematical probability, considering how many other Judies there are both domestically and abroad *(Pedantically:)*—that is, *inter*nationally as well as nationally—you might well be one of the innumerable Judies that the Fortune Teller did *not* have in mind when referring to an emotional time of romantic love in store for me in conjunction with the

SPIRITUALISTICALLY PREDESTINED JUDY

Judy whom—most probably—you're not.

JUDY: It impugns my honor and integrity to accuse us of being an imposter.

LES: My apologies.

JUDY: It would be fairer to accuse that so-called Fortune Teller of being a cheat. You paid him through the nose, and he short-changed you! *(In moral indignation:)* Where have our business ethics gone?

LES: There's one solution: to return to him—with you. As we enter his front-window-shop, located on the ground floor of a building, I'll point to you with my finger *(Acts all this out)*, and at the same time ask: "Is she the one?"

JUDY: How can you be sure he'll give you a straight answer? He sounds like a shady character.

LES: And he may very well add a steep addition to his already-added-to original fee.

JUDY: How unfair! The scoundrel!

LES: His quoted price might be prohibitively high, to such degree that I couldn't afford it. Thus, how would I *ever* know whether you're the Judy picked out in advance for me by that dynamic duo, Fate and Destiny—the Futurity twins?

JUDY: *(Dawned upon by bright solution-idea)* To avoid paying the steep price he asks, we could, as a less expensive alternative, kidnap that Fortune Teller, and charge, as ransom for his release, his telling us free—for *nothing*—whether indeed, in fact, I'm more than just a Judy with a *name*, but am also *that* Judy.

LES: *(Puzzled)* "That" Judy? *Which* Judy?

JUDY: The one designated for you, you dope.

LES: As well as, of course, vice versa?

JUDY: Of course. It's strictly equal, between us.

LES: What guarantees that?

Judy: It's in the stars.

Les: The stars!? *(Looks up and about at daylight:)* But it's daylight—this is the afternoon.

Judy: Yes, but it's night *some*where.

Les: Yes, but in some other county. What does that have to do with *us*?

Judy: Indeed. Well you may ask.

SCENE II

(Scene: Back at the Fortune Teller's front-window-shop)

Les: You mean he's dead? That's quick!

Male Surviving Relative of Fortune Teller: It was by a sudden unexpected heart-attack. It even caught him unawares.

Judy: Poor mortal!

Male Surviving Relative of Fortune Teller: Yes, but he's no longer mortal.

Les: True. The only redeeming thing about death is that at least it frees us from our mortality.

Male Surviving Relative of Fortune Teller: Yes. Some consolation!

Les: But did he leave any records behind?

Male Surviving Relative of Fortune Teller: *(Indignant)* Records!? Of course not! He was no thief!

Les: I'm not posthumously accusing him. Give me credit for *some* decency.

Male Surviving Relative of Fortune Teller: *(Apologetically)* Pardon. You look moral through and through. I was mistaken.

Les: Thanks for restoring my dignity.

MALE SURVIVING RELATIVE OF FORTUNE TELLER: My pleasure, sir. Any former client of my departed relative is surely entitled to courtesy.

JUDY: *(Impatient)* Will you two stop bickering in niceties?! It's getting us positively nowhere!

LES: Nowhere?! But aren't we *(Looking about)* already *here?*

JUDY: Yes, but what good is "here"? That so-called fraudulent Fortune Teller—a cheat in business to boot—apparently took irresponsibility to die without leaving any record as to whether I'm—of all the Judies both national and international—the one whom the destiny-fate combine has inked with you as your one-and-only intended—not to mention, of course, vice versa.

MALE SURVIVING RELATIVE OF FORTUNE TELLER: *(Echoing with obliging politeness)* Of course.

LES: There's only one recourse we have in our present difficulty, for solving our ticklish problem.

JUDY: Yes? Don't leave us in the dark. Pray tell us what it is.

MALE SURVIVING RELATIVE OF FORTUNE TELLER: In other words, share it with us.

LES: *(To MALE SURVIVING RELATIVE OF FORTUNE TELLER)* I'd rather share it with Judy than with you.

MALE SURVIVING RELATIVE OF FORTUNE TELLER: Snob!

JUDY: Well, what is it?

LES: We'll go down to the cemetery where the ex-Fortune Teller's unfortunate remains are buried. We dig up what's left of the poor sod, and we inquire of his corpse whether you *(Looking pointedly at Judy)* are the exact Judy—in fact, the *only* one—that the dead old seer had meant by—

JUDY: *(Impatiently cutting in)* Yes, yes, we know. But your plan is impractical.

LES: Why cynic?

JUDY: Dead men can't talk. This is a well-known fact; and it applies well, in *this* case.

LES: Well, we'll just have to adjust. He'd have to use sign language. We'll study the deaf-and-dumb manual before paying our graveyard visit. We'll—so to speak—*bone up*. Anything, to "get through."

JUDY: To reach him?

LES: Yes. It's urgent. We must pull out all the stops, to ascertain the truth or falsehood of whether you are *my* Judy, or *not mine*.

JUDY: *(Agreeing)* Yes, we'll have to be ruthless. Even to stop at nothing, in tracking down which single Judy the dead Fortune Teller had in mind—

MALE SURVIVING RELATIVE OF FORTUNE TELLER: *(Interrupting)* I hate to dash cold water on your ardent quest for truth, but, at the risk of your deeming me a spoilsport or killjoy, I must report that the pseudo-science cites only one way know to man—or woman, for that matter—of communicating with those departed from our realm of sensory earth.

JUDY: *(Harking)* What is that one only way?

MALE SURVIVING RELATIVE OF FORTUNE TELLER: *(Interrupting)* Table-hopping.

LES: *(Puzzled)* What!?

MALE SURVIVING RELATIVE OF FORTUNE TELLER: *(Correcting himself)* I mean table-raising: the extrasensory occultistic spiritualism, in the spooky formalism of a seance parlor. There alone have you the *"ghost"* of a chance to raise a posthumous report from my recently dispatched relative as to which of all Judies he was referring to, when doing his live job on you, Sir—one of his last clients of his noble scientific career in service to humanity's doubts and trepidations in bowing to the awe and majesty of that mysterious unknown thing we call—for want of a better word—the future.

LES: *(Indignant)* He cheated me! The scum! He overcharged. And to compound his infernal negligence, he left no record behind—curse him—to prove or indicate whether the Judy by my side is indeed *the* Judy.

MALE SURVIVING RELATIVE OF FORTUNE TELLER: You should have asked him—while he was still alive.

LES: He would have charged me extra!

MALE SURVIVING RELATIVE OF FORTUNE TELLER: *(Taking umbrage)* You're maligning my sentimentally sacred memory of my revered departed benefactor! Were I not in possession of the good taste to avoid creating an embarrassing display, I'd copiously weep in ostentation of solemn grief and flamboyant show of how I mourn my relative in gratitude for his generosity toward me in the legacy of his *will:* which singled me out as the exclusively favored survivor, while I mixed my tears of grief with the overjoy of delirium in greed of ecstasy to be made materially secure on the inherited bounty of my comfort by the fortunate stroke of his heart's timely attack.

LES: So he left all of his money—ill-earned by unfair extortion and cheating malignancy—to you? *(Threatening:)* Well, I demand back the considerable extra fee he levied on me!

MALE SURVIVING RELATIVE OF FORTUNE TELLER: Ah, that's a dead matter, I assure you. A wise motto is: "Let the past bury its dead." The transactions between you and the late lamented are strictly, in a professional sense, "buried with him." Bygones enforce an armistice or moratorium or amnesty waiving regrets aside. What was past is now all ancient history, not to be tampered with. The dust has settled. *(Warning:)* At you own infernal risk, at your eternal peril, go ruffle the white linen shrouds of ghostly imperturbability!

JUDY: *(Taking LES by the arm; prudently:)* He's right, Les. Let's not interfere in a dead matter. However ill-begotten by his benefactor, this man's *(Indicating MALE SURVIVING RELATIVE OF FORTUNE TELLER)* legacy is by legal will incontestable by us for damages and malpractice and sharp unfair dealing by said benefactor in the conduct of his once so-called business affairs that are done and over with.

LES: But I rankle with resentment that—

JUDY: *(Interrupting)* Choke it down! Swallow the bitter pill!

LES: *(Insistent)* No!

JUDY: *(With forceful reasoning that will prevail and win its point)* Let's take this man's *(Indicating* MALE SURVIVING RELATIVE OF FORTUNE TELLER*)* advice—we can't take his money. He won't be bargained with. He doesn't know if I'm the true Judy: only his dirty old dead relative does. It profits us naught to remain in this shop, which is closed forever in the context of its former palm-reading use. Why beat a dead horse? We'll move with the times. Let's clear out and consult a seance agent of otherworldly spiritualism occultly extrasensory in mystic realms of mystery; and by table-raising, invoke that fraudulent cheat's evil spirit: to petition that spirit, with the tactful supplication and delicately phrased inquiry, for the withheld secret. *(Pause. Optimistically:)* The Fortune Teller is beyond the mendacity of money cupidity now; he'll turn nostalgic with charity, and dole out a posthumous slice of his defunct old business for charity, in leniency to us who invoke his undoubtedly repentant ghost in belated kindness to atone for flint-heartedness when that cold dealer was alive, mean, sharp, hard, and cruel in extracting what he could—bleeding you in the bargain—for the pseudo-scientific pronouncement of his palm-reading divinations culled from powers veiled in the presence of an awesome mystery.

MALE SURVIVING RELATIVE OF FORTUNE TELLER: *(To LES)* She's right, Sir—as so am I. Go raise my relative's vocal visage in the approved channel. Good luck in tracking down the real gospel truth of which single woman of all those name "Judy" is nominated beyond the nominal to be, by joint destiny and fate's decree, meant indisputably for you—not to mention, of course, vice versa. I hope my benefactor's ghost will be easier to deal with—and more generously co-operative, rewarding, forthcoming, and fulfilling—than that ghost's live former self who cheated you of what's *so* vital and essential for you to know, that you must make these belated labors to see whether *this (Indicating* JUDY*)* woman is intended to give you an emotional time of romantic love (not to mention vice versa), or whether an as-yet-undiscovered woman of the same name is darkly held in reserve to provide you with such mutual privilege.

LES: You and Judy—*this (Indicating JUDY)* one, whoever she is—have prevailed on me. Well, *(Looking at JUDY)* let's go off to make contact—and no ordinary contact, I assure you—with that old fraud, to pump his old mental well of the relevant information. And let's go about it in a hurry. True love avenges those tardy to pluck it in its ripe aching mystery's perfect moment of time discovery.

(LES and JUDY, exchange mimed goodbyes with MALE SURVIVING RELATIVE OF FORTUNE TELLER, exit in strides of determination and hope)

(Curtain. End of Act Two. Intermission)

ACT THREE

SCENE I

(Scene: Seance parlor. Blackness and uncanny effect on stage, suitably atmospheric to what's going on)

FORTUNE TELLER'S GHOST: *(Unseen, from vaguely above/about; in deep, eerie, cracked voice)* Stop bothering, perturbing, raising me. I want peace, to be left alone! *(With banality, as in nasal New York vulgar accent:)* Oh, you're so annoying!

LES: I won't stop annoying you—or for that matter, bothering, perturbing, raising you—till I extract from you the requisite information, the quest for which drove me to the considerable trouble and pains—not to mention the expense—I've taken, Oh Spirit, to raise you via the formal occult baloney and hocus-pocus of this ridiculous spiritualist seance session at a seedy and disreputable parlor dedicated professionally to exploit at a profit people's yearnings to hold on to, or regain contact with, departed souls they had formerly known.

SEANCE PARLOR PROPRIETOR AND PERFORMER: You demean my craft, and belittle my esteemed trade. I'll punish you financially. Just as I've *raised* the spectacle of the Fortune Teller's horrid ghost, so too shall now be officially *raised* the price you're compelled stiffly to pay me for performing this weird, otherwordly, multi-dimensional translation of your Fortune Teller's victimizer from peaceful death's vacuous oblivion, to his currently agitated state as summoned forth ceremonially to give account to you in atonement for professional transactional neglects and misdeeds perpetrated in his earlier phase of life conducted by business.

LES: But I paid you already! You'll raise the fee? That's extortion worthy of the very ghost you've raised! As you've summoned that ghost, so shall I summon, summarily, the police.

SEANCE PARLOR PROPRIETOR AND PERFORMER: *(Blasé)* Don't bother. They're in my pay.

LES: Oh. Then the ghost is up. *(Looks up at emanation of* FORTUNE TELLER'S GHOST *in visual pun on is last verbal sentence)* Thus jacks up the pay you criminally extract, from my purse already previously enfeebled by the living earlier self of the phantom visage you've raised to my additional cost.

SEANCE PARLOR PROPRIETOR AND PERFORMER: How fitting! In that, I *do* resemble him! In a sense, it's poetically apt, smacking faintly of divine retribution, poetic justice, and some fun on the side.

LES: *(Wounded, glum, beaten)* The fun's certainly not on *my* side.

JUDY: *(Countering with note of urgent practicality against preceding semi-metaphysical linguistic banter)* Hurry, Les. The Ghost is raised *now*, but he seems flutteringly impatient, looking anxiously already homesick for the recent comforts of his spirit world. He may bolt from our view, in a wisp of vapor, leaving us groping with the pale blankness where now still lofts his white specter. Should he leave as he so longs to do, evaporating into escape by heaping the magic of disappearance onto the magic of his appearance—*before* granting you an unwilling audience so that you may address this costly apparition for which you've already paid this chiseling seance operator *(Looking at, indicating, Seance Parlor Proprietor and Performer)*—then, to get another chance, you'll be forced to repay at a special re-raise rate at such bitter expense as to be barely a bargain.

Les: Oh money, money, there's less and less of you!

Judy: Still hovering with resentment and reluctance on the enchanted black air of this disreputable seance parlor is that fraudulent so-called Fortune Teller's annoyed, disturbed, and not very friendly ghost. *(Having been looking up to it)* The specter aches to get away—he hates being called up here. With a quick address of words, fix him to his spot, impale him there, before he flutters loose outside visibility's peering range and beyond audibility's surge of wave.

Les: *(With desperate, aching yet somehow impotent)* Oh, the urgency bids me to hurry! I'm in a frantic panic to address him, in an excrutiating suspense of belated haste!

Judy: *(Simultaneously urging Les on and delaying him)* Should that elusive, wavering visage make good on a sudden escape he longs for with all his bodyless soul, then, for the difficult exertion of re-raising him, the seedy seance operator here *(Looking at, indicating, Seance Parlor Proprietor and Performer)* will be all too glad to cheat you by heaping an extra additional sum of surcharge for such service on the original steep fee, thus sadly depleting your already sagging bank account to such mathematical degree of diminished funds or balance, that you'll face financial ruin and will be so broke that not even poverty itself could reverse the downwardness and falling decline of monetary kerplunk, to the flat bottom of penniless, nickleless, dimeless, quarterless, and by all means dollarless pecuniary embarrassment that beggars all description and impoverishes the meaningless power of words.

Les: *(Covering both eyes with his hands; melodramatically:)* Oh horrible contemplation!

JUDY: *(Looking up at GHOST)* This flickering apparition of that former thief, the Fortune Teller, looks hardly welcoming, forthcoming, or pleased to be here. He's been dragged here, with great reluctance, like a surly, unwilling captive. Speak now to him, ere he vanish on the magic spot of his wavering: which will cause your miserable wallet to undergo further reduction by a re-raising surcharge by this extortionary excuse *(Looking at, indicating, SEANCE PARLOR PROPRIETOR AND PERFORMER)* for a Seance Operator, a knave equal to the former live self of the raised ghost.

LES: *(In excruciating panic of belated frantic haste; to GHOST, who has half vanished:)* Oh Ghost, oh Ghost—Heed me!

> *(Too late—the GHOST, unreplying, has now totally vanished)*

LES: *(His desperation calmed into reminiscently contemplative despair and resignation)* The desperate agony of tardiness: excruciating panic of belatedly frantic haste. That ghost failed to co-operate. Prodding him when first he came, by dreary magic, to ear ere view, my only satisfaction was this complaint: *(Imitates accurately FORTUNE TELLER'S GHOST'S deep, eerie, cracked voice:)* "Stop bothering, perturbing, raising me. I want peace to be left alone!" *(Then, in banal, nasal New York vulgar accent)* "Oh, you're so annoying!"

As it turned out, though he came out into a sort of view *(Looking up to where specter had been)* and stayed there in his white patch for a bit, those words were all he blessed me with. Instead of forcing more talk from him, leading to my eliciting from the vital information for which I came to this unholy place and have been paying, I was delayed and interfered with by foolishly getting into various sort of conversations of counter-accusations with you two *(Looking at, indicating, both JUDY and SEANCE PARLOR PROPRIETOR AND PERFORMER)*. Were those delaying tactics? Whether deliberate or not, they stalled me from further verbal stalking, querying, inquisitioning that taciturn excuse for a ghost, and from wrenching, from dragging, the all-too-obscured truth I've had him—at drastic expense, I do fear—raised for: whether you *(To Judy)* are the Judy he meant in reference to his prophecy that there was *a* Judy meant truly, only, for me—not to mention, of course, vice versa as well, it goes without saying. But the responsible blame lies not only with you two—*I'm* at fault, too. The ghost was "there"—in his captive availability. I fooled around, I didn't get to the point with him. I should have pushed, followed through, insisted—with the opportunity temptingly there. I lingered overlong. I didn't plague him enough—or *soon* enough. The chance is lost—at what cost?

(To Seance Parlor Proprietor and Performer:) For re-raising that vanished drop of vapor, what re-raising of a fee would you reasonably levy on me?

Seance Parlor Proprietor and Performer: I'm in the driver's seat, with all the bargaining power, at a commanding advantage to squeeze and exploit you quite dry. It's *my* market, and I have you over the barrel, or by the balls. You'll dance to the jig of my financial tune command. You'll know poverty first-hand!

Les: *(In dismay and horror)* Spare me! I beg—

Judy: *(Interrupting in pity)* Poor Les! All this trouble!—just for me!

Les: *(To Judy)* I don't know if it *is* for you yet. It's over *some* Judy, I know. If not *you*—then where *is* she, in this wide—

Seance Parlor Proprietor and Performer: *(Interrupting)* You're being technical, and scrupulous. Obviously, you're being very fussy when it comes to your Judies!

Les: Naturally. The *right* Judy, and only she—no other, certainly no *(Looking queryingly, suspiciously at Judy)* imposter!—opens the key to the lock of my private romantic love life. Which is no minor matter, in the universal scale of phenomena, as a value of heavenly proportion to the scheme of life's perspective for the world.

Judy: Well, I *do* hope, in that event, that it's *me*. Being Judy used to seem so simple, so easy, so natural. It was like breathing or falling asleep. I never even *thought* about being Judy. I just *assumed* it, and *was* it.

Now, its turned into a self-conscious exercise in metaphysical speculation, as a conundrum in the labyrinth of a probing inquiry into what constitutes one's own identity, in the eyes and specifications of another person keenly interested—or not—depending on whether one is *exactly* in the mold of the requisite being that the other person requires one—in no uncertain terms—to be.

LES: That's because finding one's true love—and not accepting any approximate substitute or even close replica—is the least trivial of all preoccupations in life's relentless pursuit of its own inwardly occupied industry. Emotionally, finding one's true love so heavily outweighs—

SEANCE PARLOR PROPRIETOR AND PERFORMER: *(Interrupting with parental-like authority)* As to the matter at hand—which let's return to, from the mounting clouds of your endless theories from juvenile notions and romantic emotions on the nature alike of life and love. We'll resume the practical. Let's put abstractions aside, and got down what's called "brass tacks." Any unpleasantness that such reversion to harsh reality may let loose—well, be hard, not soft, and face up to where the consequences may, with brutal chance, alight.

I refer to *material* considerations. And what's more material, in fact—or at least potentially so—then money itself?

(LES and JUDY shift uneasily squirming, apprehensive. SEANCE PARLOR PROPRIETOR AND PERFORMER continues:) A rule sacred, in long custom and practice, to my occult profession, shared by all in the seance trade adopt in the transwordly craft, goes as follows: Once a specific practitioner (*me*, in just this case) has, by official capacity, initially raised any one particular ghost, then he alone, and no other operator in the entire seance field, may ever *re*-raise that particular ghost previously raised. Thus, your only access to another chance with the fled Fortune Teller's ghost, is by way of *me* alone. You're stuck in dealing only with me, *through* me, in your desperate agonized plight of needing vital information from the ghost that only *I*—no one else—is by law of my guild, able and entitled to set before you. *(Triumphantly*

with glee:) And I can charge any price I please—in the "bargain," bleeding you quite dry!

LES: Oh, sadism! I've already been bled pale: first by that scoundrel whose ghost has been risen once but in vain; then by you, who rivals and far surpasses that ghost's former self, in greed of opportune extortion in wrenching a gain by pain from a client's dire need, extracting maximum cost heedless of all humane decency by the fair clemency of transaction!

JUDY: *(To LES)* That's bad news from *him (Indicating* SEANCE PARLOR PROPRIETOR AND PERFORMER*)*, Les. To compound your woes, let *me* add in *further* bad news for you.

LES: What! Stabbing me when I'm down already?!

JUDY: That's when it's the most fun for the stabber.

LES: What's *your* blow?

JUDY: You want desperately to ascertain whether I'm that unique of all Judies whom fate and destiny dearly wish to bestow on you in the solemn permanence of love (vice versa, naturally, as well). Only this man *(Indicating* SEANCE PARLOR PROPRIETOR AND PERFORMER*)*—mercenary beyond belief—can help, by his occult craft, to provide you with whether my identity matches to precise measurement the specifications of that special Judy. He'd charge you what the market could bear, and you'd pay through the nose. You'd be cleaned out, in pursuit of clearing up your Judy-obsession problem puzzle.

LES: That's true. It's all for love. At and cost, I *must* find out.

JUDY: Well, if you *do* find out—no longer will it, I'm afraid, do you any good.

LES: But why?—you one Judy to eliminate all other possible Judies in supreme confirmation of your being that one Judy, possibly—why?

JUDY: Because in the process of finding out, you will have turned into a pauper. Your monetary status will thus have plunged—if it hasn't already by now plunged—below my minimal marital requirements for a husband candidate. You will have financially—if you haven't already done so—priced yourself below my modest principles for decent household and living maintenance. To love a poor man—even if it did turn out that I chanced to be that poor man's only Judy of all my hordes of namesakes—would be, for practical purposes, pure folly. My ideals for self-respect, societal approval, even social survival, are too considerably high to permit me to fall below my stiff materialistic standards in choosing, for marriage partner, a mate who'll support me in the style I wish to be accustomed to. My expectations proudly must be met and upheld by my marital partner's substantial bank balance. To betray my principles by marrying beneath myself would permanently impair my self-esteem. So as not to prize myself at too humbly debasing an estimate, I withdraw my love from consideration: even were it to come to light that I prove to be, as the possible Judy of all Judies to your impoverished demands, the very Judy herself, the actual and only one with whom your love dreams find sanction as the fitting match properly approved by the deities who preside in ratification.

LES: That's terrible treachery. You've stood by me *so* far. We came to this seance parlor together. And *now* you're pulling out?

JUDY: What do you take me for?! My principles are lofty in the standards of self-respect. *(Haughtily:)* You're *much* too poor for such as I! Especially if you persist in the expense entailed of steep surcharge in getting another shot at that morosely taciturn former Fortune Teller swindler in spirit presentation. You already had your chance, and flubbed it: you didn't badger and hound the spook to talk, with the maniacal aggression you would have needed. That unearthly lump of mental air should vigorously have been prodded. But possibly the Seance Operator and I delayed you, in the verbiage of our urging and pratter—that is, prattle and chatter. You're nearly out of pocket. Your income is meager and meek. Your bank account dawdles to the dwindling point. The upshot, or anti-payoff and non-jackpot of your reduced circumstances, with what you want restricted by your lowered powers in this pitiless world of materialism and heartless pit of human indifference, is that you're in a pointless bargaining position without effect or influence in the odds of persuading others. It's no longer a compelling matter to me that, despite the long-shot odds of mathematical improbability, I *may* be the Judy of the star of your destiny as foretold by the fatalistic rites of that Fortune Teller. Palm-reading is offensive from the scientific point of view, to true truth-seeking. Destiny and fate are hokus and pokus. Free will, individual choice, decisions based on self-determination—independence from superstitious old rot: Those, finally, are what I believe.

LES: Isn't it late in the day for you to tell me that? After all I've gone through . . . You pledged yourself: we were in it together. It was on trust and faith that I—

JUDY: *(Interrupting)* I misled you? No, I followed along to see where things would lead. No pledge, vow, or oath did I commit myself to. I hung around, and gave you a chance. I was intrigued by all this weird once-in-a-million "Judy" business. It was a challenge, before the nonsense element came leading in to make it sloppy and slippery and a masterpiece of scientific implausibility.

LES: You turncoat!

JUDY: Here in this Seance Parlor you let things slip through your fingers once your well-paid-for opportunity set things into the possibility of motion. But as I disbelieve in Fortune Telling, so too do I in table-rapping or table-raising or any other crystal ball pseudo-magic. Spirits don't exist, in ghost-form. Nor do *I* exist, as even a remote chance of being your love. I've rejected men *before: too* much. They were romantic victims. I thought of trying a cure. I gave you a chance: which you proceeded—in this dingy seance parlor grubbiness, following the degrading Fortune Teller's Surviving Relative interview of equal shabbiness—to flub. So reluctantly, I return, in your sordid new case, to my old man-rejecting ways—from which I had vowed to reform. I discard you to the rubbish heap of my former victims. To break that habit, since *you* won't do, I won't waste further time here, but freely turn away and leave. Whatever Judy I am has now become an academic, pedantic footnote to the meandering text of out-of-focus irrelevancy. The Judy I am is *my* business: no longer yours. *(She leaves)*

LES: *(Sadly looking at her last vacated exiting space)* I had supposed it was, jointly, *our* business.

SEANCE PARLOR PROPRIETOR AND PERFORMER: And what's your business to *me*, now?

LES: Withdrawn. Leaving unfinished business sadly incomplete forever. I'm poor already. No incentive remains to compensate losing *more* money to you. Judy abandoned me. My quest is pointless, to pump the Fortune Teller's ghost or further information he should have supplied me with when alive—the scoundrel. I'll trouble you no more. *(While leaving:)* My life removes itself, crippled into temporary collapse. I'll start anew, to pick up the pieces, or with new pieces. I'll resort to no Fortune Teller any more. I'll seek and find a *non*-Judy, this time, without aid from fate, destiny, or prophecy. I won't appeal to the occult. Concurrently, I'll seek remunerative work to replenish my depleted, slender purse of barely solvent funds. I'll rebound, from all this: my recent as-it-turned-out nightmare. Life and fortune will favor me, if I regain a foothold and attempt new twists, other angular avenues than those down which I bungled to damn despair with you; the ghost you abortively raised; that ghost's former villain self; and that false Judy—or technically the right one it might be but now never will I know, since she's removed from my caring, but rather we join to mingle the distasteful cups of our contempt in the sour lost mutual waste of retrospect, as we both forget what bitterly united us and then propelled the mixed blessings of our release, asunder down separate ways, coupling with others instead of each other. *(Leaving)*

SEANCE PARLOR PROPRIETOR AND PERFORMER: *(To leaving LES)* Sorry you won't need my refined services any more. Refer me, recommend me, to others of desperate plight, who sorely might need to be put into an outside-earth communicative merger with anyone dead I'd be glad to conjure up—for, of course, a considerable fee. My line of work isn't the least common. It's in the rare, aethereal nature of specialization. I'm no crook. My supernatural talent should be paid in a kind of coin—

(LES *has now left, out of hearing. End of Scene. Darkness, curtain*)

ACT FOUR

SCENE I

JUDY: *(Alone, somewhere, sitting down)* Well, I didn't get the more of Les, I got the less of him—more or less. So here I am—back, in a sense, where I started from. I add another rejection to the men I've victimized—I add Les, to that inglorious heap of discards and of "never-was"es. And I'm alone—lonely. I've got to curb or cure that. I want permanent love in romance. The question is: who with?

There are men galore. I'll go to parties and find my future husband. But the unknown plagues or haunts; I can't bear the suspense of this mystery, as to the identity of "the man for me."

I'm strictly scientific as well as logical. I abhor anything occult or superstitious, exploitative of our human weakness for magic. Despite this, however, I'll go to some Fortune Teller (not the one who's dead that Les went to—that one is out of commission—but a new one, somewhere else, for *me* to find out who my true love is going to be, as well as, of course, how to go about making the meeting happen. I'll learn from past failures. I'll do the job right—not the way Les bungled it. That poor man.

How's he doing, I wonder? Time has been going by since I gave up on our odd sequence of events together. I faintly carry a lingering affection for him. He must, by now, have forgotten me—somewhat. *Apart* now, *together* before, we are linked by our never knowing, finally at all, whether the particular Judy for him was going to happen to coincide with me myself. It seemed useless to continue.

The money factor is important to me. Les was being squeezed dry of funds. Nor was he in a good position to compensate by earning more. For me, romance and poverty don't mix. I want love in conditions of financial comfort. That was a prime reason for my rejecting poor old Les.

(Getting up, preparatory to leaving) Now, to try a Fortune Teller. That's a step toward stopping making life lonely for myself.

If can't have Les, then let me have, at least, more. *(Leaves)*

(End of Scene. Curtain)

SCENE II

(Scene: JUDY in street-window-shop FORTUNE TELLER'S parlor)

FORTUNE TELLER II: *(Examining JUDY's palm)* According to your past, you have a personal history of having victimized men. You made them—or let them—love you; but you didn't requite or reciprocate their smitten affections. This process or cycle or pattern is a habit hard to cure. But now a cure is at hand. You have a zeal to reform.

JUDY: How clever! That's accurate. *(Encouraging:)* You're on the ball, and rolling up momentum. Keep going.

FORTUNE TELLER II: I see a man in your very near-by, close-at-hand future, with whom you'll try mighty hard to break your old ways.

JUDY: Can you describe him? Tell me, as well, how I should go about making sure I'll actually *meet* him.

FORTUNE TELLER II: That's practical of you to take precautions so as not to let slip loose your lifeline chance of a true romance!

JUDY: I'm earnest and seriously intent on love and marriage. But what's his money status.

FORTUNE TELLER II: Not so hot, at the moment. But he's trying. Give him credit. He's getting a job for a professional career, meaning working and earning. It's promising.

JUDY: Good. Now, describe him, as well as explain what name he has.

FORTUNE TELLER II: That will cost you more money.

JUDY: *(Indignant)* But I already paid you! I'm outraged to be so cheated.

FORTUNE TELLER II: The price or fee, or charge, is only being slightly increased or raised, in accordance with your stepped-up interest and desperation, which afford the opportunity to take advantage of your intense passionate concern, and monetarily to exploit your vulnerable expression of need, want, desire, and general tonic of emotional urgency.

JUDY: You're foul!

FORTUNE TELLER II: I'm in business for greed. *(Pronounces, enounces following deliberately:)* Take heed: the need you plead will lead, indeed, in speed my greed to feed—on *(Stumbling, pondering, sputtering)*—on—on the need you plead!

JUDY: *(Pleading)* Take pity. I can't afford much. Virtually I'm broke. I can only get occasional part-time work. That's why the man in my dreams—as soon as you reveal his identity by disclosing my dreams—must have money: or be soon to obtain it by being clever to earn profit from a line of business in steadily increased raises of salary by proving of value to his boss in efficiency in discharging his post or position in the profit-making firm's inner machinery structure hierarchy of coordinated key personnel.

FORTUNE TELLER II: *(Resigned)* I'll quote the flat sum of one final fee, within even the modest range of your budget's hungry diet. For that, I'll tell you the name of the man destined for you, and describe his physical and facial features. As to *how* you're to meet him—that requires extra work on my part, which you can't afford, so we'll have to skip that practical and active aspect of my Fortune-Telling sleuthing. You'll have to do without knowing just how to meet him: in *that* category, you'll strictly be on your own.

JUDY: *(Also resigned)* Well, I'll realistically have to settle only on the name and description of my dearly intended, not to mention destined, true love. Then I'll have to use my wits—lacking your witness—as to the logistics of locating him: that innocent elusive one, for whom my faded soul forevermore yearns to pant.

FORTUNE TELLER II: First, as to his name: It's no more than *Les*.

JUDY: *(Excited)* Les! Yes, but *which* Les?

FORTUNE TELLER II: Why, it's more or less the one I said.

JUDY: Is it *more*—or *Les*?

FORTUNE TELLER II: *(Showing insight divining power)* You seem already to know a "Les." The Les *I* have in mind for you may be—more or less—the identical Les that you already know.

JUDY: If *identical*—or not—depends on how you identify him. You promised not only to divulge nominally the revelation of his *name*—which you've given as "Les"—but moreover, *more* have you to reveal or divulge: his physical descriptive characteristics, in his own bodily and facial unique molds.

FORTUNE TELLER II: *(Impatiently; looking at the waiting room)* Other clients or customers are waiting to patronize my secretive services. I've already given enough time, for so low a flat sum of fee as meets the slim and slender supports of your tiny purse capacity financially to barely afford. Enough. We're quits! Go!

JUDY: *(Outraged; indignant but firm)* You cheat! No, I'll hold you to our strict measure of agreement. You've said his name; but that's "less" *(a pun on "Les")* than you promised.

Our bargain stipulated more: you're to throw in pertinent descriptions of face and body, such as I'd need for the accurate specifics of recognition. There are many *more* Les'es than only, for all *I* know, the Les *I* know. Is the Les *I* know the Les *you* have in your mind of occupational foresight? I won't leave until you answer this in full substance with unmisleading unmistakableness.

Implant, then, the imagery data details for me to gain a mental picture on my imaginary visual apparatus to vividly conceive what Les you have in store for me: which immediately gets compared with a man by the same name whom I recently rid myself of, walked out on, when he was in a jam—the latest on my chronically long list of rejected suitors.

FORTUNE TELLER II: *(Looking again at waiting room—which is presumably full of waiting patrons)* I mustn't keep them waiting any longer. I don't want to lose any patron, client, customer, by—*(In self-congratulatory tone:)*—in my thriving little shop, my flourishing service of prophecy—making those troubled folks (loaded with money) be kept waiting. *(Turning to JUDY:)* So I'm eager to dispense with you quick. I haven't extracted much money from you, so I'm in a haste to be done and cut down the waste of spending more time on *your* case, when people who can *pay* far more than you are kept in a stew of waiting.

JUDY: *(Now with upper hand, in driver's seat)* All right, describe him!

FORTUNE TELLER II: *(Leaning toward JUDY, preparatory to "delivering the goods")* Here's how he looks like: as to first the features of his upper facial oval; then what physically there is of him below that crucial human dividing line, the neck, ending below at the bottom of his ground-hugging feet. *(Looks anxiously in direction of waiting room again)* Forgive my haste: listen, and then depart.

JUDY: *(In full advantageous ascendancy)* I want his characteristic salient details such that will make the key procedural recognition-identification act an instantaneously simple cinch for me, an easy lark, once he comes commandingly into view for Love's altered, educated, informed, prepared eyes gleamingly, on the spot, to spot but, head-on. *(Commandingly:)* Fill me in! Let's have it. Come on; give! Spill it!

> *(In haste, FORTUNE TELLER II leans close to JUDY with look of confidentiality, and pours out—visually: unheard to audience—the description. While listening, JUDY gradually shows on her face, with more and more conviction, the taking in and realizing that the LES being described is the very same unmistakably identical LES to the LES of her experience in this play.*
>
> *Her dawning, gradual recognition is accompanied by smile that increasingly grows beaming and ecstatic the closer she grows to complete conviction that the LES*

described is her LES whom she recently betrayed, abandoned, and rejected.

At end of her listening the ardor of love—contrite love—gleams in her eye. With this is a look of determination to make amends for her recent rejection, betrayal, abandonment of LES, in full devotional compensation of loving self-redemption.)

(Finished with his description, FORTUNE TELLER II gets up, prodding JUDY up from her ecstatic trance of love. He requests in mime, and takes, the agreed-upon fee from her, then curtly business-like takes her by the elbow to show her briskly to the door. At same movement, with newly put-on expression of professional obsequiousness, he approaches direction of waiting room, looking ready to apologize profusely for the delay to those waiting, and to beckon in for immediate consultation the next in line.

Thus ignored, solo wrapped in rapt, ecstatic gleam of love for LES, JUDY exits as though floating on visitation and blessing of a suddenly stunning, all-transforming dream.)

(Curtain, darkness. End of Scene)

SCENE III

(Setting: Business office. LES at desk. He's dressed conspicuously "better" than in all his previous appearances in play, indicating that he's been doing well at his job and is embarked on prosperous phase of life, commercially and materially speaking)

LES: Except that I still think of her constantly, I've put Judy completely out of mind. She's in my past: before I got this job I've been doing so well at that, thanks to me, the company has expanded and taken on a new smokestack plant to put increased profits back into further productivity based beneficially on my efficiency improvement innovation schemes.

Judy *had* taken exception to my being poor and devoid of reasonable business prospects. That's why she pulled out, and broke faith. Well, if she could see me now, *(Looking up and around his well-appointed, important-looking office)* in my handsome new place, condition, position, situation, post, and status,—then naturally she'd renew my love rank in her emotional business organization.

My well-appointed office *(Looking at it admiringly)* and well-groomed self *(Looking at self in similar manner)*, show I'm well on my way toward personal prosperity. Were Judy to throw in her lot with my rising fortunes and join in marriage my promising executive march to commercial prominence, it would be a far cry from our poor old days of before.

To hell with fortune tellers and seance operators, with destiny and fate in occult prophecy by spiritualistic hocus-pocus. She was never "intended" for me by magical preordainment in the mystical star-kissed galaxy of trumped-up superstitious device. We met and liked each other, that's all—not by deep-layed design, but by accident and a mutual personal preference in elective affinity. *(With sudden conviction and decisiveness, as though braving fate with daring challenge:)* Who cares even that her name is Judy at all? *(Dramatic pause after such a startling contradiction of previous behavior)* To show my mature indifference, I'll have her name completely changed to a non-Judy name: which will erase the curse and stigma of our being stuck by a bond of fear to a Judy-identity-obsession in servitude to a pseudo fortune teller and his subsequent ghost as raised by that phony seance operator. Both of them—not the ghost—were in it for monetary greed, using emotional blackmail to cheat me, to impoverish me, till finally I got wise and landed on my feet *(Looking around office)* with this job I've been handling so well.

Of course, I do owe in the first place ever having met Judy to that now-dead fortune teller and the naive belief I placed in his forecasting of a Judy for me, though only in the nominal sense of her name alone, backed up by no further identificationary clue.

Now having discharged my acknowledgment in credit-giving to that unscrupulous fortune-telling crook, I hereby proclaim my emancipation from any further gratitude and posthumous obligation to the scoundrel—he forced me to pay him exorbitantly, at any rate. To hell with whether *my* Judy is the Judy *he'd* had in mind. I dispense forever with that superstitious scruple. In enlightened liberation from spiritualistic nonsense, I now transfer my trust to a less nervous, less anxious, less dependent, less fatalistic, less pitifully passive source of judgment and decision: *(Grandly, proudly:)* my own feelings, by spontaneous will!

I've thus regained the confidence and self-reliance, the innate dignity, of freedom!

Now I have no need for that stubborn, curly, uncommunicative ghost to be re-raised. The irony and paradox is that I'm so placed now *(Looks around impressive office again)* as to be quite more than well able to afford the seance operator's outrageous fees on that score for such dubious service. Thus time plays tricks—monetary pranks—on a person's changing outlooks.

> *(With complex suddenness, JUDY comes rushing into office in wild glee; in eagerness to get at LES, she jumps on desk and lands sprawling over other side onto him in his chair, both of which are knocked to floor in confusion, violence, and scurry or scuffle. Following dialogue takes place from floor disarray:)*

JUDY: I kept inquiring where you were, and put clues and hints together, into leads by which I traced the unknown lost time of your life's succession in my absence: the succession of events that's led to your eventual success. *(Raising arms)* And to top it all off, here you are!

LES: Your finding me has enabled me to find you! You by active means,

I by passive, arrived at *this* result. *(They soak each other in, by visual embrace, though bodily apart.)* You're you—but not Judy.

JUDY: *(Alarmed)* Not *which* Judy?

LES: Not *any* by my decree: I pronounce the name "Judy" irrelevant, so change it.

JUDY: *(Relieved)* Legally?

LES: *Marriage* is sufficiently legal to do it.

JUDY: But marriage can only change the bride's *last* name, not her first. Are you in such flight from the past, that you'd eliminate a vestige of all our former foolishness, the name "Judy"? No need. I recently learned that you're the precise "Les" for me.

LES: I am. But how did you learn?

JUDY: Through a new fortune teller. He predicted a "Les" for me. I pinned him down to *"what* Les?" The description—facially as well as bodily as well as improvement in financial conditions—fit you in all regards, matching each respect, respective of your true actuality, as confirmed by such physical features; and circumstances now, in this well-appointed office *(Looking around at it)*, and by your expensive grooming *(Admiring it)*, as proclaims you to all the world, *(Shouts:)* "Executive!"

LES: That's a change in me, for the good. What about a positive change *you've* needed?

JUDY: I'm better, I'm reformed. No longer do I reject or victimize men—or rather you're the permanent exception. No longer will I *need* to reject or victimize men: other men are out of the question. You've put a halt to all that. *(Pause)* And you cure us of something *else*, too.

LES: What may *that* be?

JUDY: By marrying me, you cure me of being poor.

(They embrace, still on disarray floor, near upturned desk chair)

LES: What's left? *(Half looking at audience)* A happy ending?

JUDY: Certainly. With such a sorrowful world, what's wrong with *our* happiness?—*(Consolingly:)* it won't last.

LES: Its not lasting is *later*: maybe *much* later. For now, shouldn't this *(Indicating their office-floor situation)* suffice?—followed, in formal rites, by a wedding?

JUDY: That's the sequence of steps. *(Stares at LES:)* But how did my recent fortune teller *know* about you? How was he so accurate? Magic? Divination? Uncanny insight? How?

LES: He named me? And described me?

JUDY: But neglected to say how we'd meet. I told him I couldn't afford it—which was true. Other customers were waiting. He wanted no more delay. I paid him for naming and describing you, then left—he was eager that I leave, knowing I couldn't pay more for his further divining how I was to find you.

LES: How *did* you find me?

JUDY: I'm psychic!

LES: *(Expression changing to worried frown)* Then will you exploit me? Those psychic professionals I resorted to—without exception— exploited me, bleeding me, as far as they could. *(Suspiciously sternly:)* Will that be true of you too, though amateur?

JUDY: *(Affectionately clever)* Not if you and I turn into "one."

LES: One what?

JUDY: One married couple.

LES: A pair?

JUDY: A team of two mates, in one.

(They embrace, still down on floor)

LES: *(With worried look of apprehension, misgiving)* Still, married people, at least after a while, come to conflict and strife.

JUDY: We'll weather it.

LES: Weather it? But I'm well off enough so we'll be indoors.

JUDY: I'm worth the risk. Let's try it. Financially, I have nothing to lose; but you do, and more and more, as your salary improves. But markets are never quite ideally equal. *(Abruptly:)* You're my Les!

LES: But I change you from Judy!

JUDY: What to?

LES: To Ruth. *(Looks at her:)* My Ruth!

JUDY (Now RUTH): *(Tenderly)* But you're no *less, (pun on "Les")* what you were before.

LES: Together, we're...

LES AND JUDY (Now RUTH): *(Together, in determined, ruthless tone)* Ruth-less!

JUDY (Now RUTH): But names are only tags, or labels.

LES: But they come to mean a lot.

JUDY (Now RUTH): But the meanings come to change, though the names *(Looking at LES)* remain—

LES: *(Completing her sentence looking at her)*—Or not.

> *(They rise tightly entwined so closely together as to appear momentarily to be one person, which symbolically they are, temporarily. Leaving upturned chair on floor they exit, closely locked in step, as one. Office remains, in its silence of inanimate expensive businesslike materials.*
>
> *Reappearance of LES—without JUDY (now RUTH))*

LES: *(Picking up chair, putting it back at desk place; remaining standing, half-facing audience)* I gave Ruth money to buy herself new attire and stuff to make our wedding upgraded, in keeping with my new business prosperity.

How did she locate me here? She wanted to badly enough, and whether by magic or not, she found the way.

My work has been well, and now love completes my life, at its current state. Whatever's to come, at least I have this.

At this moment, it's all I ask. Any mystery that's left, will find the magic to appear only when I let this moment go. What went before, led to this. Darkness stops this up, and despite what may fall, I'm preserved. I pause and stop. The rest will be; but first I suspend my good fortune in this state favorable to bright rest. Let blackness keep it safe.

(Curtain, total blackness on stage. End of play)

ANTI-NUCLEAR LOVE
or Love Unfairly Tested
(A full-length play in only one act)

Characters:

> BETSY: who loves and lives with TERRIBLE TONY
> CARL: who loves BETSY and is jealous of TERRIBLE TONY
> TERRIBLE TONY: who loves and lives with BETSY
> POLICEMAN: who benevolently serves to help to solve BETSY's and TERRIBLE TONY's problems, but not CARL's

(Setting: Main room of BETSY's and TERRIBLE TONY's apartment (in a city), which includes a door for both coming into and going out of that apartment. Time: Approximately now [1982])

(BETSY (attractive and idealistic) is alone in apartment, eagerly but nervously expecting someone at door. She opens door; CARL enters. He looks at her with shy longing, but covertly, aiming to conceal it. She motions him to sit down anywhere. When he sits, she sits opposite, leaning forward, earnestly. CARL waits for her to break their tense silence and speak; she doesn't, but looks anxious)

CARL: *(Finally breaking the ice)* Is Terrible Tony here?
BETSY: No. He's out.

(Pause)

CARL: You summoned me here? *(Tenderly:)* Something to do with us?

BETSY: *(Making an announcement)* Terrible Tony's sanity is of universal importance.

(Pause, to let that sink in on audience)

CARL: *(His tenderness disappointed)* That's an exaggeration. *(Jealously:)* His sanity is of no concern to *me*, for example.

BETSY: *(Scolding)* But he's your friend!

CARL: Sure, but his craziness is nothing to worry about. For years, his friends have accepted it as harmless: It hasn't bothered him, and we ignore it. We all remain loyal, and *(Sadly, looking at BETSY:)* go on as before.

BETSY: Something has changed.

CARL: *(Ignoring that)* We know all about him. I'm not concerned.

BETSY: *(Portentously)* You *will* be, once I tell you why his sanity is vitally essential to the whole world.

CARL: *(Perks up)* Did you say something's changed?

BETSY: Terrible Tony, as you know, is a diabolical genius.

CARL: *(Let down; half yawns)* Nothing new about *that*. That's long been a known fact. *(Politely:)* But meanwhile, why is his sanity any great matter?

BETSY: *(Letting out her bombshell)* He's invented his own personal private microscopic little nuclear bomb.

(Pause, to allow that to sink in on audience)

CARL: *(With indignant outrage)* But that's illegal! Only an entire *nation* is allowed to own—at whatever size—a nuclear bomb!

BETSY: *(Speaking knowingly about* TERRIBLE TONY*)* Since when has Terrible Tony obeyed—or even respected—international rules? He's such a law unto himself, that not even *national* rules, much less *international* ones, earn any respect from him.

CARL: Is his own personal private microscopic little nuclear bomb that he in his genius has invented . . . capable of as much damage as a nationally owned *big* version which has a government seal of official authenticity on it?

BETSY: Because Terrible Tony *is* such a *diabolical* genius, the answer to your question is "yes."

CARL: Now I can understand—considering the devastatingly lethal, potentially catastrophic power in the amplified private personal mini-bomb that he's invented for his own possessive use at his own discretion—why Terrible Tony's sanity is of considerably universal importance.

BETSY: *(Her worry now moderated by logic)* Of course, even if he's insane or becomes so, that's fortunately no guarantee that he'll definitely *use* the bomb.

CARL: *(Taking up some of the burden of BETSY's worry)* Yet, he remains a national—even international—risk. He's a hazard to the survival of the human race. Potentially, he's a liability to life itself, by his mere *possession* of that ultimate of all weapons.

BETSY: *(Glad to have gained CARL's agreement, so that he'll share her burden)* He endangers security, we can't take a chance.

CARL: That's why you summoned me?

BETSY: Can there be a more major reason?

CARL: *(Hiding his disappointment)* Naturally, not.

BETSY: *(Rhetorically)* What shall we do about Terrible Tony?

CARL: Our course seems unequivocal. We should, as responsible citizens of the global community, not to mention our specific country, turn him in.

BETSY: It's our duty to report him to the authorities, such as (*Counting off absently on her fingers:)* police, detectives, secret service intelligence, bureau of federal investigation, or what the C.I.A. initials mean: civil information administration; or to any one of the armed forces, or even to state troopers, or whoever's in charge, like sheriffs, magistrates, and suchlike officials publicly concerned with the propagation and perpetuation of peace.

CARL: What's the protocol or procedure, that's regularly used in the case of someone discovered to be armed with the recent invention of a private personal weapon of international knockout power fatal to all our species?

BETSY: This is an unprecedented case, by law. What prophet, seer, or soothsayer could have predicted what even that diabolical genius, Terrible Tony, would come up with?

CARL: *(Suspiciously)* Who *told* you what he invented?

BETSY: *He* did.

CARL: But why did he confide such a private matter, such a hush-up secret . . . ?

BETSY: Loved ones confide in each other. Nor is it a secret from the world that for years he and I have been intimate lovers right here in this apartment, where we live together most intimately unmarried.

CARL: But—are you not betraying him?

BETSY: *(In anguish)* Of course—at great personal sacrifice. But: what might doom the world if left unchecked, neglected, unlocked into, is, by any humane scale, more important than just his and my—two people's—love happiness.

CARL: That's so unselfish, you might become, in the due course of events, recognized as a saint, martyr, savior.

BETSY: *(In dignified tone of heroism)* My reward will be simply this: the world will have been spared. Beyond that, I don't care for petty medals of fickle fame, rosy glory, or silver renown. Those are but tinsel emblems of vanity, when set against—

CARL: Mankind's survival?

BETSY: You're so right. So in spite of my love for Terrible Tony, I'll go—

CARL: *(Interrupting)* With my co-operation—

BETSY: *(After grateful look, continuing)*—report him to have him disarmed of that all-too-potent toy, his recent invention.

CARL: *(Building up his daring)* When he's in jail—for I presume a very lengthy sentence in the interests of everyone's security—your love bond with him might become a mortal casualty, due to long interruption. *(Pause. In bold shyness:)* Since secretly I've felt a concealed love for you, may I now announce it to you, in the hope, possibly, of taking his place?

BETSY: *(Unsurprised, having already suspected CARL's love for her)* No, Carl. How can you replace such a diabolical genius as Terrible Tony?

CARL: By matching him in one particular.

BETSY: *(Blasé; knowing what's coming, but playing along)* Which is?

CARL: Love for you.

BETSY: But that's trivial, compared to the critical urgent priority of our first joint task: to deprive Terrible Tony of the freedom to be at large to maybe become insane enough to promote fierce damage by way of his recently invented toy.

CARL: *(Calculatedly bargaining)* By helping you succeed at that high priority, will you reward me—

BETSY: *(Interrupting; annoyed)* Set that consideration aside. *(Chiding:)* Such bribery or blackmail betokens corruption. *(Defiantly:)* Nor do I need your assistance in reporting—

CARL: *(Repentant)* I'm sorry.

BETSY: A potential madman, ferociously armed, may be on the loose. Let's get him tracked down, and put away—out of harm's way, for all our sakes.

CARL: *(Once again, dauntless)* Love of *humanity* may be *your* motive; love of *you* is *mine*.

BETSY: Let's go to our local law-enforcing agency quick. *(Stringing him along:)* Let's leave this *other* question for another day.

CARL: *(Naively)* What other question?

BETSY: *(Stringing him along, to ensure his co-operation)* The one you yourself made so bold as to introduce: the replacement by you of Terrible Tony as my partner in love, once the latter is forcibly imprisoned for having been diabolical genius enough to invent what, when allied to possible insanity, might endanger not only love, but life, and limb, for *all*.

CARL: Unarguably, let's proceed. *(Pause. Upon considering:)* But did you not try to convince Terrible Tony to give his violent invention up to the authorities, as a safety measure for the public?

BETSY: *(Sadly, bitterly)* Thus I argued; he refused.

CARL: Then, giving up on him, you summoned me?

BETSY: You're first his old friend, and lately mine too. It might seem more credible to the police if we made a *joint* report on such a grave matter. But expect no reward from me, other than gratitude, and your honorable sense of serving humanity at a crisis. *(Firmly:)* Your help is unconditional; there's no "deal" involved. Either I depend on you, or I'll act alone.

CARL: *(Not letting go his hope)* Let me assist you to alert the authorities. Eventually, by your own sweet will rather than my coercing, you might grow to love me once he's safely tucked away in jail, out of even a harmless kiss's reach.

BETSY: *(Lofty)* Let's put aside the question of "us." For love of life itself for everyone else, including all the unborn, let's go and make our grim report. Duty calls most uncommonly, for the common good.

CARL: *(Still persisting)* Though we take this urgent step—may I yet love you, Betsy?

BETSY: You've already taken, without permission, that liberty. This is scarcely the time to be delayed by what's so private that it seems petty, when haste is urged by so pressing a public affair: when it's *our* mission alone to rescue a *world* from a danger it doesn't know.

CARL: My love for you then will have to wait.

BETSY: *(Sighing with exasperated impatience)* First let's secure the world's safety from Terrible Tony's misuse of diabolical genius by the possible violence of insanity. *Then*, we'll entertain—

CARL: *(Ardently, imploring)* May I hope?!

BETSY: *(Annoyed; single-mindedly; on the move out of apartment, shoving CARL out too)* Please, Carl! We'll rush out headed in a hurry to our nearest local precinct to give the police sergeant at the desk such a surprise that let's hope he has a steady heart that wouldn't succumb by the shock of our news to a fatal stroke.

CARL: *(Carried away)* Let's act in unison! This is exciting! We'll be glamorous heroes! Television and newspaper cameras will couple us in joint heroic roles! Our names will be paired; the world will expect love of us! We'll become a famous couple!

BETSY: *(Getting him and herself out of the door; angrily)* More is at stake than the pettiness of personal publicity, whether paired or separate. Please appraise your priorities!

CARL: I love glory, I love you!

BETSY: I love humanity. Come with me. First let's save the world from Terrible Tony. *(Contemptuously:)* Then, go pursue the vanity of your glory, by exploiting our double deed—letting *me* off the heroine pedestal—to carve for yourself a self-loving label: "hero."

CARL: *(In amorous excitation)* A hero having earned the highest trophy, the grandest tribute, the most floral laurels: *(In ecstasy:)* your love!

> *(On the way out of the door, they're intercepted by, coming in, TERRIBLE TONY, who's just overheard, to his horror, CARL's last speech)*

TERRIBLE TONY: *(Suspicious; alarmed)* What have I heard?! And why the hurry?!

CARL: *(Caught off guard; guiltily)* What are you doing here!?

TERRIBLE TONY: (Indignant) *Doing* here! I *live* here!

BETSY: *(Flustered; to* TERRIBLE TONY*)* We were just on our way out.

TERRIBLE TONY: *(Testing them)* But what haste! You act like furtive lovers, dashing out, on impulse or calculation, to elope!

CARL: *(Guiltily)* Of *course* not!

BETSY: Naturally not, Terrible Tony! Don't misunderstand us!

TERRIBLE TONY: Then what have I just heard? And why, in unison, this unseemly hurry? You both share telltale looks of guilt, and hasty stealth!

CARL: *(So guilty, he loses his head and blurts out:)* It's not to elope and thus betray you in your love for Betsy—no, that's not it at all . . .

TERRIBLE TONY: *(Laying the trap)* No? Then how do you explain . . .

CARL: *(Stupidly thoughtless)* We're only just on our way out . . .

TERRIBLE TONY: *(Sensing something)* Yes?

CARL: *(Blurting out before frantic* BETSY, *sputtering, can interrupt him)* . . . to the authorities to report on your having invented your own personal private microscopic little nuclear bomb, which, if allied to potential insanity on your part, might empty the world of its long legacy of human life!

(Pause. BETSY *looks horrified, being exposed)*

TERRIBLE TONY: *(To* BETSY, *accusingly)* You've babbled! I've entrusted a secret in you on strictest confidence, which you've betrayed to Carl, our mutual friend. To further compound your treachery, you've enlisted his assistance to—*(In betrayed surprise)*—to turn me in! *Me*, your one and only love! That's indefensible!

BETSY: *(Recovering her defiance)* It is defensible, on the grounds that a grave public danger—an ominous global menace—is constituted by your diabolical invention of your own personal private microscopic little nuclear bomb, which, if detonated, could spell—

TERRIBLE TONY: *(Interrupting)* Cut out the histrionic melodramatics! Your dread that what I've concocted will blow up the world, is blown up out of all proportion. Let me explode such a notion!

BETSY: You had no explosive intention?

TERRIBLE TONY: I'll *de-fuse* your pessimistic alarm. Don't dabble, darling, in morbidity!

CARL: But Terrible Tony, why *did* you invent that collectively lethal little micro-toy?

TERRIBLE TONY: For peaceful purposes!

CARL: What a lame excuse!

TERRIBLE TONY: *(Angrily, to CARL)* Keep your head out of this! I just heard you declare love to my woman! *(To BETSY:)* It's truth I speak!

BETSY: *(In hope)* Your invention wasn't meant diabolically?

TERRIBLE TONY: When I confided my creation, did I imply it would be monstrous?

BETSY: No; I *assumed* it would be. You keep it concealed, and refuse to tell me its hiding place. I suspected—

TERRIBLE TONY: *(Hurt)* What do you take me for! Haven't our years of love, living and sharing together, given you sufficient insight into me to reveal my basic good will and peaceful intentions?

BETSY: I've known you to be unsteady; even . . .

TERRIBLE TONY: *(Wincing)* Unstable?

BETSY: Enough so, to worry how sound your sanity was. And your hiding the whereabouts of your invention seemed ever to confirm—I brooded. Then I summoned Carl, to help me protect the world population, and all of posterity, from your possible annihilative threat.

CARL: *(Cutting in; jealously frustrated and disappointed; to TERRIBLE TONY)* I wish we *could* turn you in. I wish there *were* grounds to distrust the "peaceful" intentions of your diabolical invention, so that Betsy and I could go ahead with our original plan of getting you arrested as a menace to world safety, with your micro-bomb confiscated by governmental officials as constituting a danger in your unsteady hands, and so you'd be put out of harm's way, confined from liberty, leaving then the coast clear for Betsy to treat my love with tender—

BETSY: *(Angrily to CARL)* What have you given away by your imprudent babbling? And what are you so rashly fabricating, so falsely insinuating? It's not Terrible Tony, but *you*, who've lost your head! You're a cheat, and a fool!

TERRIBLE TONY: *(Accusingly, to CARL)* I was, then, initially right, on intercepting you two in your flight. You're exposed! You *do* love my loved one, and were planning to elope with her!

BETSY: *(To TERRIBLE TONY)* To be strictly accurate: *He* loved *me* but *I* didn't love *him!* To elope with him stood remote from every emotion I have!

TERRIBLE TONY: *(Perplexed: theatrical, melodramatic)* What am I to believe!?

BETSY: *(To TERRIBLE TONY)* What am *I* to believe?! I care for mankind's universal safety. So I mention the intention behind your invention. Its potential is explosive. By such *dynamite*, we may all *die-by-night*. Terrible Tony, we've lived and loved together for years. If your motive wasn't destructive, then why did you make what you did?!

TERRIBLE TONY: Don't you trust me?

BETSY: Not with the world's fate at stake.

CARL: *(Longingly, amorously, to BETSY)* Betsy—is it *him* or *me*?

BETSY: *(Annoyed, to CARL)* Stop interfering. I wanted your assistance in what I felt to be a dire emergency. I needed someone to share so acute a burden: but you became a nuisance, and mess my cause with mischief. *(Still addressed to CARL, but aimed for (with glance at him) TERRIBLE TONY's ears:)* Certainly I don't love you! I love universal mankind, and Terrible Tony.

CARL: *(Wrathfully, to BETSY)* I'll get revenge. Your love for universal mankind is incompatible with your love for Terrible Tony. I'll exploit that incompatibility, by exposing him and his concealed little monster-toy to the rightful authorities: to rid the world of him and his threat by having him be put away; and to rid *me* of my rival for *you*, in love's name. *(Threatening:)* I'll replace him, yet!

TERRIBLE TONY: *(Furiously, to CARL)* This confirms what I overheard you say to Betsy on your way out when I came in. You *were* our friend; now, I'll kill you!

CARL: *(Taunting)* And along with me, the whole world as well? By one little mighty explosion?

BETSY: *(Frantically)* Please, you two! Let's restore sanity!

CARL: Yes—but whose?

(Pause)

TERRIBLE TONY: *(To CARL)* You've enraged me—even infuriated me, to such a point, that I'll give myself away. You were right, and caught me in a lie when I protested that what I created was with a peaceful purpose.

CARL: *(Triumphantly)* Hah! You did create what could only destroy— contrary to your lame excuse! You're a fraud—but a fright!

BETSY: *(In horror, to TERRIBLE TONY)* You live up to "Terrible Tony," as a prophetic name?!

CARL: *(Vehemently, to BETSY)* He lives *down* to it. Let's deprive his name of his *actual* terror, and restrain his name from potential act, by having the *owner* of that name disarmed and legally stripped of the evil freedom to convert the harm of his name into the grave alarm of a deed!

TERRIBLE TONY: *(His back to the door, alert to prevent CARL from leaving; to CARL)* My name is doomed to be your destiny. Now, let me be explicitly nasty: My invention is subtler than you think. It's not only tiny compared to those blunt devices that *nations* own; it's also—thanks to my diabolical genius—selective.

BETSY: Selective? How?!

TERRIBLE TONY: *(To both BETSY and CARL)* The blunt large earlier versions, owned by nations, blow up everyone *indiscriminately*. But my polished streamlined sophisticated model, pocket-sized, is only *selectively* destructive. With subtlety, I can *control* the violence. *(To CARL alone:)* To illustrate, Carl, I'll start with you: I'll eliminate you, and you alone, through a moderation-chamber of my weapon. This will assuage the rage you've put on me.

CARL: *(Trying to run to door, that's blocked by TERRIBLE TONY; but first restrained by BETSY)* Help! Help! A madman wants to kill only me!

BETSY: *(Restraining CARL from attempting to reach door)* But Carl—be reasonable!

CARL: *(Pausing from struggling)* How?

BETSY: *(Again showing her genuine love of humanity)* Better that *you alone* should die, than *everyone!*

CARL: Better?

BETSY: Of course!

CARL: For *you* it is! For *him* (Indicating TERRIBLE TONY) it is! For others it is! But—*(Breaks loose from BETSY; only to be restrained in turn by TERRIBLE TONY)*—but not for me! *(Struggles in grip of TERRIBLE TONY, at door)*

TERRIBLE TONY: *(Panting to BETSY)* He's hardly the humanitarian type!

BETSY: *(To TERRIBLE TONY)* He's no ideal model for humanitarianism, no. *(Challengingly:)* But you—are *you* any better?

TERRIBLE TONY: *(Still clutching CARL; at the end of his patience)* Betsy, I can't stand your doubting me always. Your continual doubting poisons the soil of love, at the roots of love.

BETSY: You sound like our love is a farm or a garden. Terrible Tony: what *have* you invented?

TERRIBLE TONY: I'm contaminated by *your* distrust. I won't tell you, for I don't trust you!

BETSY: You trusted me *before* with the revelation that you'd made, to perfection, your own private personal miniature model of a nuclear bomb that works. For humanity's sake, I *must* misplace that trust!

TERRIBLE TONY: Look, Betsy—*(He starts to gesticulate, in explanation, but in so doing inadvertently loosens his restraining hold on* CARL, *who bolts away to open the door and flee from apartment, yelling to* TERRIBLE TONY *in flight while soon leaving sight:)*

CARL: *(Then, soon, only his voice)* I'll report this to the authorities. You threatened my life; singled me out, while sparing the rest of the whole world. That's discrimination; I'll have you arrested on the rap of selecting me for unique murder. And that whole complex instrument of yours that you've invented: Scientific officials will wish to place it under examination to determine the potentially potent extent of its destructive capacity when the *selective* mechanism is off and the switch turns on to the devastating holocaust of the wholescale massacre, indiscriminately, of our entire human species, ending our evolved cultural traditions alongside the prospects of unborn posterity, all in one annihilating blast! *(Jealously:)* Terrible Tony, shouldn't Betsy's love have contented you? Did you have to become greedy, and add everyone's death—as their killer—to the triumph of owning Betsy's love? You've gone too far! I'll report you! *(*CARL*'s voice thus ends, after his sight had already vanished)*

TERRIBLE TONY: *(At open door: calling after the vanished* CARL, *who might or might not still be able to hear him)* Too bad I don't happen to have my own personal private microscopic little nuclear bomb *handy*, to turn on its "selective" device, so as to eliminate specifically you! Now you've fled to report me to the police. They might think you crazy and not believe you. *(Pause. With worried frown:)* But they might believe you and come hunting for me. You'll tell them where I live. *(Turning to* BETSY:*)* Betsy, this place *(Indicating apartment)* is "hot." Let's you and I flee, to "lay low." We'll stop at my workshop, which is where I've secreted my invention. Unexpectedly, I may have to use it prematurely in self-defense.

BETSY: *(Horrified)* Terrible Tony, my worst fears are confirmed! You *did* make that ugly little toy! You *are* a diabolical genius!

TERRIBLE TONY: I already confided in you as to my creation. But you betray my confidence as well as our love, by having intended to turn me in. You've done the damage. You blurted my secret to Carl, who at this moment is busy reporting me to the authorities. Is it *all women* who aren't to be trusted, or just *you alone?*

BETSY: Don't scold me, Terrible Tony. I considered it my duty to mankind to rid it of the peril you've put it under. I *am* giving my frantic warning signal to the world, as to your danger to it, via the proxy of my messenger, Carl!

TERRIBLE TONY: *(Anguished; poignantly)* Then you've betrayed me—my love!

BETSY: I betrayed you for humanity's good, so that life will survive. Meanwhile, I love *you* still.

TERRIBLE TONY: *(Suddenly changed by her last sentence)* In *spite* of my invention?

BETSY: In my heart, yes.

TERRIBLE TONY: *(Finally letting out the truth)* Oh Betsy—I was only testing your love for me!

BETSY: You mean you *didn't* invent that alleged invention?

TERRIBLE TONY: No, it was a hoax—to test your love.

BETSY: By so extreme a measure?!

TERRIBLE TONY: You failed the test—I'm being sought by the authorities, thanks to Carl now, and ultimately thanks to you! I'm a hunted man! I'm legally being hounded down!

BETSY: Oh Terrible Tony: Let's flee if we think the police will believe Carl; but remain if we think the police will laugh at Carl as being merely crazy.

TERRIBLE TONY: Which is their more likely response?

BETSY: At a hazard, we could only guess. Oh Terrible Tony—what a terrible test to put my love to!

TERRIBLE TONY: It was found wanting: you love humanity more!

BETSY: How will you punish me?'

TERRIBLE TONY: By leaving you.

BETSY: How cruel! I love you! What will become of me?

TERRIBLE TONY: *(Viciously) Carl* is all too willing to replace me in your affections.

BETSY: But I don't love *him*—I love *you*.

TERRIBLE TONY: Yet you *betrayed* me to him!

BETSY: *(In angry horror)* I was right! You *are* unstable! How paranoiac of you to concoct and devise so cruel a bluff to test my love! You insult my love's purity, and degrade its nest of trust.

TERRIBLE TONY: *(Pointedly)* You've *failed* that test!

BETSY: As you're of unsound mind, your test must be invalid, unfair! I wanted to protect the human race, which you led me to suspect would be placed in jeopardy by what you'd claimed to invent. Your convincing bluff placed me in a horrible position, a cruel dilemma. I made my choice—being forced to choose. I proved my love for humanity in my willingness to sacrifice your love. But for all that, I love you no less than before!

TERRIBLE TONY: *(Cruelly)* Wrong choice! *I* come first!

BETSY: That's selfish of you! *Humanity* comes first!

TERRIBLE TONY: *(Testing her again)* At my expense?!

BETSY: *(Defiantly)* Yes!

TERRIBLE TONY: At our love's expense?

BETSY: *(Miserably)* Yes, unfortunately.

TERRIBLE TONY: *(Violently decisive)* Then consider our romantic affair *over! (Heads for door)* **Goodbye!**

BETSY: *(Chasing after him)* But Terrible Tony—you haven't packed!

(As TERRIBLE TONY *is leaving apartment, pursued by* BETSY, *he's intercepted by* POLICEMAN, *who enters with* CARL*)*

POLICEMAN: Are you Terrible Tony?

TERRIBLE TONY: *(Puffing)* Admittedly, yes.

POLICEMAN: Is this man *(Points to* CARL*)* crazy?

TERRIBLE TONY: Yes, officer.

POLICEMAN: *(With grateful praise)* The world *needs* more people like you.

CARL: *(In outburst)* No it doesn't!

POLICEMAN: *(To* CARL, *threateningly)* Enough of you. I'll add gagging your mouth to your already being handcuffed, if I you make another outburst. You've meddled enough in people's lives, and harassed them. *(Pause. Stares in silence at* TERRIBLE TONY *and* BETSY, *studying them. Still addressing* CARL:*)* It's obvious that pair love each other. *(*CARL *winces in tortured and frustrated jealousy)* My insight into human nature is well respected in the Force. They're *crazy* about each other, those two. *(*CARL*'s tortured reaction intensifies)* And *you're* crazy too—period.

TERRIBLE TONY: *(In confessing tone)* It's true, officer: I love her!

BETSY: *(Sweetly open)* You're right, Officer: I love him.

POLICEMAN: Such mutual love as I see between you two makes it a crime not to be married. *(Stares at their fingers)* My sense of observation instructs me that you two are devoid of wedding rings. *Why?!*

TERRIBLE TONY: *(On the defensive; apologetically)* We never got around to it, Officer.

POLICEMAN: Is it an invasion and violation of your rights to privacy to inquire if you've been living together, and if so, for how long?

BETSY: *(Eagerly co-operating, seeing POLICEMAN as being a kind ally)* We *have* been living together—in this very apartment—for the last couple of years, Officer.

POLICEMAN: During which time, has your love had occasion to increase?

TERRIBLE TONY: Mine for her has, Sir.

POLICEMAN: *(To BETSY)* And yours?

BETSY: Similarly, Sir.

POLICEMAN: *(With decisive authority)* Then I hereby constitute it a crime of omission to stay unmarried. I give you a week to rectify that omission. My headquarters precinct is in this district here. I'm making a note, *(Does so, with pen and pad, while non-writing wrist remains handcuffed to dejected CARL)*, to come back in a few days for the progress report I expect. Should you disappoint me, I'm sufficiently schooled in the wiles of corruption to concoct charges against you which you'd find it impossible to refute, thus leading to terms of separate imprisonment!

TERRIBLE TONY: *(Gladly docile)* Obediently, I'll marry her, Sir.

POLICEMAN: *(To BETSY)* And you?

BETSY: *(In eager gratitude)* Similarly, Sir.

CARL: *(In muttering outburst)* This is a fraud—a frame-up!

POLICEMAN: I already warned you. To gag you would take up time awkwardly. Then let *this* silence you! *(Knocks CARL out unconscious (but still on feet) with billy-club)*

TERRIBLE TONY: *(Radiantly)* Officer, may we invite you to our wedding?

BETSY: *(Enthusiastically)* Please, Sir, we'd *love* to have you!

POLICEMAN: *(Proudly modest)* I'm honored! Moreover, I'm touched!

TERRIBLE TONY: *(In sudden inspiration)* Will you witness this, Sir?

POLICEMAN: *(Puzzled)* Yes? What?

(TERRIBLE TONY *goes down on his knees, in traditional posture of time-honored formal proposal of marriage, to* BETSY. *The miming should be realistic and convincing*)

BETSY: Oh Terrible Tony—may I call you "Tony"?

TERRIBLE TONY: Why not? That'll simplify matters.

(CARL *revives*)

CARL: *(Protesting to* POLICEMAN*)* It's a fraud, officer! They're bluffing! He's paranoiac! She secretly loves me, but is afraid to let him know!

POLICEMAN: *(To* BETSY*)* What do you have to say to *that*, Madam?

BETSY: It's not worth commenting on.

POLICEMAN: You'd not dignify it with a reply? *(Making ready to hit* CARL *on head again with outraised billy-club)*

BETSY: *(Intercepting* POLICEMAN, *by taking hold of his club-bearing arm)* Officer, please don't harm him! He's demented. He needs more pity than punishment. He needs tender understanding, Sir. He's got to find sympathy—from somewhere!

POLICEMAN: *(Putting away his billy-club in holster)* You're very humane, Madam.

TERRIBLE TONY: *Too* humane!

POLICEMAN: *(Alertly taking* TERRIBLE TONY *up on that)* How so, Sir?

TERRIBLE TONY: *(Complaining)* She's so humane that she puts humanity first and me second.

POLICEMAN: *(To* BETSY*)* Is that true, Madam?

BETSY: *(Candidly)* It's been proven to be, Sir. *(Looks toward* TERRIBLE TONY*)* I've been tested, on that score.

POLICEMAN: *(Heading toward door to begin leaving with handcuffed* CARL; *to* TERRIBLE TONY*)* You're a very lucky man, Sir.

TERRIBLE TONY: How so, Officer?

POLICEMAN: I'm a student of human nature. I'm never wrong in my appraisals. She's a lovely, humane woman. The priority of her love for humanity in general, confers even greater value on her love for *you*.

TERRIBLE TONY: *(Seeing the light and justice of that remark)* You're wise, Officer.

POLICEMAN: *(In last stages of leaving with CARL)* All in the line of duty, Sir. I'll check when the wedding is.

BETSY: *(Parting after POLICEMAN at door to intercept him; impulsively)* Oh officer—this is no bribe—but will you accept this little gift?

POLICEMAN: *(Surprised)* What?—

(BETSY hugs and kisses him. While she does so, handcuffed CARL suddenly puts his face in the way of BETSY's kissing of POLICEMAN, to conspicuously intercept one of her kisses for himself)

CARL: *(To TERRIBLE TONY and POLICEMAN, in "proven triumph")* There! —I told you she loves me!

POLICEMAN: *(Showing forbearance, restraint, to CARL)* I promised her I'd humanely spare you, so I won't knock you out again. You can thank her humanity that, as I drag you away in custody, you're coming along consciously and not unconsciously. She's right that you need pity, sympathy, and understanding. You also require tenderness, and loads of love. But all that will have to wait till you're released either from your jail cell or from your mental asylum room. Whether you'll be *able*, upon release, to get what you need is perhaps problematical.

BETSY: *(To CARL)* Choose your woman more wisely, next time. One who'll be a most willing source of the tenderness, sympathy, understanding, love, and generous pity you sought from *me* so pathetically in vain!

CARL: *(Semi-lucidly)* All your love was used up on humanity and Terrible Tony, with nothing left to spare for me?

BETSY: Humanity *includes* you. But circumstances made things difficult. Situationally, I had to deprive you. In addition, I was temperamentally disinclined toward you, as a romantic candidate. And I had already emotionally committed myself. Consider this advice: Choose a more likely woman, next time, one *(Looking with mischievous smile at* TERRIBLE TONY:*)* unencumbered in the disposal of her affections.

*(*TERRIBLE TONY *puts his arm tenderly around* BETSY. *They look the perfect image of a betrothed couple: almost as though, beamingly, they're posing for a conventional engagement or marriage photo)*

POLICEMAN: *(Looking approvingly on* BETSY *and* TERRIBLE TONY *in their joint role he's helped to enforce)* I'll see you shortly, so you can fill me in on the wedding details. *(Proprietarily; with, maybe, a broad or knowing wink:)* I take a paternal role, in all this. The conventional marriage unit is hereby sacredly conserved. You've observed it just in time. Without it, you would have broken apart.

BETSY: *(In tone of reverence)* Our love is preserved, thanks to you, dear Sir, and that institution we'd neglected: marriage; to which, in the law's wisdom, you guide us with stern supervision as our love's second father and divine preserver. You're our love's god by nature: to which we submit our devout souls amorously saved by your kind intervention.

POLICEMAN: *(To* BETSY:*)* You overwhelm me! *(To both of them:)* Return to the prosaic level, with less lavishly embarrassing rhetoric! Or I'll subject you to verbal arrest! I merely serve you this injunction: marry!

TERRIBLE TONY: *(Obediently prosaic, but grateful)* Officer, to let you down *would* be a crime.

BETSY: *(Admiringly grateful)* Officer, you not only defend and uphold justice, but you *create* it!

POLICEMAN: *(Caught between modesty and agreement)* I improvise where I see fit. *(Pause)* I'm too hard-boiled, and allergic to sentimentality, to linger overlong now. I'll take temporary leave, in company of the culprit. *(Finally exits, in flustered flourish, with handcuffed CARL)*

BETSY: *(Ecstatic)* Oh Terrible Tony! *(Embracing him)*

TERRIBLE TONY: *(While they're embracing)* Do call me just "Tony," to simplify matters. We'll need to economize, and generally trim things down, now that our love enters the domestic institution and turns marital.

BETSY: *(Still while embracing)* Marital, yes. *Martial,* no. Love's *balm* beats any *bomb.*

> *(They continue embracing, while curtain falls, to end play)*

TOPSY-TURVY

Characters:

WILBERT WILLS: (Later a.k.a. THE GRAND DUKE OF WILBERTANIA.) Novelist, age mid-fifties.

THADDEUS: (Later a.k.a. PRINCE GLITZ.) Age 21. Very graceful and handsome, in the romantic hero mold.

SY: Age early fifties. Suntanned L.A. Assistant T.V. Producer under MORTON RAY.

BRUCE WAIN: Age mid-thirties. Hard-boiled, no-nonsense Private Eye.

ROXY: Age 21. Beautiful, innocent aspiring actress.

MORTON RAY: Age late fifties. T.V. Producer, suntanned, L.A., rather small of height.

MARCONI: Age mid-thirties. Homosexual. Casting Director.

MAGGIE: Age early thirties. T.V. Associate Producer under SY. Beautiful but cold and calculating.

VITTORIO: Age early forties. Italian émigré. T.V. Director.

CELIA SEE: Age thirties or forties. Feature writer for T.V. & show biz gossip magazine, "Peep-hole Magazine."

Note: So that no extra actors or actresses are needed, various of the above characters can be doubled with the following minor, miscellaneous characters:

Waiter, Scriptwriters, Announcer, Set men, Reporters, Photographers, Studio technician, Lighting people, Camera crew, Cameraman, Assistants to Director, Wardrobe people, Policemen.

SYNOPSIS

WILBERT, a "pure" novelist whose aesthetic muse has dried up, is commissioned to write an episode for a prime-time, mass-market vulgar T.V. series by his former old friend SY, now the series' Assistant Producer. WILBERT is to inject new blood into the commercially flagging series by creating a new character, a young romantic male lead. But that character, THADDEUS, suddenly disappears from WILBERT's working script. WILBERT accuses SY of having THADDEUS kidnapped, but SY denies it. WILBERT hires a tough Private Eye, BRUCE WAIN, to find THADDEUS. Meanwhile, THADDEUS, who has amnesia, meets a lovely young would-be actress, ROXY, in Sardi's; they fall in love. BRUCE WAIN arrives too late at Sardi's: THADDEUS has gone to be auditioned for, coincidentally, the same role for which WILBERT had created him. The producers fly THADDEUS, whom they rename PRINCE GLITZ, to L.A. to be filmed in the T.V. series, amid press media hullabaloo. BRUCE WAIN follows him there, then ROXY, as well as WILBERT. The latter three find themselves also cast as characters in the same T.V. series, along with the series' actual producers, director, etc. Thus the drama merges on two levels: the actual action and the T.V. series acting. These two levels coincide and become one.

ACT ONE

SCENE I

(N.Y.C.—WILBERT's East Village apartment.)

(WILBERT, feverish excitement in his eyes, leaves his paper-cluttered desk and rushes out of the room, and out of his flat, and out of the building. Silence. Then from below paper-cluttered desk, a weird slow-motion crashing-through occurs: the figure of THADDEUS

emerges, breaking through not only the desk but also the room walls)

THADDEUS: Some force beyond myself lifts me away from here, toward—unpredictably what? I'm being impelled, compelled, propelled—but not expelled. A double mystery perplexes me utterly: where am I going to, and where am I coming from? Between those two mysteries, in passage, I lack a stable definition, I lack a secure identity, with a blurred future, a blurred past, and an undetermined me. As I live, I wish to give my life some consistent shape. To that end, I rush—whither? From whence?

Outward bound, I whizz away from this unsatisfactory "here," to forge some self-realization in fulfillment of an as yet undefined urge. I'm curious what I'm to become. Both the curiosity and the becoming are now in process, starting with this escape.

SCENE II

(5:30 P.M. on same day as in Scene One. SY's New York hotel room. WILBERT, carrying briefcase, greeted at door by SY.)

SY: So Wilbert baby, come on in, sorry I'm in a rush, big dinner party tonight, the T.V. division of Paramount up at Helmsley Palace. But come in, I'm expecting something you got in that little briefcase. It's good seein' you again. What's it been, four, five years? You lost a little weight, but you're lookin' great. When you get to be our age, a few pounds loss is always a good plus. Sit down, my home is your home.

WILBERT: Sy, it sure has been a while.

SY: *(Slapping WILBERT on back, half-embracing)* Good to see ya, old pal.

WILBERT: *(Eyeing SY up and down)* You look in sound health.

SY: Never felt better. How do I look, huh? Southern Cal has done this to me. Bought a little place along the ocean, a little get-away, two tennis courts, pool, hot tub. I tell ya, this series has been good to me, real good. You know I'm real happy that I could cut *you* in on some of the action.

WILBERT: Thank you.

SY: By the end of the season we'll be number one. If things work out *(Looks at WILBERT's briefcase)* and Morton is happy with your work, maybe I can get you on the staff: it'll be an income like I know you never even saw yet, with all your lifetime struggling as a writer, you poor sap.

WILBERT: Here I am—there you are. How changed we are from those old days when we started out together in the glow of youthful ideals.

SY: Yeah, we sure go back, don't we. But when I think about it, it was another incarnation, Wilbert. Another time and another space. It sure don't stack up against what I got *now*.

WILBERT: I've stuck to my guns nobly till recent years when my Muse dried up, thus sucking the life out of potential new novels.

SY: Had a bad day, huh? This city is no good for the psyche. Maybe you've been havin' women trouble. I'll get you a drink. Scotch, right? *(WILBERT doesn't answer; SY prepares a drink.)* As for me, you know what? I can't even remember some of the titles of those novels *I* wrote! Poetic rubbish.

WILBERT: You willfully, ignominiously sold out years ago.

SY: *(Vigorously, in self-defense, self-justification)* Sold out? Bought in! Look at me now: I'm paid too much, do little work, get to travel a lot, have friends and fawners in abundance—*(Forcefully, emphatically, rubbing it in:)* I have fun and still I reach twenty million plus a week! *(Complacently, as though that settles it:)* Now tell me, what more can we ask for in this life, right?

WILBERT: You've become a weary cynic, a conformist in the commercial exploitation of the lowest popular taste. It's a sad sight!

Sy: *(Laughs, to maintain superiority)* Same old Wilbert! The starry-eyed idealist: *(Claps him on back, with mock-affection.)* It's really good to see you, guy!

Wilbert: You depress me. I despise—

Sy: *(Interrupting)* You're serious, aren't you *(Condescendingly:)* You got to learn to lighten up—you'll live a lot longer, and get more women. Consider the evolution of the species, Wilbert baby, and learn what it takes to survive!

Wilbert: *(Angrily)* Don't sicken me! You talk cheap!

Sy: *(Overriding Wilbert's anger)* Take a look at yourself. Now I only say this—I take the liberty, the license of an old friend—but who are you? Some quasi-poetic "pure" novelist? What does the public care for your precious fiction—your careful prose? Am I right? Or who's wrong?

Wilbert: *(Angry)* You little fink!

Sy: *(Overriding Wilbert)* Look here . . . *(Fingering Wilbert's clothes above waist)* Take stock. Just look at yourself. *(Wilbert makes a gesture of pushing Sy away, but Sy persists.)* Shoes there untied. Your tie has your lunch on it, I see you still go for that veal Parmesan. Shirt missing a button. *(Musses Wilbert's hair despite Wilbert's warning look of annoyance.)* You sure do need a haircut. *(Fingering Wilbert's jacket:)* This sport coat *was* very stylish—in the fifties! *(Finally Wilbert wriggles out of Sy's grasp and shoves Sy away. Wilbert looks grim.)*

Wilbert: Who are you insulting?—You trendy little creep!

Sy: *(Sneering)* Sure, you've made some sort of name for yourself—a little high-fallutin' critical fame in literary circles. But Wilbert, dear boy, face it—the times have changed!

Wilbert: All right, so why'd you hire me?

Sy: You still don't get it, do you?

Wilbert: What's there to "get"?

Sy: The real world, Wilbert baby. Rise and shine. We put your name on the credits; your name elevates our show-biz mass-market commercial classiness with the imported extra clout of your contribution to our product: your pseudo-intellectual literary pretentiousness. We'll get the cover story from *T.V. Guide* at least, and the highbrow press will fork over promotional coverage.

WILBERT: I was hired for that? Is my name worth that much? Then I *do* have credentials! My devotion to pure writing *has* been vindicated!

SY: You poor slob. Don't let it go to your head. All your hard work, your dedication to your so-called craft, makes you—you know what?—a nobody! Nobody recognizes *you* on the streets, but they're beginning to recognize *me*. I have a limousine, too.

WILBERT: You've sunk as low as a snake in the grass. Your sneer has lowbrow slime written all over it.

SY: Is that an example of your gratitude? I love you, we're old friends, so why come at me like I'm doin' something wrong?

WILBERT: *(In ominous tone, to accompaniment of musical chord)* Because you are—you've done *great* wrong! Where's my character?

SY: *(Perplexed, puzzled)* Where's my what? Are you crazy? I throw a nice fat series commission at you, for old times' sake, and you make out like I stole your soul.

WILBERT: *(Staring at SY; still taken aback, finding new SY unrecognizable from old one)* Are you human?

SY: So Wilbert baby—*(Eyes WILBERT's briefcase)* ... Where's the script?

WILBERT: I knew you would mention it—hypocrite!

SY: Don't be spiteful.

WILBERT: *(Sarcastic)* Old friend!

SY: *(Earnest, busy, trying to get back to point)* I love you, Wilbert, but another time. I have this dinner party, then I fly back to L.A. tomorrow afternoon. Come out there and spend some time pool-side. Do you play tennis yet? *(Eyeing briefcase:)* So let's have it.

WILBERT: *(Mocking)* Sure, "let's have it."

Sy: That's how it is. Morton gets on my back and puts me on to your back.

Wilbert: How quaint. We're all a bunch of slimy frogs on each other's backs in a mating ritual of a pecking order of a T.V. production's creative department's hierarchy, splashing in the pond, counter-croaking a daisy-chain ritual . . .

Sy: *(Eyeing briefcase; forceful)* I love it, Wilbert, but I *don't* love it.

Wilbert: *(Deliberately stalling, to spite Sy's impatience for script)* For protecting me from backsliding into effete intellectualism, what do I owe you?

Sy: Don't lay that on me. Appreciate where I'm coming from. *(Pressing Wilbert physically:)* This one episode *(Eyeing briefcase)* you're about to hand over will put you into the living rooms of twenty million Americans sitting on forty million buttocks. What's the sales figures on all your novels put together? If this episode *(Again eyeing briefcase)* hits, you can write your own ticket. You'd make out like crazy in L.A. The dames save their special stuff for writers. *(Eyeing briefcase:)* Now hand it over. I can't be late tonight.

Wilbert: *(Being perverse by deliberately stalling)* With ill-earned T.V. script-writing money, I could afford to stop this degradation into the gross taste of mass popular demand and return to true art's loftier simplicity.

Sy: Money's not only the bottom line—it's everything!

Wilbert: *(Interrupting)* I'll make a comeback, resume the Muse, turn her juices hack on, and be my old true self. Then I won't have to put up with the likes of you and Morton Ray.

Sy: *(Goes over to Wilbert's briefcase and picks it up)* I'll take the script now.

Wilbert: *(Yelling)* That's mine!

Sy: The *case* is yours. The *contents* are mine.

Wilbert: Now look—there's something I want to ask you. That character—

Sy: *(Interrupting, impatiently)* Yes, yes, fascinating, I only wish we could relax and have a chat, for old times' sake if for nothing else, but I gotta get ready.

Wilbert: *(Sarcastically)* Oh how disappointing for poor abandoned me.

Sy: *(Interrupting)* I'll read the script on the way to L.A. and give you a call.

Wilbert: *(Snatching back the briefcase)* It's all your fault—you damn kidnapper!

Sy: Is something wrong with the script?

Wilbert: Stop pretending you don't know what I'm talking about.

Sy: Wilbert, I love you. But this is no time for jokes!

Wilbert: Who's joking?

Sy: Be professional, baby.

Wilbert: Professional? I, at least, still have a profession! What's yours?—Prostitution?

Sy: You disappoint me.

Wilbert: Sy, you and I—we go back a long way together.

Sy: I don't have any more time to give you. Right now, I need this *product*. *(Pointing to briefcase in WILBERT's possession.)*

Wilbert: *(Still stalling, to be spiteful, in power play)* "Product!" I'm not some prefab-cranking piece of mass machinery. Respect me, I'm an artist, even if it takes me years, even though the script is commissioned by your time-bomb deadline—respect me—

Sy: Look, baby, what are you trying to pull on me? You're getting me all tensed and stressed out. In this situation I'm in control, I'm the associate producer.

Wilbert: You're not in control of *this* *(Pointing to self)* exploited peon scribbler! *(Sy aggresses, WILBERT pushes him away.)*

SY: So you had a problem with the script? Is *that* why you're so defensive? You couldn't finish? You had a block? All right, let's not get childish and cry over it. I own a staff of writers, they'll finish it, they'll patch it up. We won't blow this thing out of proportion and quibble like babies. Pretend you're a man.

WILBERT: You're low and cheap, Sy. And sly. I thought a kidnapper had more guts.

SY: *(Sighing, shrugging)* Oh Wilbert, what are you doing to me?

WILBERT: What have *you* done to *me*? Or more to the point, what have you done to my *character*? *(Angrily:)* Answer!

SY: Hey, I just copped a half ounce of the highest grade coke; want a blow? You're grounded now, but it could put you right back in the saddle again.

WILBERT: Betraying me into betraying my own ideals to T.V. Babylon's tawdry corrupt rot!

SY: *(Preparing the cocaine)* You signed that contract by your own free will!

WILBERT: By free will? By economic necessity! Yet I upheld artistic honor, integrity, by creating such a character that you had to steal him!

SY: Raving again? *(With cocaine.)* Take a blow, Wilbert baby. Nothing like this high-grade Bolivian. Come on, it'll resume our friendship. *(Snorts the cocaine, while WILBERT declines some for himself.)*

WILBERT: *(Bitterly contemptuous)* You sniffling, sniveling, snide—

SY: I can't believe it! Other writers would lavish booze and flowers on me for the contract I made the mistake of throwing away on you! A good turn—that you turned on!

WILBERT: Sy, I'll level with you.

SY: Be reasonable, within reason, *(Sniffling the coke.)* What's with the story? Talk to me. I can deal with it. What's the problem? Having trouble with that new young romantic lead?

WILBERT: *(Paranoiacally confirmed in his suspicion)* You little sneak!

SY: *(Ignoring WILBERT's tone)* Did you develop him okay?

WILBERT: *(Blowing up)* You took him! You helped yourself!

SY: Take it easy: Would another drink tone you up?

WILBERT: Under intense pressure to meet today's deadline, I was working away—

SY: *(Interrupting, conciliatory)* If all you could manage was a rough draft, that would be acceptable.

WILBERT: I worked myself to a frenzy of exhaustion, till sorely needing a rest break to curb my whirling head.

SY: I didn't ask you to write an epic.

WILBERT: Anyway, to clear my fiery head I left off writing to go for a walk, to breathe the free and open air so far as this ever-crowded city would permit, with its big buildings bulging together to close me in with my head bursting out.

SY: The script, Wilbert!

WILBERT: Returning—somewhat refreshed and calmed down, ready for renewed exertions, in the ardors of verbal battle, I turned to the manuscript with a glorious glow, only to discover—

(Pause and organ chord.)

SY: Yes?—Discover what?

WILBERT: The brazen crime of an old and former friend, now ruthless and amoral!

SY: What the hell are you talkin' about?!

WILBERT: *(Staring fixedly at SY)* You play dumb so convincingly ... Braced by my head-clearing walk, fortified to the restored levels of working energy, I took up my pen, angled my typewriter to the ready ... first surveying my pages already written by dint and stint of brow-sweating labor ...

SY: So what happened?

WILBERT: *(Accusingly)* You know it, all too well!

SY: *(Angrily)* Know *what?*, damn you!

WILBERT: That's right—where's Thaddeus?

SY: Who the hell's Thaddeus? *(Flash of discovery on face:)* Oh, I get it—he's our new character?

WILBERT: *(Picking up on "our")* "Our" new character?! *My* creation!

SY: *(As to a lunatic)* You've been working *much* too hard.

WILBERT: There he was, all sketched out, his personality portrayed, given a place in the universe all his own, uniquely original, and blessed with striking dialogue!

SY: So what's the problem?

WILBERT: He's lost. Gone.

SY: Look, we have a strict shooting schedule.

WILBERT: It's no use, Sy.

SY: *(Impatient)* Where are those pages, Wilbert?

WILBERT: Don't raise your voice at me like you're innocent! All the script pages are accounted for, numbered in pagination, carbon and all.

SY: Well, he's *there*, then.

WILBERT: *(Lifting his briefcase)* Yeah? I'll show you something magic—before your very eyes. Blank empty spaces where Thaddeus had appeared! Want to see?

SY: Sure, show me.

> *(Finally opening his briefcase, WILBERT snatches the script pages, flings them at SY and then, in despair, into the air.)*

WILBERT: *(Becoming upset like a bereft parent in seeing the pages)* See where he's vanished—see here—see here—see here—not a trace!

SY: *(Picking up some of the pages and inspecting them anxiously)* It's terrible! How could this happen? Blank spaces, more blank spaces! Some magic vandalism. Some leprechaun, some negative occult deity. The context reveals all the places he has to appear—and they're gaping holes!—white, wiped of type!

WILBERT: *(Himself re-examining a few pages)* And *here!* And look *here!* Gone and stolen, bodily, from all these multiple places. I—*(He looks ready to cry, in despair.)*

SY: This is like "Twilight Zone."

WILBERT: Why me? Why Thaddeus?

SY: Look, keep cool. *(Tremblingly pours himself a drink, gulps it. Tremblingly, reaches for phone.)* I'll phone L.A. They'll know how to . . .

WILBERT: *(Coming out of his grief-stultification)* You know what they've done with him.

SY: *(Confused)* What?

WILBERT: I'm convinced by the conviction of logical intuition that the culprit stands before me—he's you!

SY: Don't joke about it.

WILBERT: *(Taking over)* No joking. Only a few questions. *(Pushes Sy into a chair.)*

SY: Hey, what—?

WILBERT: Not you—me, *I'm* the one to ask the questions.

SY: *(Protestingly)* Look—

WILBERT: *(Interrupting decisively)* Where were you at three-thirty this afternoon?

SY: You think I have the key to your apartment?!

WILBERT: My character—he's lost.

SY: *(Accompanied by organ chord)* Are you sure you even *had* a character?

WILBERT: Extracted, lifted—bodily, entire, with all his soul's potential still immature but ripe in the brilliance of promise—from those script pages. *(Pointing to pages scattered about.)*

Sy: My ass is on the line, too! I gotta call L.A. My career's at stake, my pool, my tennis courts, my expense account, my dames... Where's that phone? *(Sy tries to get out of his chair to get to phone, but is pushed back into chair by Wilbert.)*

Wilbert: *(Tough)* Look me in the eyes, buddy boy!

(Sy extracts sunglasses from inside jacket pocket, and puts them carefully on. [This should get a laugh.])

Sy: Wilbert, I don't have time for this.

Wilbert: For years you've been anxious of my characters. And now —my boldest, truest conception—

Sy: *(Pleading)* I got to call LA.

Wilbert: Your T.V. series needed new blood—a well-fashioned young male to capture some of the younger market—

Sy: But why would I *take* your character? We hired you to write him.

Wilbert: Fearing that I would render Thaddeus too exquisitely literary for your coarse audience, you had your network hoods abduct him to be stereotype-transformed into T.V. banality before I could wean him to the sublime maturity he's destined for, inherent to his created nature, high above the vulgarization mold you plot for him. I've seen it happen to other great literary creations—lobotomized, robotized, mangled flat out of recognition. And that's your intention for my precious Thaddeus!

Sy: Wilbert, you're out to lunch.

Wilbert: Pretending you needed the script as per deadline for production schedule, was a dodge to keep me from rightfully suspecting your engineering of the evil abduction of my Thaddeus.

(Sy has meanwhile sneaked away out of chair and gone for phone, but Wilbert recovers and seizes the phone

before Sy *can.)*

Sy: *(Yelling)* It's *my* phone!

WILBERT: T.V. pillager! Stealing Thaddeus out of envy, spite, malice, and crass commercialization, you pilfered my soul's alter-ego, my noble created other self, the purity of my heart!

Sy: Search my whole hotel room, search *me* even.

WILBERT: Your network hoods did the dirty work and have him in their clutches. I want him released—*(Threateningly:)*—or—

Sy: *(Calmly, regaining control)* Sit down and relax before you burst a blood vessel! Let *me* take over.

WILBERT: *(Irate, aggressing on Sy)* Arch enemy of art! You commercialized meddler, you character-flattener! This cynical tampering by envious, world-besotted villain—

Sy: *(Warding WILBERT off)* Behave yourself. Wherever he is, we'll find him.

WILBERT: How?

Sy: By assigning some reliable writers, and helping you patch up the script.

WILBERT: "Patch up!" my belovèd character! *(Wails like a wounded animal.)*

Sy: Wilbert, why not just fill in the blanks with a new character?

WILBERT: You've lost all concept of the true writer's art. "Just fill in the blanks!"

Sy: But why not?

WILBERT: There can never be another Thaddeus, the whole world over. He was once-in-a-lifetime—a unique entity, irreplaceable, unduplicable.

Sy: Oh, come on, now!

WILBERT: *(Earnestly)* In him I'd found my own consummate character, the delicate alchemy of self idealized into the miracle of fiction.

SY: Relax!

WILBERT: No rest till he's found. Till then, no moment will be peaceful.

> (WILBERT *has turned as if obedient to an inner voice that calls him out of the room.* SY *had already gathered up the loose script pages.*)

WILBERT: *(In a mesmerized voice, while leaving)* No peace.

SY: *(Calling after* WILBERT, *waving aloft the few pages he's already picked up)* Hey wait! The script! Is this all there is? I paid you for it! It's mine by rights, by contract! They'll have my neck!

WILBERT: *(Offstage, as if into far distance)* Can you hear me, Thaddeus? Can you hear me?

> (SY *takes phone and dials hurriedly.*)

SY: *(On phone)* Hello, A.J. . . . Sy here. I just had the strangest scene with Wilbert. Is Morton in? *(Indignantly)* No, no, do I sound like I'm kidding?

SCENE III

> (*Messy office of* BRUCE WAIN, *private eye.*)

WILBERT: Mr. Bruce Wain, private eye?

WAIN: Yeah? Who's looking for him?

WILBERT: I, as a matter of fact.

WAIN: Yeah? Who are you?

WILBERT: Wilbert Wills, fiction writer, in the flesh.

WAIN: Yeah, I believe you. Come in. Sorry the place is a mess.

WILBERT: I need your help, please, and I'll pay promptly.

WAIN: Make yourself at home.

WILBERT: I have what must be the most unusual case you, in your professional capacity, have ever been asked to handle.

WAIN: All my cases are unusual.

WILBERT: Mine is truly extraordinary...

WAIN: I'll tell you how extraordinary it is after I've solved it.

WILBERT: Good. I was told you're precisely the man for the job.

WAIN: What's the problem, Mr. Wills?

WILBERT: You must realize how difficult it must be for me to discuss it.

WAIN: I've heard them all.

WILBERT: This has been a most upsetting experience.

WAIN: Relax, sit down.

WILBERT: *(Sits down)* Thank you, Mr. Wain.

WAIN: Cigarette?

WILBERT: Thanks, but I don't smoke.

WAIN: Chewing gum?

WILBERT: No, I can't—dentures.

WAIN: So start from the beginning.

WILBERT: You see, I'm a novelist, poet, short story writer, and occasional essayist by profession. In addition, my lecture tours...

> *(Both WAIN and WILBERT go into fast action as WILBERT indicates his life history. Sound of WILBERT's sped-up dialogue comes over the P.A.)*

WAIN: You really make a living doing that?

WILBERT: I do eke out a living, yes, not the best one...

WAIN: Okay, that T.V. stuff—what gives?

WILBERT: Well, I was commissioned to write this series episode. Struck with a wonderful burst of blind inspiration, I poured out a volume of notes, outlines, a character profile. Then the other day, disaster struck.

WAIN: Oh yeah? What?

WILBERT: Helpless, I realized...

WAIN: Go on.

WILBERT: A different medium had now enveloped me.

WAIN: Uh huh.

WILBERT: Uh huh.

WAIN: And that's when you noticed this guy was missin'?

WILBERT: After my inspired gush of writing, I needed to clear my seething head, and went for a walk. While walking, a weird apprehension came over me: that here was altogether a different medium, and I was in it! In eerie panic, I rushed home to resume working on the script. Back at my desk, I discovered the mystery: my newly created character had vanished!

WAIN: He wasn't there?

WILBERT: No, sir.

WAIN: Nothin' else was touched?

WILBERT: No, nothing! Everything else was intact, every comma, exactly as I had left it.

WAIN: You contact the police?

WILBERT: No! No! Please, no police. That's why I came to you, Mr. Wain. All I want is to locate my character again, take him back, and quietly continue with my work. Please, you must consent.

WAIN: I understand, Mr. Wills.

WILBERT: This has all been so upsetting to me. I can't sleep nights.

WAIN: This ever happen to you before?

WILBERT: Of course not! What kind of writer do you take me for?

Some novice hack?! I've written dozens of characters of every shape, color, size, period, style, and philosophical inclination. My works are well-respected and—if I do say so—elegantly formed. Because they haven't received a popular audience has no bearing on their aesthetic merit. Undoubtedly my fame awaits me, in the tardy irony of the posthumous.

WAIN: What's this guy's name again?

WILBERT: Thaddeus ... dear, poor Thaddeus.

WAIN: *(Spelling it)* T-H-A-D-

WILBERT: *(Finishing spelling)* D-E-U-S: "Thaddeus."

WAIN: Last name?

WILBERT: I didn't get that far yet. I was on the verge—

WAIN: Keep calm. I'm here to help you.

WILBERT: Sorry, sir. I had just begun to render him. The blood was beginning to flow. From my volume of notes I had introduced him to the script. He embodied the ideal hero. He was to become lifelike, real. This lost love of my soul was spontaneously developing into the distillation of all my toil and literary development. The culmination of my lifetime nurturing of genius, he was arriving, he was coming—

WAIN: Uh, Mr. Wills ... ?

WILBERT: Certainly—yes?

WAIN: You and this Thaddeus guy ... *(Mimes homosexual gestures: limp wrist, etc.)*

WILBERT: (Indignant) Mr. Wain!

WAIN: Then what *was* your relationship?

WILBERT: Simply that of creator to creation. It's the consummate relationship.

WAIN: I *see*.

WILBERT: I doubt if you actually do.

WAIN: *Look*, Mr. Wills, you gotta help me find him—*see*?

WILBERT: I'm sorry. I do sincerely apologize.

WAIN: Okay, now down to some hard facts.

WILBERT: Yes?

WAIN: What's this guy look like?

WILBERT: I—I—I have just a general idea.

WAIN: That don't help me.

WILBERT: You see, I first sketch in the essence, the soul, of a character, and build from there outward to the physical characteristics last, that come to externalize the core.

WAIN: Any photos?

WILBERT: No, but I was about to depict him . . .

WAIN: That don't help me now. How old is the guy?

WILBERT: —Ahh—Certainly he's young, handsome, and brilliant. The idealized, aesthetic paragon of our blighted age.

WAIN: How old is that in years?

WILBERT: *(Deciding on the spot)* Twenty-one. Yes, twenty-one would be the right age for him. But far from the peak of his powers.

WAIN: You ain't makin' my job easy.

WILBERT: I'm sorry, but I'm a high-class fiction writer, not some reporter on the New York Post who writes for idiots.

WAIN: Unless you get more precise with the information, Mr. Wills, I don't know . . .

WILBERT: Excuse me. I've been inappropriately highbrow.

WAIN: How tall?

WILBERT: Five-eleven. No, that wouldn't do. Six feet, at least . . . I have it: Six feet-one. *(Proudly possessive:)* That's my Thaddeus, to the inch!

WAIN: Weight?

WILBERT: Ahh . . . one-seventy-five pounds . . . Yes, that's perfect. No superfluous fat.

WAIN: Build?

WILBERT: Build?

WAIN: Yeah. Build.

WILBERT: An interesting problem. Medium. Well-toned, but not too muscular. Like a Michaelangelo figure in the heroic mold ... Or rather, Bernini: slender, supple.

WAIN: Hair?

WILBERT: Soft, slightly curly.

WAIN: I mean the color.

WILBERT: Black! ...

WAIN: Black?

WILBERT: Of course not! What was I saying?! Blond. And, of course, natural.

WAIN: Eyes?

WILBERT: Blue!

WAIN: Beard or moustache?

WILBERT: *(Severely)* Nothing of the sort. He's a classical inspiration, not a cartoon strip!

WAIN: Birth marks, identifying scars, tattoos?

WILBERT: How fortunate you mentioned that!

WAIN: *(To himself)* Oh brother!

WILBERT: What was that?

WAIN: No brothers?

WILBERT: No, not the least.

WAIN: How about family?

WILBERT: He's the last remaining heir of a long and noble line ...

WAIN: Huh?

WILBERT: The long-lost last prince of an ancient royal duchy. Due to an unfortunate case of amnesia, little does Thaddeus realize the distinction of his ancestry. He must assume his rightful place to carry on the great tradition. That's why his long-lost uncle, the Duke of Wilbertania, seeks him. *(WAIN looks at him with cynical lifted arched eyebrow:)* Don't ask *me*—I didn't write the plot outline!

WAIN: No scars, then?

WILBERT: Please, Mr. Wain: No banality, please.

WAIN: *(He's been jotting things down in his notebook)* Any other distinguishing marks?

WILBERT: I'll consult my notes upon my return home.

WAIN: Where does he live?

WILBERT: I never got that far. The Village? Why not? . . . No, that's not quite right. Soho is the place. On Prince Street.

WAIN: Address?

WILBERT: 122 Prince Street. Apartment 3F.

WAIN: This guy an artist?

WILBERT: Artist? . . . A much better idea. However, the script outline requires that he be an actor.

WAIN: Friends, relatives?

WILBERT: Not yet. Give him time.

WAIN: This guy screwin' any broad?

WILBERT: To overlook your reductivist coarseness, let me reply that romance is certainly in the air, given Thaddeus' magnificent good looks and passionate though intellectual nature; not to mention that this is a nation-wide television serial or, to be blunt, a prime-time melodrama, with expensive advertising rates; so most assuredly romance is in the air—as soon as it will be *on* the air.

WAIN: Who's the dame?

WILBERT: Being under contract, I had to semi-vulgarize my unique originality of scenario plot and story line.

WAIN: Who's the dame?

WILBERT: As pre-established, she's an ongoing character, an aspiring actress, a starlet in the making.

WAIN: Name?

WILBERT: Nothing *I* would choose. I suppose it's perfect for T.V. Catchy, sexy, actressy. How they meet . . .

WAIN: What type of a guy is this Thaddeus?

WILBERT: *(Indignant)* Type! How dare you! What do you take me for? I create unique original individuals, not—

WAIN: Describe him.

WILBERT: Brilliant. Articulate, well-mannered. Highly artistic, innately cultivated, distinguished superior. But tough, worldly, practical, too. Confident, self-assured, quick to act. Magnetic. Electrifying. In short, dynamite.

WAIN: Where was he last seen?

WILBERT: In the scene I put him into. Late afternoon, sitting in Sardi's. That's where I had left him . . .

WAIN: Any chance he left on his own?

WILBERT: What?!

WAIN: Maybe he *wanted* to leave.

WILBERT: *(Indignant)* He'd never be so ungrateful as to leave me—his creator—when only half-developed!

WAIN: Mr. Wills, you're in a different medium now, where anythin' can happen.

WILBERT: *(On his knees, frantic)* Promise me you'll find him! Promise me!

WAIN: Cut the hysteria. *(Pause.)* One last thing.

WILBERT: *(Getting up)* Yes?

WAIN: What was he wearin' the last time you saw him?

WILBERT: You *would* be that practical! I never thought about his garments—the turn of the story hadn't suggested as yet what he'd have on . . . *(Thinks.)* I supposed he must be attired in some of my own clothes. Where else could he have acquired anything to wear? I'm his parent—I'm both his parents. *(Preens:)* Naturally, he's dressed as stylishly as I am. *(This is an obvious self-delusion, for* WILBERT *is dressed sloppy and unkempt while being ignorant of that fact.)*

WAIN: *(Mostly to self or audience)* This is gonna be a tough one to crack.

SCENE IV

(Tuesday, lunch hour in Sardi's. Sounds of bar music and subsequent bar crowd. Having a draft beer, and wearing glasses, THADDEUS *sits at table by himself contemplating quizzically his surroundings. The customers are stage-set papier-mâché dummies.)*

THADDEUS: *(Looking around)* What is this place, where I find myself? From the egocentric point of view, surely it's this moment's center of the universe. However, the world is broader than only here. Nor is this place typical of all other places.

(To audience:) How did I get here? Did some outer force plop me down here at random, or plant me here for a purpose?

I feel so incomplete, undeveloped, half-baked: perhaps vulnerably passive to whatever—or whoever—might chance to impinge upon me now.

What was my boyhood, who were my ancestors—from whence have I arrived? Where, if anywhere, do I "belong"?

*(*ROXY *enters in the distance.)* Here, drowning in my own loneliness, uncertainty, incompleteness, I'm being furtively approached by this pretty girl. She'll offer me a destiny good as any: I'll let her take me over, she'll lead me into an aspect of the world, thus momentarily filling this vacuum of availability I'm currently embarrassed to be in. *(*ROXY *has finally arrived at his table, standing near him.)* This ends my solilo-

quy, for it now becomes appropriate—sane—to change my monologue into a dialogue: losing, in the process, that solitary isolation called loneliness.

> (ROXY, *having entered Sardi's looking for someone else, but seen and been impressed by* THADDEUS, *has glided or sidled over to his table.*)

ROXY: Hi. Mind if I join you? I'm waiting for somebody—you know how it is to wait for somebody.

THADDEUS: I've been waiting too.

ROXY: Really? Who for?

THADDEUS: You, perhaps.

ROXY: Oh no, don't get me wrong, mister. I just thought—

THADDEUS: How opportune you are! I was just feeling so self-pityingly lost.

ROXY: (*Sitting down at* THADDEUS's *table*) You don't talk like you look.

THADDEUS: How so, my beauty?

ROXY: (*Blushing at what* THADDEUS *called her*) Are you some professor or something like that? I went to acting school, because I'm destined to be an actress. I just can't wait!

THADDEUS: You're the messenger, the go-between. I'm so grateful! I adore you!

ROXY: (*Surprised, not unpleasantly*) what made you say that?

THADDEUS: I don't know ... I'm not me. Are these words my own? Or am I a mouthpiece—

ROXY: But we've only just met—

THADDEUS: Something destined us to meet.

ROXY: Now look, you're putting me on, aren't you?

(WAITER *enters.*)

WAITER: *(Wearing a white jacket, comes over, with an insolent attitude)* I can take your order now.

ROXY: *(Compassionately)* You're so busy today.

WAITER: *(Rudely snappy)* Why shouldn't I be? Why don't you just give me your order?

ROXY: *(Too caught up with meeting* THADDEUS, *to be too stung by* WAITER'*s curtness)* I'll take a beer too.

WAITER: *(Writing in pad; to* THADDEUS*)* Another draft beer? *(*THADDEUS *stares blankly into space.)* Two draft beers. *(*WAITER *turns and exits severely.)*

ROXY: *(Mildly hurt by* WAITER; *then, noticing one of the customers)* Oh, you see that man over there?

THADDEUS: *(Turning in direction* ROXY *indicated)* Yes—?

ROXY: Don't stare. That's Hugh Raymond, in the flesh!

THADDEUS: Sorry, I—

ROXY: Sure you know him—you're just pretending not to!

THADDEUS: *(Smiling)* I am?

ROXY: *(Annoyed)* You mean to say you can sit there and actually not know who Hugh Raymond is? Where have you been?

THADDEUS: *(Meditatively)* Where *indeed* have I been?

ROXY: Don't tell me you're not an actor!

THADDEUS: I suppose I *must* be an actor. . . Is he *(indicating direction of "Hugh Raymond")* an actor?

ROXY: *(Scandalized at* THADDEUS'*s naiveté)* Where have you been?

THADDEUS: If this is life, then life is exceedingly strange.

ROXY: You sound like you just came from another planet.

THADDEUS: But do tell me who he is.

ROXY: *(Exclaiming, as to a child)* He's the biggest star of all soap opera. He's in—don't tell me you haven't seen it!– "As All the Guilding World's Hospital Turns with Hope."

THADDEUS: Bombastic, pretentious title.

ROXY: I think you're fabulous.

THADDEUS: Why, thank you.

ROXY: The minute I saw you, when I first walked in, I knew you were the maximum! I *knew* it!

THADDEUS: You insist so convincingly, out of such conviction . . .

ROXY: What's your astrology sign?

THADDEUS: I feel as if I'm being taken over. But it's a pleasant feeling—with *you*.

ROXY: *(Passionately)* Oh darling! *(She impulsively kisses* THADDEUS; *then backs off, looking abashed and self-conscious at what she's just done. Recovers herself, sighs romantically.)*

THADDEUS: My life is a vacuum. Why don't you fill it?

ROXY: *(Begins to respond warmly, but then spots someone)* Oh look! There's Tony Evans!

THADDEUS: Sorry, I—

ROXY: He produces movies and T.V. *(Looking at* THADDEUS's *no-recognition expression:)* Where have you been?

THADDEUS: *(Affectionately mocking)* "Where have you been?!"—Your refrain, from which you couldn't refrain.

ROXY: You're a real smoothie!

THADDEUS: Pardon. I didn't realize—

ROXY: *(Taking out a pack of cigarettes)* You want a cigarette? *(Puts one in his mouth and lights it.)* You know—you're really odd. Are you from L.A.?

THADDEUS: L.A.? L.A.? That has a familiar ring to it.

ROXY: *(Teasingly, not accusingly)* Are you schizophrenic? Maybe you just got out of Bellevue.

> *(Before THADDEUS can think of an answer, WAITER re-enters severely and condescendingly with a tray on which are two draft beers.)*

WAITER: *(Condescendingly, contemptuously)* Two draft beers. *(He puts them on table with ostentatious contemptuousness, then condescendingly exits.)*

ROXY: *(Too smitten with THADDEUS to bother to mind WAITER's offensiveness, she holds up her beer glass to salute)* Well, here's to us. *(They drink.)* But you're so weird.

THADDEUS: How?

ROXY: You're funny. We'll consult my astrology chart later, if you're free to come with me.

THADDEUS: Of course I'm free. All *too* free . . . Freedom—that's all I have, right now.

ROXY: *(Ignoring his words; staring amorously at THADDEUS)* What's your name?

THADDEUS: Thaddeus.

ROXY: Oh.

THADDEUS: Do I fit the name? Or does the name fit me? I don't know *where* I belong—or who, even, if am. Perhaps you'll help me latch on to something. I'm cut off from my past, severed from roots; isolated in time. Undeveloped, I'm devoid of structure or purpose. I'm floating, moorless, in the passive quandary of a vacuum. I'm all dressed up with nowhere to go. I need to hook on to the world. I'm helpless. Help me.

ROXY: *(Passionately)* Oh, Thaddeus! I'm Roxy. *(She leans over table to embrace him, not only amorously but protectively and possessively.)* I'll take care of you!

THADDEUS: Thanks.

ROXY: *(Fervently)* We'll *always* be together! We'll be inseparable! We'll be known as the *team*—like Lunt and Fontaine, like Hepburn and Tracy, like Taylor and Burton, like—

THADDEUS: I was drowning, but you've pulled me ashore.

ROXY: *(Ecstatic)* This was fated to be. Co-stars! Hollywood's top romantic pair! *(In rhapsody:)* I can see it! I can see it!

THADDEUS: A lovely vision. And you're a vision in loveliness.

ROXY: *(Turning more coy)* What a line! You don't waste much time, do you?

THADDEUS: *(Philosophically)* What, then, is time?

ROXY: *(Literal-mindedly)* Oh, don't worry. *(Looking at her wristwatch.)* It's still early.

THADDEUS: You'll take care of me?

ROXY: *(Worldly)* If this is an act, I can tell you—it's working.

THADDEUS: Maybe it *is* an act. Am I playing a pre-ordained role? Am I being directed by some invisible hand? Am I, unwittingly, performing a part, in character, in some drama larger—or smaller—than life?

ROXY: *(Sympathetically)* Don't let it bother you.

THADDEUS: I'm being enveloped—taken over—I'm weak—I'm hungry. . . Marconi.

ROXY: Marconi! Do you know Marconi?! He's the biggest casting director in New York! I've been hoping to get in to see him for a year!

THADDEUS: I have an appointment with him.

ROXY: What?! When?! Where?!

THADDEUS: *(Pulls out a business card, shows it to Roxy)* Here.

ROXY: Two-thirty! Fabulous! He's only seven blocks away. We'll go together, he'll cast us as a team! Wait for me, be back in a jiff, just going to the little girls' room to powder my nose and fix my hair.

(She exits enthusiastically in a hurry. But instead of waiting for ROXY, THADDEUS, *as though pulled and impelled by a fate beyond his knowing, leaves the restaurant alone to keep his appointment, as though* ROXY *had never asked him to wait for her.)*

SCENE V

(Tuesday, 4:00 P.M. WILBERT's *East Village apartment.* BRUCE WAIN, *having just missed* THADDEUS *and* ROXY *at Sardi's, confers with* WILBERT.*)*

WAIN: So then a dame named Roxy came by.

WILBERT: Roxy did you say?

WAIN: Whats-a-matter?

WILBERT: The script's plot specified a certain "Roxy" whom Thaddeus was to meet at that same "Sardi's."

WAIN: That so? The waiter said this dame was a sexy would-be actress type, good-lookin', talented, but not smart enough to play the game of show biz.

WILBERT: That's precisely her description as she's to be depicted as per the script. It's the splittin' image of the Roxy of the series—the same one. How odd! What else were you told?

WAIN: *(Reading from notes)* She joined him about two o'clock. The fag waiter said he was talkin' to himself before she came over. Then they started talkin', they even kissed, then he left the place like in a hurry, while she was in the ladies' room.

WILBERT: Poor Thaddeus! This is my living nightmare! We must find him!

WAIN: There's more, Mr. Wills.

WILBERT: *(Brought up short)* Yes, of course. Please go on.

WAIN: Then I proceeded to—

WILBERT: *(Interrupting)* It's truly possible: Roxy is their instrument: a sexually alluring device planted by them to tempt my unsuspecting Thaddeus away from me—permanently.

WAIN: Then I proceeded to—

WILBERT: *(Interrupting)* Mr. Wain—excellent detective work!

WAIN: —To one-twenty-two Prince Street, that address you had for him.

WILBERT: Yes?—yes?

WAIN: No cigar. I had to rough up the super a little, so he spilled what he had and it wasn't much. Apartment 3F is vacant, been for some time. He swore he don't remember any guy of Thaddeus's description bein' there.

WILBERT: All this—it's too upsetting.

WAIN: It's only the tip of the iceberg, Mr. Wills.

WILBERT: The dreadful possibility occurs to me that, this very moment, my Thaddeus is being corrupted, contaminated, by the company of actual T.V. characters in person!

WAIN: Yeah, it sure could be. Got anythin' on the dame?

WILBERT: Not me. I gave you all I had on her. They saddled me at the onset with her basic character outline to work from; but as for her particulars apropos of our desperate quest of Thaddeus; I'm at a loss.

WAIN: Yeah? What happens next in the "plot"?

WILBERT: *(Admiringly)* Of course! How logical you are! I knew I hired the right man! *(Goes to desk and piles through his papers.)*

WAIN: Cut the flattery, Mr. Wills.

WILBERT: I was assigned by plot requirement to follow Thaddeus on appointment to a leading major T.V. casting agent, for Scene Three.

WAIN: What name you got for that guy?

WILBERT: He too, is an ongoing character in the series. *(Finds name at desk:)* Marconi.

WAIN: Spell it.

WILBERT: M-A-R-C-O-N-I.

WAIN: Maybe Mafia?

WILBERT: Do you suspect a conspiracy of magnitude—an international plot?

WAIN: Looks like Thaddeus's only the tip of the iceberg.

WILBERT: Your cliché, through repetition, becomes a cliché.

WAIN: What about the rest o' the plot?

WILBERT: Of course . . . *(Obediently fumbling through his papers.)* The outline is here somewhere . . . it *ought* to be . . . ah, *here* it is!

WAIN: *(Roughly)* Gimme that. *(Grabs script from WILBERT.)*

WILBERT: Sorry. It's embarrassing how awkward I can be at times.

WAIN: *(Reading)* It says here, "Scene Three, Thaddeus at casting agent Marconi's office, Thaddeus cast as new romantic lead in T.V. series . . . "

WILBERT: *(Incredulous, horrified)* It says that?

WAIN: You didn't read the outline?

WILBERT: Having invented my marvelous Thaddeus, his development distracted me, it consumed me, it obsessed me—

WAIN: *(Reading)* "Scene Four, Thaddeus now Prince Glitz. His uncle, the Grand Duke of Wilbertania from Europe, arrives in New York, hires a private eye to locate his *(Has trouble pronouncing it:)* amnesia-ridden nephew."

WILBERT: That part I remember! Yes, the Grand Duke realizes how vulnerable, innocent, unprotected his nephew, the long-lost heir . . . Oh, I should have read that plot more carefully. Mr. Wain, it's urgent— we must find Thaddeus *now!* What's the next Scene? It should afford us a clue, and that's our cue—quick, what follows?

WAIN: That's it.

WILBERT: No! There *must* be! *(Takes the outline; reads; disappointed:)* You're right: it says, "To be continued in L.A."

WAIN: Who gave you this Plot?

WILBERT: Sy did—he's the associate producer, and story editor, of this series.

WAIN: Then he's the man we want.

WILBERT: When I first discovered my hero's disappearance, my suspicion pointed to Sy as the one behind it.

WAIN: If it's that guy's plot, he's the one we're after.

WILBERT: The villain—I can see him controlling, manipulating Thaddeus at the evil promptings of his whim, for slick commercial gain.

WAIN: *(Making aggressive gestures)* Where do I find 'em?

WILBERT: He lives in Los Angeles, but is at a New York hotel at the moment. But hurry—he's due to fly back to Los Angeles very soon.

WAIN: Why would he want to take Thaddeus?

WILBERT: The survival of his series—in fact of his career—depends on his getting his greasy paws on a well-drawn character to degrade into the vulgar appeal of stereotype.

WAIN: *(Philosophically—for him)* It's dog eat dog, all right.

WILBERT: T.V. is notorious for its plundering, pillaging of truly original characters and stories: they're stolen, raped for all they're commercially worth, then discarded broken, uselessly vulgarized, drained of soul and substance.

WAIN: How come you didn't mention Sy before?

WILBERT: You see, Sy, in years gone by, had been my friend; and for an old friend to stab me in the back—

WAIN: Those are the ones that'll do it to ya.

WILBERT: Before desperation turns to despair, we must pull out all the stops, leave no stone unturned, nor guilty nose unbroken, pursuing a single goal—get Thaddeus back to me, intact!

WAIN: Like I told ya, it's only the tip of the iceberg! *(Making ready to go.)*

SCENE VI

(Same day, 3:00 P.M. MARCONI's glitzy office, show-biz decor, on Lexington Avenue in the Sixties. THADDEUS dashes in, MARCONI greets him.)

MARCONI: It's about time, young man! Thaddeus, I presume?

THADDEUS: It's I, if you think so.

MARCONI: *(Circling around to ogle THADDEUS)* Funny, but cute to the point of devastating! You know, honey, that we've all been waiting for you?

THADDEUS: For me?

MARCONI: We've heard so much about you, and here you are finally! *(Ogling:)* Not bad, not at all bad! And what sweet buns you have! Anyone ever tell you that, baby?

THADDEUS: If so, I don't remember.

MARCONI: *(Noticing his clothes)* What's with the rags?

THADDEUS: *(Uncomprehending)* Rags?

MARCONI: *(Turning bitchily severe)* You're not here for an artsy theater audition, this is no Public Theatre on Lafayette Street, or *[name of actual theater where this play is being currently performed]*. Let me set you straight. You're here for a T.V. audition—big money, good looks, glamor, Hollywood Boulevard. Get it? So what gives?

THADDEUS: Sorry, I didn't know what my appointment was for. I'm not sure—

MARCONI: That's not *my* problem, go scream at your agent. They're looking for a leading man—not some character actor who occasionally pops out of the background!

THADDEUS: They are? Where? . . . Is that who I am? I've been at a loss, pondering my identity.

MARCONI: *(Melting)* You're sweet, dumb, and innocent—just the way I like them. But really—you *must* do something before I let you go in there. *(Scolding like a parent:)* Just look at you!

> *(MARCONI takes it upon himself to adjust THADDEUS's clothes to make him look up-to-date fashionable: takes off his glasses, puts his collar up, etc.)*

THADDEUS: I'm feeling awkward.

MARCONI: Don't worry, my infant, big daddy will be there to help you. *(Backing up to inspect the "new" THADDEUS:)* Now you look more like the hunk you are, my gorgeous piece of handiwork!

> *(MARCONI stares at THADDEUS, till THADDEUS finally, self-consciously, has to break the silent staring spell.)*

THADDEUS: Something else wrong?

MARCONI: *(Shaking his head—incredulous with wonder)* I just can't get over it!

THADDEUS: Over what?

MARCONI: You look exactly like the character breakdown! It's incredible!

THADDEUS: How happy I am, at last, to be rounding out into *some* identity! I feel I'm in good hands. What should I do next?

MARCONI: That's the boy! Now, take this side and read it over. *(Leaving.)* I'll be right back out and they'll be ready to audition you, dear.

THADDEUS: Read this? But you took my glasses.

> *(MARCONI exits. THADDEUS tries to read by holding the paper close to his face. MARCONI enters again.)*

MARCONI: My sweet thing, they're all ready for you!

THADDEUS: *(Concerned)* But I haven't been able to read this yet.

MARCONI: *(Breezily)* Just fake it.

THADDEUS: *(Pleading, earnest)* But why am I here? What am I doing?

MARCONI: You're adorable when you look so serious, so earnest! You're reading the part of the new romantic lead in that fabulous T.V. series, "Fantasy Life." That turn you on, you sexpot? Now let's go, we don't want to keep the money people waiting, do we, darling?

> *(MARCONI coquetishly shoves THADDEUS into next room, where seated are SY, VITTORIO, and MAGGIE.)*

MARCONI: *(Whispering to THADDEUS)* Now's your big chance! I don't have the slightest doubt in you. *(Pinching THADDEUS on behind.)*

THADDEUS: Big chance? For what? *(Looking about. To himself:)* Yet this room fills me with instinctual foreboding: a dreaded doom it's too late to avert, as the die is cast, as though here destiny and I meet at the crossroads of our rendezvous. Marconi's my Virgil, at an underworld's portal, escorting me—closing all doors behind me forever—to—ah yes, where is he leading me? Across this threshold, my first station, my first stage—in this, a journey I'm blindly led to undertake.

MARCONI: You just have to *read*, my child: they don't need you to do a *monologue*.

> *(The CASTING TRIO has risen and are now standing behind their table.)*

MARCONI: Well folks, here he is. Thaddeus, I'd like you to meet Sy, the Assistant Producer in charge of casting and script development.

SY: *(Shaking his hand)* My pleasure, Thaddeus. Just relax, now.

THADDEUS: Thank you, sir.

MARCONI: This is Vittorio, the series Director.

VITTORIO: Buongiorno!

THADDEUS: Placere, Signor.

MARCONI: *(Surprised)* Oh—you speak Italian?

THADDEUS: Huh?

MARCONI: And this is Maggie, the series' Associate Producer.

THADDEUS: The series?

MARCONI: Isn't he fun? So Sy, would you like to fill Thaddeus in a little on the scene?

SY: We'll just lay a few things on you; then you can take it from there. It's about a guy just like you: a good-looking guy, name of Prince Glitz, he's found wandering around New York—and he doesn't know who he is, or where he's from.

MAGGIE: *(Husky sexy throaty voice in all her speeches)* And in this scene he wanders right into Sardi's, sits down, and has a beer.

VITTORIO: *(Italian accent in all his speeches)* A lovely, universal scene! So touching! He is right in the middle of a pure, pure identity crisis!

SY: And right then, this dame Roxy comes in—looking for somebody.

THADDEUS: *(Recognizing)* Roxy! That's right, Roxy.

MAGGIE: *(Sexually responding to THADDEUS, to parallel her description)* As soon as she enters, without expecting to be, she finds herself attracted—immediately—to Prince as to a magnet, she's drawn to him. Why? Because of his irresistible sexual powers. He's a knockout! . . . And that's you, all over . . .

THADDEUS: *(As if by belated discovery)* Prince did you say . . . my name is Prince Glitz?

SY: You got it! That's you!

THADDEUS: But where does he come from? What's wrong with him? Why doesn't he know where he is—and why he's there? Is he in possession of his faculties; fully, to find his bearings, his orientation, and to locate himself, at the core of identity?

Sy: Take it easy. Not so fast.

Thaddeus: Fast? Why not?

Sy: My script staff hasn't finished this scene yet. A certain writer—you see, we had some difficulty with him. Not to worry, though. In a few days he'll be all fleshed out . . . and so will you . . . we're working on your character.

Thaddeus: Can you fill me in more specifically for the time being?

Maggie: He has amnesia. He's from European royalty. From a long, illustrious line of nobility, he has just one living relative left: his uncle, whose title is—I know it sounds funny, in this day and age—"the Grand Duke of Wilbertania."

Vittorio: You see, you—Prince—is the sole remaining heir to a noble heritage.

Sy: You got it? And the uncle—

Maggie: —the Grand Duke, that is—

Vittorio: —he come looking for him, he help him find himself, and realize his destiny.

Maggie: That uncle, he's miserable, for he misses his relative: the uncle is lost until he can find Prince!

Vittorio: And Prince,

Sy: who's amnesiac,

Vittorio: must to shake off his amnesia, to relate to the real world,

Sy: to become well-adjusted;

Vittorio: he is bewildered by the world he is found himself in—and he is looking—

Maggie: —Just like his uncle is looking for *him*, *he's* looking for *himself*.

Sy: That's right—get it?

Thaddeus: I'm beginning to—to find myself.

SY: Great! We love it!

THADDEUS: *(Indicating script)* Let's read this. I've got to know more.

SY: Yeah, you'll find your way, you'll make your own way.

THADDEUS: I'm dying to! Please!

SY: That's the spirit! You're getting there!

MARCONI: Thaddeus's right—let's get back to the script. He can feel his own way.

THADDEUS: I can!

MARCONI: I'll be reading the part of Roxy, the pretty girl who's just come into the restaurant.

THADDEUS: Yes, Roxy—it's coming back to me.

SY: That's terrific, Thaddeus baby.

MAGGIE: *(Winking at THADDEUS)* We're ready if *you* are.

THADDEUS: *(Reading with some difficulty)* Where am I? Oh, how did I get here? Why . . . I must be lost! But how, how? Ah, why am I feeling this way? It's tragic! I'm overwhelmed! Who am I?

> *(MARCONI, in playing ROXY, unwittingly imitates and mimes her precise voice, gestures, mannerisms, etc., as she was in previous scene, Scene IV:)*

MARCONI: *(Playing ROXY; reading)* Hi. Mind if I join you? I'm waiting for somebody—you know how it is to wait for somebody.

THADDEUS: *(Reading)* Why of course, baby. Sit down and make yourself at home. You've chased all my loneliness away! You make me feel like a man!

MARCONI: *(Playing ROXY; reading)* Oh no, don't get me wrong, mister. I just thought—

THADDEUS: *(Reading)* You sure are good-looking. Let's have a little chat. Who knows—it could lead to romance!

MARCONI: *(Playing Roxy; reading)* You don't talk like you look.

THADDEUS: *(Reading)* How easily you've dropped into my life! Like a princess from the clouds! Well, now that you're here, let's make the most of it!

MARCONI: *(Playing Roxy; reading)* But we've only just met.

THADDEUS: *(Reading)* Come on, baby.

MARCONI: *(Playing Roxy; reading)* You want a cigarette? *(Puts one in THADDEUS's mouth and lights it.)* You know—you're really odd. Are you from L.A.?

THADDEUS: *(Reading)* Why do you say that, my lovely?

MARCONI: *(Playing Roxy; reading)* You're a real smoothie!

THADDEUS: *(Reading)* I'm fascinated! Tell me more! How do I look? In fact—

MARCONI: *(Playing Roxy; reading)* I think you're fabulous.

THADDEUS: *(Reading)* Oh, am I?

MARCONI: *(Playing Roxy; reading)* If this is an act, I can tell you—it's working.

THADDEUS: *(Reading)* Ah, if—

SY: *(Cutting in)* Thank you, that's all we need to hear.

(The CASTING TRIO gather closely in a huddle, buzzing in hushed conversation.)

MARCONI: They just loved you. *(Winking sexually)* I know *I* sure did.

THADDEUS: I could barely see the lines.

MARCONI: *(As though that proves THADDEUS's rare talent)* You're a natural!

(The CASTING TRIO conclude their conference.)

SY: Thaddeus baby, are you under contract now?

THADDEUS: What?

MAGGIE: How much camera work have you done?

THADDEUS: What?

VITTORIO: Is that you natural hair color?

SY: Thaddeus, you see this paper?

THADDEUS: Of course. What is it?

SY: I'll tell you what it is. Now listen.

THADDEUS: Please.

SY: It's a two-year contract to play the leading man in our T.V. series, "Fantasy Life." Happy to have you aboard. Will you sign it, please?

MAGGIE: We think the role was made for you.

VITTORIO: You and the role fit, like the snug together.

SY: Yeah, there's no difference. Sign, baby.

THADDEUS: I'm not sure. I'm somewhat scared by all this—taken aback, somewhat. Apprehensive. My *life* is at stake. My whole life.

MARCONI: *(In confidential, intimate tone)* Darling, take it. They're making you a wonderful offer.

MAGGIE: Yes, just think: for the next two years you won't have a thing to worry about!

SY: Your slightest needs will be taken care of. You'll have tons of money, and future financial security.

VITTORIO: Every week, twenty million Americans soak you up, they drink you in—you get fan mail!

SY: You're star material. We'll smooth you out—polish you up. A little shading, here and there—presto!—you *are* the role! You're a star!

MAGGIE: You'll fit it perfectly. *(Erotically suggestively:)* You're a perfect fit!

THADDEUS: I'm overwhelmed, it's too wonderful to be true. But—

VITTORIO: Si?

THADDEUS: But where's the rest of the script? I'd like to know where I stand, in it. It's essential. What am I to be? How will my life go?

SY: Don't worry about a *thing!* It's all taken care of. Right now, I've got my writing boys working on it. And as soon as you get to L.A., you'll know where you are, who you are, where you're going.

MAGGIE: Other actors can only *dream* of what *you're* actually being offered.

VITTORIO: Next week we start shooting.

THADDEUS: I'm not sure—I'm uncertain—what should I do next?

SY: All you have to do is sign right here. That's the beauty of corporate media, see? It's as simple as that.

THADDEUS: Really? I see—so *that's* what comes next.

SY: You just fall in with it. It's all for your benefit. It's like music.

THADDEUS: That's what follows?

SY: Hollywood is next, big boy, then the starry heavens. It's the big time!

> (THADDEUS *goes to the contract, hesitates while the others hold their breath—which they release with relief when he finally signs.*)

CASTING TRIO PLUS MARCONI: Bravo! Congratulations! A star is born!

SY: *(Taking the contract and checking it)* No champagne now, don't have time—things to do and places to go. Maggie, you're in charge of Thaddeus. *(MAGGIE responds with look of sexual joy.)* Get him some new clothes, get his hair done. I'll arrange the press for when he hits L.A.. We can get a lot of coverage out of this. We have a hot superstar in the making, it's good timing, there happens to be a vacuum in the public hero worship right now, a slot made for a Prince Glitz. He's the unique product everyone's looking for. Marconi, you'll call and make sure the limo is downstairs for me. *(To everyone:)* Let's get hustling.

MARCONI: Sure thing, Sy.

SY: Vittorio, you and I have that five o'clock at LaGuardia, or we'll miss our meeting with Morton . . . Thaddeus, here's your copy of the contract. *(Hands it to THADDEUS.)*

THADDEUS: Oh, thank you.

> *(THADDEUS puts the contract in a pocket, but it falls out and onto the floor, unnoticed by himself and the others.)*

SY: Maggie, make sure Thaddeus sees video tapes of the series, get him caught up to date; get him loosened up for the shooting, he seems a little stiff. Make him natural, at home—you know what I mean, baby. *(Pets MAGGIE on her behind.)*

MAGGIE: *(Winking)* Will do, Sy.

> *(As SY, MARCONI, and VITTORIO leave in a rush:)*

SY: See ya in L.A., Thaddeus baby!

> *(MAGGIE and THADDEUS then follow, together.)*

MAGGIE: You don't know how lucky you are, Thaddeus. Your day has come.

THADDEUS: So I'm Prince Glitz now?

MAGGIE: *(Keeping close, clinging; to him physically.)* You got it, sweetheart. You've met your destiny now. Isn't it sweet?

> *(MAGGIE and THADDEUS exit, and now everyone's gone. After a moment, the sound of breaking glass is heard. From the shadows BRUCE WAIN, Private Eye, enters the office quietly, looking carefully around. Beginning to*

> snoop, he notices THADDEUS's accidentally fallen contract on the floor, and picks it up. Reading it over, he looks up in direction of exit)

WAIN: L.A., huh? Well, me too.

SCENE VII

> (Wednesday morning, L.A. airport. Even at airport, L.A. is shown—as fantasy-land, etc.—in startling contrast to previous N.Y. scenes, and will continue to be shown thus for remainder of play (this Scene and all of Act Two). Grouped on one side, waiting, are reporters, photographers, and a T.V. video crew.)

ANNOUNCER'S VOICE ON P.A. SYSTEM: Now arriving, Flight 807 from New York's LaGuardia Airport, at Gate Seven. Flight 807 from New York's LaGuardia Airport at Gate Seven.

> (THADDEUS, now known publicly as Prince Glitz, and MAGGIE enter from direction opposite to the waiting media group on the other side. They're carrying hand luggage. THADDEUS has been transformed into Prince visibly: dressed stylishly up-to-date, sporting a new haircut, etc.)

FIRST REPORTER: There he is!
SECOND REPORTER: Over there, guys!

> (The media group all rush over to THADDEUS and MAGGIE.)

MAGGIE: *(Taking charge)* Hello, guys. Well, here he is: meet Prince Glitz. Isn't he gorgeous?

(There's a flurry of flash photos.)

MAGGIE: We only have time for a few questions. Prince has a very busy schedule.

FIRST REPORTER: How does it feel, Mr. Glitz, to be cast in "Fantasy Life"?

THADDEUS: A new world, a new life, is opening up for me.

SECOND REPORTER: Is this your first major network role?

THADDEUS: Very possibly so. The past is somewhat murky.

THIRD REPORTER: Who's your designer, Prince?

THADDEUS: For now; whoever's writing the script.

FOURTH REPORTER: What do you think of the "Fantasy Life" series so far, up to where *you're* climbing aboard?

THADDEUS: I'm here to be directed. I'll do the best I can. I won't rock the boat.

FIFTH REPORTER: Will it fit comfortably on your own style?

THADDEUS: I'll learn my lines. I'm a good adapter. One can get used to just about anything, I guess.

MAGGIE: *(Beaming proprietorial, possessively)* Isn't he charming, guys? He's the goods, isn't he?

FOURTH REPORTER: How was Prince cast?

FIFTH REPORTER: Was it a difficult choice?

MAGGIE: Our Prince was selected only after the most exhaustive, nation-wide search for the positively absolutely right and perfect character.

FIRST REPORTER: How many were auditioned?

MAGGIE: Literally thousands! It was like an all-points manhunt! But once we saw Prince, we knew that we had no choice—he made it seem inevitable.

SECOND REPORTER: Do you predict he'll push "Fantasy Life" back into the number one ratings slot?

MAGGIE: I'd stake my life on it.

THIRD REPORTER: Prince—what's your astrological sign?

THADDEUS: Huh?

FOURTH REPORTER: Were you trained for the stage?

THADDEUS: For the stage?—*what* stage?

FIRST REPORTER: Maggie, could we have you two stand a little closer together?

MAGGIE: Glad to oblige. He's a heartbreaker, isn't he?

>   (MAGGIE *pulls* THADDEUS *closer to her. Flash photos flash in a flurry.*)

FOURTH REPORTER: You two aren't an item, are you?

MAGGIE: (*Deliberately ambiguous, for P.R. intrigue*) Maybe, maybe not. Now don't you print anything, I'm still married. I don't want any scandal-mongering.

THIRD REPORTER: Prince, do you plan to settle in Hollywood?

THADDEUS: Hollywood?

FIRST REPORTER: Do you think life on the West Coast is different?

FOURTH REPORTER: How does it feel to be the romantic lead opposite some of T.V.'s most yummy glamor girls?

SECOND REPORTER: When does the shooting start?

THIRD REPORTER: What kind of contract are you under, Prince?

FOURTH REPORTER: I don't mean to pry into your personal affairs, but you wouldn't want to mention any figures, would you?

THADDEUS: I—I—the contract?

THIRD REPORTER: Who's your agent?

FIRST REPORTER: Who's your hairdresser?

FOURTH REPORTER: What's your definite opinion about the current political situation? What are you for? What are you against?

THADDEUS: The political situation? Which one?

SECOND REPORTER: What's your hobby, Prince? What sports do you go in for?—heh heh, I mean *outdoor* sports.

THIRD REPORTER: Prince, who's number one in your love life?

FIRST REPORTER: When did you first fall in love?

SECOND REPORTER: What's your personal opinion about bisexuality? Does it agree with your own lifestyle? Or are you shy about it? Is it a closed secret?

THIRD REPORTER: Have you ever been in love? I mean *truly* in love, with all the trimmings? What advice can you give on the subject?

FOURTH REPORTER: Ever been married, Prince? For how long?

FIFTH REPORTER: How many times?

FIRST REPORTER: Who's your favorite pop star?

SECOND REPORTER: Prince, what do you *really* like to do in your spare time? Be frank!

THIRD REPORTER: Have you ever had a mystical experience?

FOURTH REPORTER: Next to acting, what's your favorite activity?

FIFTH REPORTER: Would you like to direct some day, Prince?

FIRST REPORTER: Any tips for aspiring actors who are just setting out, Prince?

SECOND REPORTER: Or words of caution?

THIRD REPORTER: What's the worst thing that ever happened to you? Be honest!

FOURTH REPORTER: What about your past, Prince?

THADDEUS: My past—my past? It's sort of a blank right now.

FIFTH REPORTER: *(To MAGGIE)* Can you tell our "Entertainment Tonight" viewers anything about this prime-time heart-throb new mystery-man?

> (*The T.V. cameras get in close. A reporter comes up to hold microphone close to* THADDEUS.)

MAGGIE: Prince will tell you a little about himself, then we really have to go, we have a tight schedule. Go ahead, Prince.

THADDEUS: What handicaps me in trying to come to terms with my past, is the dimness of my recollection of it.

SECOND REPORTER: Was it too painful, Prince? Try hard to remember. We're all on your side.

THADDEUS: It's so vague! Only one thing is clear about my past. Cultivation, high culture. The best in literature, art, theatre, music, opera. It was a proud upbringing. Classy, you might say.

THIRD REPORTER: Boo! So you turn out to be a real culture snob, eh? Would you call yourself too good for Hollywood, T.V.—the *popular* arts?

THADDEUS: My lineage is aristocratic, from high nobility.

> (*This last statement produces a hush, hum, buzz, uproar, perking up the group of media people. As the T.V. cameras, in the sensational revelation of this media event, move up closer,* BRUCE WAIN, *private eye, is seen in the background.*)

FIRST REPORTER: Could you tell us more about that, Prince? It's what we'd all like to know.

THADDEUS: (*Innocently, not boastfully*) I'm the last of a long and noble line. As the sole remaining heir to the Dukedom of Wilbertania, I'm nevertheless delighted to have arrived in Hollywood, where "Fantasy Life" is filling in the blanks in my life, and covering over my identity-void with the acquisition of new true substance. Before "Fantasy Life,"

I confess to having been confused, undirected—in a fog. The lines of my script—my role—have given fresh meaning to my life, as I replace my former vacuum with what comes next in the episodes to come. This serial *is* my life. I draw my vitality from it, and owe my identity to it. My veins of blue blood are nourished red by the characterization in the script. I'm wedded to my job—at one with it. Acting is my whole life.

> (*This speech is treated as a great sensation-revelation by the media group. Uproar.*)

MAGGIE: Sorry, guys, but that's it for today. We've got to be on our way now.

FOURTH REPORTER: Ah come on, Maggie—after what he said, you *got* to let us at this guy!

THIRD REPORTER: It could be the story of the season!

FIRST REPORTER: You can't let us down!

FIFTH REPORTER: Yeah, give us a break, Maggie!

MAGGIE: You'll just have to make do with what you've got this morning—and that's plenty!

> (*Groans and cries of protests come from media group.*)

MAGGIE: You poor deprived babies! You're greedy! Well, I promise you a press conference next week, so you can save your ammunition for Prince for then, till then.

> (*As groans, moans, outcries greet this, MAGGIE and THADDEUS start to exit. Reporters hound, surround, follow them as they exit. Photos flash madly. A reporter desperately tries to get in a question.*)

> (*BRUCE WAIN, straight from airplane, still wearing his N.Y. duds, goes to telephone booth, dials a long-distance*

number.)

WAIN: *(On phone)* Hello, Wills? Wain here.

WILBERT'S VOICE ON PHONE: I've been waiting desperately for your call. Where have you been? Any development?

WAIN: Sure thing. I'm in L.A. now.

WILBERT'S VOICE ON PHONE: *(Alarmed)* No!—don't tell me! No!

WAIN: Sit tight, now. They got your boy here. *(Scream heard from WILBERT's voice. WAIN holds hands over his ears.)* Screams won't get you nowhere, Wills, but an airplane ticket will. Yeah, they got him. We might have to do something illegal. *(WILBERT's voice sputters.)* Sounds desperate? So is the case, Mr. Wills.

ACT TWO

SCENE I

(L.A. studio script development department for the T.V. series, "Fantasy Life." Four SCRIPTWRITERS sitting around a large table writing, as SY enters in a rush.)

SY: Okay, gang, here we go! I was just in with Morton. He knows our backs are against the wall—but he and I have faith in this staff!

ALL SCRIPTWRITERS: Gee, thanks boss!

SY: Good enough, sweethearts. So this is how it stands. The artsy-fartsy writer we commissioned for the episode couldn't deliver. So it's a patch-up job—we'll tie scraps together, fill in blank spots. Our priority is getting the last scenes finished up by our shoot deadline.

SCRIPTWRITER ONE: Lay it on us, boss!

SCRIPTWRITER TWO: No problem.

SCRIPTWRITER THREE: A piece of cake!

SY: Okay! Alright! Some background first. *(Waves a paper aloft.)* See this here? Know what this is?

ALL SCRIPTWRITERS: What, boss?

SCRIPTWRITER TWO: Don't keep us in suspense!

SY: It's market research survey our sponsors have just hit us with.

SCRIPTWRITER FOUR: Oh, tell us, what does it say, boss?

SY: *(Reading)* The ratings are down two points from the beginning of the season.

ALL SCRIPTWRITERS: *(Taking blame hanging their heads in shame)* Sorry, boss!

SY: *(Part-reading)* It also says that eighty-five percent of our audience share is middle-aged or older. That's no good, since our sponsors are desperate to project a youthful image in their lines of products and appeal to the upscale, upwardly mobile market.

ALL SCRIPTWRITERS: We'll go young, Sy, we'll aim for the kids and the yuppies.

SY: That's right—give the money people what they want.

ALL SCRIPTWRITERS: What *do* they want?

SY: More action, more romance, a more exotic setting, glamor, intrigue, adventure, excitement, passion. That's what'll sell their products. Guys, have I been heard?

ALL SCRIPTWRITERS: Loud and clear, boss!

SCRIPTWRITER ONE: Let's get going!

SCRIPTWRITER TWO: We introduced Roxy two episodes ago.

SY: A good move—that's a step we can capitalize on now.

SCRIPTWRITER FOUR: She's young, sexy, but innocent.

SCRIPTWRITER THREE: We still need a male romantic lead in her age bracket to play opposite her but who'll turn out too good, too big, for her. That's what we need!

SY: Not any more—now we've *got* him!

ALL SCRIPTWRITERS: We have?

SY: He's in our possession—Prince Glitz!

ALL SCRIPTWRITERS: Hurray! Prince Glitz! In person!

SCRIPTWRITER FOUR: Our problems are solved!

SCRIPTWRITER TWO: I feel lighter!

SY: He's in our hands, to make of him what we want. He can get us a number-one rating if we do *our* job—to realize his potential as the prime-time heart-throb new-wave rave, the magnet to a million new fans who'll *stay* tuned in, if only we provide him with live-wire material so he can strut his stuff and bounce all over the tube. Dig?

SCRIPTWRITER TWO: We dig!

SCRIPTWRITER THREE: You got it—we got it!

SCRIPTWRITER ONE: We're with you every inch of the way, boss!

SY: I love it! Render me the music. Run down the outline. Go on, blast!

SCRIPTWRITER FOUR: Here's what our plot gives:

SCRIPTWRITER TWO: Prince wanders vague into Sardi's, all lost, no memory. Roxy walks in, then they meet then they fall in love—

SCRIPTWRITER THREE: Then Prince abandons her to keep his appointment with Marconi—alone—

SCRIPTWRITER ONE: He's cast in a T.V. show—

SCRIPTWRITER FOUR: Next stop is stupendous L.A. in the captivity of sexy Maggie, one of the biggies behind the show.

SY: *(Urging them on, in semi-sexual cadence)* Yeah, don't stop now, lay it on, you've worked me up, don't leave me dry—

ALL SCRIPTWRITERS: *(Downward note)* Our invention pauses there, boss. We're at a loss . . .

SY: You perched long enough—now fly again—

ALL SCRIPTWRITERS: We're stuck—let's get unclogged—let's flow!

Sy: What does the doctor order?

Scriptwriter One: A romantic scene. Dreamy but devastating.

Sy: You got it!

Scriptwriter Two: A triangle—to introduce conflict?

Sy: Specify!

Scriptwriter Three: Build up suspense?

Sy: I hired you, so think!

Scriptwriter Four: Lay on intrigue?

Sy: Don't stop the music *now!*

Scriptwriter Three: How about this scene: we build on the Grand Duke of Wilbertania, who arrives in L.A. looking for his long-lost nephew, heir to the noble legacy but currently amnesia-ridden—

Sy: *(Acting like an orchestra conductor)* Fantastic! But let's not get ahead of ourselves.

Scriptwriter Four: I got it!—

Scriptwriter Three: Yeah—

Scriptwriter Two: How about—

Scriptwriter One: Roxy—she's in love with—

Scriptwriter Two: Obsessed, driven by her love for Prince,

Scriptwriter Three: She follows him—doglike—to L.A.

Scriptwriter Four: Groovy! Women become his slaves—he's an irresistible dreamboat of stunning clean-cut angelic sweet-tempered virility—

Scriptwriter One: Sy, what's our golden boy look like?

Scriptwriter Two: Yeah, boss, can you precision him?

Sy: *(Handing out identical copies to each of the Scriptwriters)* Here's the data sheet. *(Reading from his copy:)* Obvious hero type. Built in the wholesome pure romantic mold. Age twenty-one, height six feet one, weight one-seventy-five well-proportioned pounds—build not too muscular but well-toned. Hair soft, slightly curly, blond—not light blond but masculine blond, and completely natural to fit the rest of him. Eyes a piercing, but relaxing, blue. No beard, no moustache—there's nothing sinister about him.

SCRIPTWRITER FOUR: What a lowdown, boss!

SCRIPTWRITER ONE: He's all-American!

SCRIPTWRITER THREE: What about his personality?

SY: Glad you asked. Here, boys. *(Hands out more identical copies all around. Reading:)* Bright, articulate, tends to be introspective. Well bred—polite and courteous. High artistic sensibility—appreciates the finer things of life. Yet, being impulsive, can be easily spurred into action. Knows his way around town, confident in any situation, self-assured—yet not arrogant. He has no relatives except his long-lost uncle; but he's welcome among the best people, he has charisma, magnetic vitality. Whatever he does it's damn interesting and frequently leads to drama. *(Stops reading, resumes talking)* And boys, he's macho-tough. The audience will get larger and younger—a perfect cult figure that'll hurry up the puberty of teenage girls and bring back the puberty of the young marrieds.

SCRIPTWRITER ONE: He's our saviour, incarnate!

SCRIPTWRITER THREE: He'll save our bacon and zoom the ratings!

SCRIPTWRITER TWO: Boss, his clothes?

SY: Proper, stylish, smart—naturally.

SCRIPTWRITER ONE: As befits his character, boss!

SCRIPTWRITER TWO: So in the next scene, we put—

SCRIPTWRITER THREE: Roxy and Prince—

SCRIPTWRITER FOUR: Together in a sexual steambath—

SCRIPTWRITER THREE: She's been desperate for him—

SCRIPTWRITER FOUR: With a heart of gold, her love for Prince is unselfish—heartfelt—

SCRIPTWRITER THREE: In the sweet but starchy innocence of a long-lost virginity.

SCRIPTWRITER TWO: This will titillate all fledgling imaginations—

SCRIPTWRITER ONE: Of an increasingly switched-on young audience—

SCRIPTWRITER TWO: To whom our ecstatic sponsors will sell their soaring products—

SCRIPTWRITER THREE: In an expanding market of delirious consumers.

SCRIPTWRITER ONE: Lovelorn, Roxy visits Prince in his bachelor flat,

SCRIPTWRITER TWO: And love rides the saddle in L.A.!

SCRIPTWRITER THREE: Their modest whispers grow risqué!

SCRIPTWRITER FOUR: Just then—

SCRIPTWRITER THREE: Who should walk in—

SCRIPTWRITER TWO: No less, but Maggie!

SY: Music to my ears, I love it! Okay, now that *that* scene's sketched out, leading to the raging triangle in a tangle of wild passion with dreams that go boom or bust—we're hot!—so let's move on to the *next* scene.

SCRIPTWRITER ONE: The one introducing the eccentric uncle, the Grand Duke?

SY: *(Urging them on)* You got it! I didn't hire no dummies! Talk to me, make me happy.

SCRIPTWRITER TWO: The Grand Duke of Wilbertania, all the way from moldy old Europe, that jaded, decadent nest of history—

SCRIPTWRITER THREE: Arrives in clean and shining L.A., desperately seeking—

SCRIPTWRITER FOUR: his amnesia-ridden nephew, who's none other —

SCRIPTWRITER THREE: than our own local stud-in-residence, Prince Glitz—

SCRIPTWRITER TWO: Who's built along the hero mold!

SCRIPTWRITER ONE: To locate the lost Prince, the Duke has hired—

SCRIPTWRITER TWO: the toughest Private Eye he can find, built along the brutal lines—

SCRIPTWRITER THREE: of the semi-sadistic Micky Spillane!

SY: Gentlemen, I'm overwhelmed. This is truly greatness. I feel like praying.

ALL SCRIPTWRITERS: Hallelujah, boss! Let's piously keep the faith in the almighty holy media dollar!

> *(All SCRIPTWRITERS, along with SY, pause for a unison moment of prayer and meditation.)*

SY: *(Snapping them out of it, ready to crack the whip)* Okay, guys. I love it, but religion ain't everything. Let's roll up our sleeves and hammer out the greatest T.V. script in the annals of mankind.

ALL SCRIPTWRITERS: *(Variously)* Sure thing, boss! / It's in the bag! / A cinch!

SY: Put your nose to the grindstone. Let's hustle. I can smell paydirt.

ALL SCRIPTWRITERS: *(Scrambling to begin)* So can we!

SY: You have all the information. Let's be creative! We're artists, poets, of the mass electronic age!

ALL SCRIPTWRITERS: We're the collective Shakespeares of L.A., boss! By committee!

SY: Okay. Hop to it. Here. *(Hands out more script-note copies all around.)* Here's the bits-and-pieces remnants that the artsy-fartsy writer left for us. Now, make hay of this. Refine this raw material, patch it up, embroider, amalgamate, incorporate, stitch together—get going! I don't want no lazy beach-bums around here, so bloated on sun and cocaine that they're too lazy to breathe!

ALL SCRIPTWRITERS: *(Rolling up their sleeves, etc.)* We're here to work, boss!

SCRIPTWRITER ONE: We got rhythm!

SCRIPTWRITER FOUR: Momentum!

SCRIPTWRITER TWO: We're on top of the game!

SCRIPTWRITER THREE: We're *ahead* of the game!

SY: You won't let me down?

ALL SCRIPTWRITERS: *(Singing operatically in chorus)* No! A million times no!

SY: Convert this stuff to exotic magic.

ALL SCRIPTWRITERS: You got it, boss!

SY: Fulfill all romantic dreams ever dreamed.

SCRIPTWRITER ONE: In no time, boss!

SY: Will our ratings go juicy?

SCRIPTWRITER FOUR: Our ratings will ejaculate, boss!

SCRIPTWRITER THREE: Our ratings will cream in their panties with multiple orgasms!

SCRIPTWRITER TWO: Our ratings will scream themselves breathless!

SY: Well, what do I hear?

ALL SCRIPTWRITERS: "Fantasy Life"!

SY: This one's for the Gipper!

ALL SCRIPTWRITERS: Hurrah!

SY: Shall you earn your salaries by putting in an honest day's work to dignify labor in our capitalistic society?

ALL SCRIPTWRITERS: We'll do it or die trying!

SY: Then unleash your minds. Let it rip! Bang out the shooting script!

(Pandemonium is thrown loose, no holds barred: Speed-up soundtrack, speed-up visual motion. Script pages, pens, pencils, typewriters, glasses, bottles, are

thrown around in wild scene of working chaos. SCRIPT-WRITERS *animatedly, heatedly continue discussing script, plot, characterization, etc., in comical farcical zany speed-up exaggeration effects, as this part of Scene finally ends. Tempo changes. A wall clock spins, denoting passage of time. Lights dramatically shift, slow down.)*

(Tired, worn; pooped, spent, the SCRIPTWRITERS *all leave office.* SY *remains, as the responsible executive, summoning reserves of stamina and endurance, to go over his notes at his desk, and to coordinate his new notes with the* SCRIPTWRITERS' *copies.)*

*(*BRUCE WAIN, *Private Eye, enters disguised as cleaning lady with mop, bucket, etc., wearing a babushka, etc., and goes over to* SY.*)*

SY: *(Only slightly distracted; goes on working at desk)* Can you do the windows today?
WAIN: *(In falsetto)* I don't do windows. That's Josephine's department.

(After looking around, WAIN *goes to door and locks it. Then he goes to busy, preoccupied, unheeding, unsuspecting* SY, *grabs him unceremoniously by the collar, and lifts him out of his chair.)*

WAIN: Hey you. You got a minute?
SY: *(Startled)* Why—you talk like a man!
WAIN: You like the color of my babushka?
SY: You *are* a man! What a fabulous disguise!
WAIN: Tryin' a little flattery? *(Menacingly:)* Where do you think that'll get you? *(Steps up the threatening rough-housing.)*

SY: What are you doing here? Our security here is as tight as the Kremlin's.

WAIN: I ain't here for politics.

SY: What do you want?—I didn't do anything!

WAIN: Who's askin' the questions—you or me?

SY: *Please* don't hurt me—I'm too important, too responsible!

WAIN: I checked it out. The door's locked, the room's sound-proof. So I don't want no unnecessary screamin'.

SY: *(Meek, cowardly, cringing, whining, simpering)* You look like you mean business.

WAIN: I ain't here to take no vacation.

SY: *(Cringing)* I'll answer your questions! *(WAIN grabs SY.)* My nerves are delicate—my skin is too sensitive,

WAIN: Yeah? *(A mock-cordial offer:)* I can toughen it up. *(Laughs brutally. Points to notes on desk:)* Those notes on Prince Glitz where'd you get all that info?

SY: *(Helpless)* I made it up: Give me credit! I'm creative!

WAIN: Sensitive, delicate, creative, eh? You a fairy? *(Slaps SY hard.)*

SY: Were you hired by another network?

WAIN: Who's askin' *who* questions? *(Slaps SY again.)*

SY: *(Hurt with pain)* Oh! That hit home!

WAIN: So where's Thaddeus?

SY: Thaddeus? Who's *he?*

WAIN: *(Slugging SY a few times)* You're saying "who?"—*I'm* sayin' "where?"

SY: Enough spare me! I don't know who "Thaddeus" is. Obviously, you've come to the wrong department. *(Desperately trying to help, to be of service:)* You must want the "Movie of the Week" department. They're in the next studio.

WAIN: *(Slugging Sy again, then pointing to notes on desk)* Thaddeus is right there. You're messin' with somebody's character. See?—Prince Glitz!

SY: No he isn't! How can you presume—*(Silenced with another blow.)*

WAIN: You played a trick, but I'm no sucker to it.

SY: *(With hurt pride, righteously)* I!? Never!

WAIN: You changed his name. I don't fall for that stuff.

SY: I'm innocent!

WAIN: Innocent? No you ain't. Talk. *(Slaps Sy more blows.)*

SY: *(Wilting in pain)* Okay! Okay! Our script department developed Prince Glitz. We own him—outright. There's only one way for you to get him to buy the rights. But no gold can glitter our Glitz from us.

WAIN: Who do I see about the rights?

SY: I've already told you all I know.

WAIN: Who do I see? Fast!

SY: I told you all I know, already—there's nothing left—

WAIN: *(Slugging Sy, and pretending to be hard of hearing)* I didn't hear you.

SY: *(Persuaded)* Morton Ray's your man! He's our producer. He owns us all. He has all the rights—and none of the wrongs.

WAIN: What's this Morton Ray guy gonna do with Prince Glitz?

SY: Make him a famous character.

WAIN: Where?

SY: In "Fantasy Life."

WAIN: Where's that?

SY: It's our show.

WAIN: When?

SY: He'll be introduced in the next episode.

WAIN: *(Raising his hand threateningly again)* What else? You ain't through yet.

SY: *(Cowering in fear)* That's the limit of my knowledge! I swear!

WAIN: Where're they keepin' Prince?

SY: They found him a split-level—modest by Hollywood standards—a nice pool and hot tub but no tennis court.

WAIN: Yeah? What's *your* end of all this?

SY: I'm only a functionary. I have no executive responsibility. I'm an unimportant cog.

WAIN: That wasn't your tune before.

SY: I'm merely paid to do what the producer and the sponsors tell me to. My nose is clean.

WAIN: It is? *(Gripping SY by the nose, and twisting it hard.)* Seems pretty dirty to me.

SY: *(In physical agony: having difficulty talking with his nose closed by WAIN's grip, he talks in a funny way with distorted sounds and nasal grunts)* I'm personally innocent. I'm not involved. Morton Ray is the one. *(Reduced almost to his knees in WAIN's tightening grip:)* You should be doing this to *him*—all this pain is being *wasted* on me! *(Sobbing:)* How unfair, that innocence should he a martyr, a scapegoat!

WAIN: Yeah? Go on, talk.

SY: *(In agony)* I already talked. I even shouted. Maybe your babushka is too tight over your ears.

WAIN: You don't like my babushka? *(Slugs SY a final time; SY slumps over.)* Thanks for your help. I appreciate it.

> *(WAIN goes over to retrieve his cleaning gear and bucket. While exiting with them, he glances at SY out cold on the floor:)*

WAIN: Hollywood's a weirdo town.

SCENE II

(*L.A. THADDEUS's split-level: very fashionably appointed; lots of chrome and glass. He sits alone—isolated at removal from his surroundings. He's blankly staring at the T.V. set, which flickeringly reflects a blue glow across his face, seeming to absorb him into its entrails. Finally, as if in tremor; he monologues:*)

THADDEUS: Someone—is it I?—but what is *that*?—sits here in my chair, watching the blue glow flickering across his face . . . I thought certain issues had settled themselves. For a moment I was fortified by my new identity as Prince Glitz. Standing assured and confident, for a brief moment I "knew" who I was. Now doubts come questioning forth from some unknown place. Prince Glitz? It seems arbitrary, it doesn't ring true, it falls flat. For the real me, I'm called back into a past I can't recall. But where's my current identity—the me I just can't place? The answer is not in these cool flames that lash and lick up at me. This box and I both flicker agitatedly, from an inner emptiness. Our solitudes rage, both cool and perturbed.

(*Pause. Then knock on door is heard.*)

THADDEUS: I'm hearing my heart's echo, my chest's rhythm!

(*More knocks. Then knob is tried.*)

THADDEUS: This is *external* to my identity: it's the *door*.

(*THADDEUS goes over to door, opens it. ROXY enters, and immediately puts her arms around his neck.*)

ROXY: Honey—it's me!

THADDEUS: Who?

ROXY: *(Passionately)* Oh, how I've missed you!

THADDEUS: Pardon, but—

ROXY: Why did you run out on me like that?

THADDEUS: Did I?

ROXY: Don't you know me?!

THADDEUS: Sorry, I—

ROXY: This takes the cake!

THADDEUS: *What* cake?

ROXY: I came all the way from New York to find you—and this is how you greet me?

THADDEUS: *(Reflecting)* Yes—you *are* somewhat familiar.

ROXY: Thanks a lot! How can you forget your own words to me: "My life is a vacuum; why don't you fill it?"

THADDEUS: Of course—it's coming back.

ROXY: We were in Sardi's—I was looking for someone, you were waiting for someone or something.

THADDEUS: Yes—and my waiting hasn't stopped.

ROXY: Then you asked—I'll never, ever forget it—"You'll take care of me?" Oh, you were the cutest!

THADDEUS: Of course! You're—

ROXY: Roxy—my darling! *(Embraces him.)*

THADDEUS: *(Belatedly, anti-climactically finishing his own sentence)* Roxy.

ROXY: *(Looking around split-level)* Boy, look at this place! You really made out alright for yourself, didn't you? Wow! Classy! What's the rent here?

THADDEUS: Where did we meet?

ROXY: *(Laughing)* Still spaced out, huh? In New York, you were waiting at a table and your beer was getting warm. I saw you—

THADDEUS: What was—what is—my name?

ROXY: This is some sort of game?

THADDEUS: Game? Am I named Game?

ROXY: It's Thaddeus!

THADDEUS: Now I *am* confused.

ROXY: You're in L.A. a few days, already you're acting like you're born here. *(Touching his hair:)* I like your haircut; wonderful color.

THADDEUS: *(Act of remembering)* It comes back to me! Of course! I'm Thaddeus!

ROXY: How do you do? I'm Roxy, remember? I'm here to take care of you.

THADDEUS: You're Roxy? No, no, it can't be . . . But then—*(Making a recently learned connection)*—I must be Prince.

ROXY: *(Laughing)* Boy, you're weird!

THADDEUS: *(Gets script and points at parts to show her)* It says so—right here—and *here*, too.

ROXY: What's that? *(Takes script from him:)* Here, le'me see it. *(Reads it, her eyes skimming and leaping over it.)* Prince . . . Roxy . . . wow! *(Looks at script's cover:)* I don't believe this! It's the shooting script for "Fantasy Life"! *(Excitedly:)* Are you Prince?

THADDEUS: That's what I wonder about.

ROXY: Oh God, to be Roxy!

THADDEUS: But Roxy—that's who you *are*!

ROXY: You're tempting me! It's an actress's dream, to get that part.

THADDEUS: "Part"? Of what whole is it a part? A part of our whole?

ROXY: *(Enthusiastically)* Oh, Thaddeus! Us playing opposite each other in a prime-time T.V. drama! If only it *could* be!

THADDEUS: By playing your role—your part—maybe you can help me find out who I actually I am—the real me?

ROXY: You're really stuck on that, aren't you?—you're obsessed.

THADDEUS: Of course. Isn't that everyone's quest?

ROXY: Thaddeus—I understand—I want to help you more than anything! *(They embrace.)*

THADDEUS: Yes? Then all that's required is that you play *your* part.

ROXY: *My* part?

THADDEUS: Roxy.

ROXY: But I can't just *play* Roxy!

THADDEUS: You're the only Roxy *I* could play opposite to, with the full conviction of love.

ROXY: *(Melting)* Oh, if only I *could!*

THADDEUS: I'll insist that you alone play it. Otherwise I'll refuse to be the Prince Glitz they're so eager for me to be.

ROXY: *(Melting)* Are we dreaming? *(They kiss.)*

THADDEUS: And anyway—even as we're talking—you're already being a convincing Roxy: the only true authentic Roxy there can be. So go on with it, to help me discover my*self*. See: *(Pointing to script:)* It says so right here.

ROXY: *(Looking at script)* You're right—I'm the only one to help you! You're my tender crusade! *(Suddenly looking in alarm at THADDEUS:)* Oh honey—you've gone pale! Is something wrong?

THADDEUS: *(Looking pale, with eyes fixed)* A vague voice keeps uttering that I'm not what they've forced me to be: despite this script, "Prince" doesn't fit me; I'm in the wrong place; I'm in a false position. There's a different path I should have followed: somehow, I miss my calling; I've fallen into hands that misguide me. I'm led away from where by rights—if I can only locate them—I should be. You're here, so I appeal to you—can you straighten me out? My gratitude is love itself. For your love is all I can go by—my sole certainty.

ROXY: *(Having been looking at script while listening.)* Gosh! That was beautiful! I'm really awed! You memorized these lines *(Indicating script) perfectly!* *(Awed:)* You're a *natural!*

THADDEUS: You promise to help me find out who I am?

ROXY: *(As they embrace)* I promise, my poor lost darling! Oh, you're so lost! Oh Thaddeus, of *course* I'll help you. *(Glancing at script, then reading from it:)* "my pitiful love! My lost soul!" How was that? How'd I do?

THADDEUS: *Then* what happens? *(Indicating script:)* Does it say there?

ROXY: *(Reads)* "There's a knock on the door."

> *(There's a knock on door. Then knob turns: MAGGIE enters, dressed only as those in Hollywood can be dressed.)*

BOTH ROXY AND MAGGIE: *(Simultaneously to each other)* Who do you think you are? What the hell are you doing here?

ROXY: None of your business!

MAGGIE: It's obvious that the bitch that's addressing me so insolently is—Roxy.

THADDEUS: *(Pursuing his own logic)* That's right . . . if she's Roxy, I'm Prince . . .

MAGGIE: To what great fortune do we owe her presence?

THADDEUS: She's here to take care of me—in my plight, which centers around an identity problem.

MAGGIE: *(Sarcastically)* How thoroughly kind, how decent, of her!

THADDEUS: Yes, isn't it?

MAGGIE: But that's *my* job, remember?

THADDEUS: Your job?

ROXY: *(Sarcastically, to MAGGIE)* You must have made a great impression on him!

MAGGIE: Since you don't belong here, I don't acknowledge you.

THADDEUS: My memory is appallingly erratic.

ROXY: Thaddeus—don't let this woman snap our spell.

MAGGIE: She's a dime a dozen, Prince. I gave you credit for better taste than *this*.

ROXY: Say something, Thaddeus—tell her about us!

THADDEUS: I'm at a loss—I don't know what to say . . .

ROXY: Take your cue from here. *(Reading from script:)* "Prince, oh Prince. We love each other, don't we? And that's all that matters! Right, my dear?"

MAGGIE: Sorry, that's not right. Let's take it back.

ROXY: See, look. *(Showing THADDEUS the script:)* This is what you say next, Thaddeus.

MAGGIE: Let's take it back. Ready, Prince?

THADDEUS: Okay.

> *(All three actors return to original positions as they redo following lines with same inflections and gestures as before:)*

THADDEUS: Your job?

ROXY: *(Sarcastically, to MAGGIE)* You must have made a great impression on him!

MAGGIE: Since you don't belong here, I don't acknowledge you.

THADDEUS: My memory is appallingly erratic.

ROXY: Thaddeus—don't let this woman snap our spell.

MAGGIE: She's a dime a dozen, Prince. I gave you credit for better taste than this.

ROXY: Say something, Thaddeus—tell her about us!

THADDEUS: I'm at a loss—I don't know what to say . . . What am I supposed to say?

ROXY: *(Indicating script)* Let me look at it—I'll help you find your lines.

MAGGIE: Prince, we'll straighten this out later. We all make mistakes. I forgive you.

ROXY: *(Taking back script from THADDEUS)* Hey, wait a minute! You don't *own* him!

MAGGIE: Oh, is it preferable that he be influenced by some ordinary nobody—like you?

ROXY: What are you calling me? I know what *you're* after!

THADDEUS: *(Looking through script)* I'm sorry . . . you lost me. What page are we on?

MAGGIE: *(Sternly)* Prince, I don't need all this. *(Consulting watch:)* we're due at the Studio in twenty minutes. Say goodbye, and let's go!

ROXY: *(Mockingly mimicking MAGGIE)* La dee dah! "We're due at the Studio in twenty minutes." Where'd you get that accent, at Vassar or Bryn Mawr?

MAGGIE: Now look—

ROXY: *(Forcibly interrupting)* At what? You think you can order Thaddeus around because you're some Hollywood type? You're nothin' and never *will* be. You know why? Because I have what you'd give your ass to have. You know what it is?—it's Thaddeus's love! So go find somebody else to manipulate!

MAGGIE: *(Defiant)* Thanks to me, Prince is going to be a star! I'm not about to let a little nobody like you take my Prince and ruin him! Over my dead body, sister!

ROXY: Dead body? You've been dead for years! You were out of fashion before you were born!

THADDEUS: *(Finding the right page, finds his lines, reads:)* Girls! *Please* don't fight! It's beneath you! Remember your dignity. Let's not make an ugly scene.

ROXY: Thaddeus—we're in love, remember?

THADDEUS: *(Reading)* We are, my dearest. But I have to be at the Studio. I'll make oodles of money, to set off the jewel of our love in a glittering setting! Have to run now. You just keep the home fires burning, honey!

MAGGIE: Look, Prince: Your career comes first. You'll have to learn to sacrifice a few cheap temptations *(Indicating Roxy)* for the sake of your future stardom. You'll have to give up some things *now*. You need discipline, Prince—I'll enforce it.

ROXY: I wouldn't put it past you, bitch!

MAGGIE: Prince—I'm leaving now. Either you come with me, or remain behind and ruin your whole career before it even starts!

ROXY: *(Scorning)* A showdown, huh?

MAGGIE: What's your choice, Prince? Be a man!

THADDEUS: I'll be a man—but I wish I knew *what* man.

MAGGIE: We're late already.

THADDEUS: *(Reading)* Roxy! *(Takes her in his arms and kisses her tenderly.)* I'm leaving now, don't grieve, it's not forever. You must trust our love. It's sacred to me. I'll be back.

ROXY: *(Weeping)* Men are all alike. Stringing us along with promises!

THADDEUS: *(Reading)* But Roxy!—

ROXY: *(Sobbing)* You'll forget me—I *know* you will! *She* can offer you fame, fortune, glamor, excitement. But Thaddeus—*I* can help you find yourself—just give me the chance! With me, you'll find the true you: the you that only *I* can see, it's so deep within. Oh Thaddeus!

THADDEUS: *(Reading)* Roxy—I hate to, but I *must* go! But make yourself at home. Help yourself to the fridge—anything you want, especially the perishables. I'll phone later. Be patient, love!

MAGGIE: *(Proprietorially victorious)* Come on, my dear. We mustn't waste any more time.

THADDEUS: Right behind you, Maggie.

> *(As MAGGIE exits followed by THADDEUS, ROXY bravely, pathetically, heartbrokenly waves to THADDEUS.)*

MAGGIE: *(As she exits)* Tough luck, honey. Don't worry. I'll keep him nice and fresh for you.

> *(Alone in THADDEUS's split-level, ROXY sits, forlorn, crying. She turns a page of the script left behind.)*

SCENE III

> *(T.V. Studio for "Fantasy Life." WILBERT waiting nervously. He's dressed out of sync—inappropriate for L.A.: heavy tweed jacket, hat, scarf, overcoat. By contrast, BRUCE WAIN now enters dressed in sync with L.A. for first time: sunglasses, a loud tropical print shirt, white trousers, etc. The disguise is so effective that WILBERT doesn't recognize him.)*

WILBERT: Excuse me, sir, but I was looking for—

WAIN: Cut the stuff, Wills, it's me—*(Raising sunglasses, then lowering them back in place)*—Wain. Keep cool, act nonchalant. I was followed. We're probably bein' watched now.

WILBERT: Maybe it was unwise to meet here?

WAIN: We're movin' in for the kill. It's the *only* place to meet.

WILBERT: *(Looking around)* Your metamorphosis is so convincingly thorough, I'm not sure I'm even talking to the one I presume you to be—if you are, indeed, you.

WAIN: These are just some duds I picked up in the costume shop . . . You're shakin', Wills.

WILBERT: I fear the worst—that something terrible might have happened to Thaddeus.

WAIN: *(Looks around)* There's still time.

WILBERT: What have you found out? I've been a nervous wreck since leaving New York.

WAIN: We're closin' in.

WILBERT: How close?

WAIN: *(Putting his finger to his lips)* Act natural.

> (A STUDIO TECHNICIAN *walks by with a head-set on.*
> WAIN *assumes a "casual, natural" pose.)*

WAIN: *(Voice disguised, for benefit of passing* TECHNICIAN*)* So the guy says to the dame, "Well, whataya got, baby?" And the dame says to the guy, "That's not the point. The point is what *you* got." So he rises to . . .

> (*The* STUDIO TECHNICIAN *has left; Wain looks around.*)

WILBERT: Is this elaborately melodramatic caution quite necessary?

WAIN: Like you said, Wills—this is another medium, where anythin' could happen.

WILBERT: Threats abound in vague shapes of dread.

WAIN: L.A. is a nutty place. You think you got a fact; then the fact, in fact, ain't there no more—in fact, you got an illusion.

> *(They keep looking around in cautious alert suspicion,*
> *but it's always a false "alarm.")*

WILBERT: Thaddeus may be in a web of peril and all is lost if we waste a minute. What's your rescue plan, Wain?

WAIN: We got to wait now; And he ain't Thaddeus.

WILBERT: *(Alarmed)* What—!

WAIN: They gave him a new name.

WILBERT: Those tampering meddlers, manhandling butchers, identity-molesters, character-levelers, stereotype addicts!

WAIN: Keep it down, Wills.

WILBERT: What nameplate did they brand their stolen merchandise with?

WAIN: Prince Glitz.

WILBERT: How crassly banal of those nomenclature-nincompoops! How degrading, demeaning, debasing in their slimy Hollywoodizing. Beyond the nominal, what have the criminals—

WAIN: They made a T.V. star of him—they already shot the first episode.

WILBERT: *(In a comic hamming of the agonized outraged)* I've just entered the special hell reserved only for authors!

WAIN: Sy's not the guy we're after.

WILBERT: Diabolically *who*, then?

WAIN: Sy's the front man. He organized the hit but he ain't the brains.

WILBERT: You've uncovered the big fry to Sy's small fry: an ultimate mastermind villain schemer?

WAIN: Morton Ray.

WILBERT: Of course—the Producer.

WAIN: You're quick, Wills.

WILBERT: He's sullied, distorted, contorted into a hideous Prince Glitz my gallant Thaddeus. Let's restore and redeem my fine original!

WAIN: If there's still anythin' left of him.

WILBERT: A horrible vision: I can see him entwined forever in T.V. airwave network—or floating aimlessly through the dreary mediocrity of prime-time, seeking the lost substance of his pure old self, in endless purgatorial claptrap.

WAIN: Calm down, Wills. Seems like Morton Ray done this kind of dirty work before.

WILBERT: His evil must be sharpened to routine formula! How many worthy characters from actual or potential literature—not to mention the stories themselves—has he bleached of original substance, and drained dry of artistic merit, till the meaning runs out? Till one day there'll be nothing left from our literary heritage except what's crumpled to palpable pulp for popular consumption. The wreckage and remains of cultural genocide, beaten down to the idiotically plain.

WAIN: Relax, Wills. *(Looking cautiously around.)* While you're out here, maybe you oughta get a little sun.

WILBERT: Forget about me—get Thaddeus! They—

WAIN: Shhh! . . . .

> *(Like two identical mechanical dolls or toy soldiers, they simultaneously look around, then wait stock-still in frozen dummy silence for a moment—all in unwittingly comical pantomime.)*

WILBERT: *(Whispering)* What is it?

WAIN: Dunno, thought I heard somethin'.

WILBERT: Mr. Wain—I'm deathly afraid!

WAIN: Nothin's gonna happen to yuh if me and Bessy have anythin' to do with it.

WILBERT: Bessy?

> *(WAIN identifies "Bessy" by pulling out a 45 automatic pistol, then quickly reconcealing it.)*

WAIN: They got this place rigged up so eerie, yuh don't know if you're comin' or goin'. I think they hypnotize yuh with that electronic wave frequency that T.V. puts out.

WILBERT: An electronically manipulating system that's invisible, like nerve gas, chemical warfare? It's illegal!

WAIN: This is their territory.

WILBERT: A nice little predicament! What do we do now?

WAIN: We'll act like the guys that belong here. Be cool, play dumb.

WILBERT: But how?

WAIN: Don't tip 'em off with any of those big jawbreakin' words—only use small words.

WILBERT: What else?

WAIN: Don't say nothin' that makes any sense. Change the subject a lot, like you're ignorant. Never look anybody in the eye. That's the way they do it out here.

WILBERT: Such cautionary prudence! I feel gripped by a paranoiac vapor.

WAIN: Don't worry, we'll get out o' this okay.

WILBERT: *(Panicking, so that he forgets himself and speaks in normal voice)* Yes, but Thaddeus—Thaddeus—

WAIN: *(Hand roughly over WILBERT's mouth)* Keep it down—you wanna blow our cover?

WILBERT: *(Chastened; in obediently soft voice)* Where—where is he?

WAIN: They got him holed up in some split-level in Hollywood somewhere.

WILBERT: But why are we *here*?

WAIN: They gotta bring him here, sooner or later. Anyway, I gotta find *Ray*, he's the kingpin and answer man.

WILBERT: Do you propose to beat the information out of him?

WAIN: Come off it, Wills, you been watchin' too many T.V. cop stories. This is still real life, where it ain't that easy.

(WAIN *and* WILBERT *immediately, simultaneously strike exaggerated "nonchalant" poses as a* CAMERAMAN *wheels a camera by them and across stage. Once coast is clear, they resume their normal hushed, huddled, intent, suspicious, cautious postures.*)

WILBERT: Why isn't it that easy?

WAIN: There's complications. How come you never told me Ray owns Thaddeus?

WILBERT: *(Taken aback)* I own Thaddeus! Don't *you* try to mix me up, when all the elements here conspire to my befuddlement.

WAIN: You signed a contract: any characters you made for the show are Ray's property; he commissioned you to write the stuff.

WILBERT: He commissioned me to write for a T.V. show. But the character I created belongs beyond T.V.—in a literary work of art.

WAIN: It's all the same as far as these guys go.

WILBERT: This is a nightmare. My lifetime's supreme creation is lawfully maimed and tainted to the banal promptings of a gold-chained, suntanned T.V. tycoon-vulgarian without a soul to his name!

WAIN: How do yuh know he's suntanned?—Shhh!

(WAIN *and* WILBERT *look apprehensively in opposite directions; then, like clockwork, back to each other.*)

WAIN: I'm still with yuh. Nobody got a right to mess with another guy's character—I don't care how much money is behind it. I don't care if this is in the nineteen-eighties, I don't even care that this is L.A.—there's *still* rights and wrongs, right?

WILBERT: Why, Mr. Wain, what a noble manifesto, a humane proclamation, and a testament of personal loyalty that exalts me above the role of a mere paying client. It honors me—

WAIN: It ain't no big deal, Wills. Cut out the crap.

WILBERT: It affords me the timely reassurance of comfort and support at this juncture of my life's crisis when my psyche's precarious balance tilts in a fragile tremor of disequilibrium.

WAIN: *(Taking out a little bottle and offering it)* You want an aspirin?

WILBERT: No, this is a pain I must live with.

WAIN: I'm on to this Ray guy. I gotta go now.

WILBERT: *(Frightened)* Are you leaving me here?! *(Grabbing hold of WAIN's arm.)* The electronically transformationally hypnotic waves of this sinister, ominous atmosphere scare my will and threaten its self-control.

WAIN: *(Showing 45 automatic pistol)* Me and Bessy will take care of you. We'll be back soon. If anybody asks you any questions, just play along with them, make up a story, play dumb; these clowns, ain't too bright, they'll buy anythin'. *(WAIN leaves.)*

WILBERT: *(Feebly, futilely calling after)* But—but—how . . . ?

(WILBERT stands fidgety for a moment, then darts off in one direction only to abruptly stop short, turn, and dart off in another direction, in restless nervousness: confused as to what to do, where to go, etc.)

(Two SET MEN move a piece of wall into place behind WILBERT.)

SET MAN ONE: Hey, watch out there, buddy.

WILBERT: Oh, pardon. Am I in your way?

SET MAN TWO: Yeah—move *that* way.

WILBERT: *(Moving)* Here?

SET MAN ONE: No, over *there*, stupid!

(Confused, scared, WILBERT obediently moves again.)

(VITTORIO enters in a flurry and flourish, with two ASSISTANTS in tow. He goes immediately to WILBERT.)

VITTORIO: At last! Where were you? I am too busy to go chasing around!

WILBERT: I've been here.

VITTORIO: *(Surprised)* Here?! *(To ASSISTANT ONE:)* Where was he supposed to be?

ASSISTANT ONE: *(Looking at clipboard)* In Wardrobe.

VITTORIO: See? In Wardrobe. Half-hour ago. *(To ASSISTANT ONE:)* Half-hour, right?

ASSISTANT ONE: That's right, sir.

VITTORIO: So, what do you do *here*?

WILBERT: Sorry, but what are you talking about?

VITTORIO: Please, this is no time for the jokes. I am very, very busy. *(To ASSISTANT TWO:)* Right?

ASSISTANT TWO: A schedule so tight you can barely breathe.

VITTORIO: *(To WILBERT)* You see?

(SET MAN ONE enters with chair.)

VITTORIO: *(Shouting at SET MAN ONE)* You are blind! No! No! Not that color! It must be blue to show regal power! Take it off, I don't want to see it!

(SET MAN ONE obeys. SET MAN TWO enters with a desk.)

SET MAN TWO: Where should this go?

VITTORIO: Here . . . No, no, to the left. *(To ASSISTANT ONE:)* Where was I? *(ASSISTANT ONE points to WILBERT.)*

VITTORIO: *(To WILBERT)* You! You still here!

(Two WARDROBE PEOPLE enter bearing a costume.)

VITTORIO: *(To WARDROBE PEOPLE:)* Ah, very, very good! *(To WILBERT)* See, if you no go to Wardrobe, Wardrobe go to you! *(To WARDROBE PEOPLE:)* Please, take care of this man.

(As VITTORIO then turns his attention to the set, the WARDROBE PEOPLE begin to tug and take off WILBERT's overcoat, attending to him busily and professionally, etc.)

WARDROBE PERSON ONE: We were looking all over for you!—Hold still!—Where were you?!

WARDROBE PERSON TWO: You're wanted in Make-Up right after this.

WARDROBE PERSON ONE: They need to white your hair and wrinkle your hands.

WILBERT: But what for?

WARDROBE PERSON TWO: To make you old and crotchety.

WILBERT: *(Wrestling away from them)* Hold on, you're making a mistake! I'm not the man you assume you're referring to! *(WILBERT frees himself from their clutches.)*

VITTORIO: What do you want? Not ready still?

WILBERT: There's some absurd misunderstanding; I'm a victim of mistaken identity as though playing a comic part in a Restoration Comedy! They're trying to prepare me for television. This would be funny—

VITTORIO: What is funny about it? I am very busy!

WILBERT: I'm not who they think I am.

VITTORIO: You are crazy?!

WILBERT: *(Blurting out)* I'm here to find my character—that's my sole purpose for being here! Otherwise, I'm back in New York!

VITTORIO: I am no interested in character motivation—I want the results. *(VITTORIO's attention is drawn away to the set. To SET MEN:)* No, no, I tell you before, you don't listen! Producer's desk to be cluttered with work—he is busy making deals! Hurry! And bring the lighting! Do what you are told!

> *(The two WARDROBE PEOPLE have resumed their hurried, professional pawing at WILBERT.)*

WILBERT: *(Resisting again)* Stop! Leave me alone! I'm not who you think I am!

VITTORIO: *(To ASSISTANT ONE)* My distractions are being interrupted! What is this?

ASSISTANT ONE: *(Pointing to WILBERT)* He's acting up.

VITTORIO: *(To WILBERT)* Professional standards I insist here! Unions or no Unions! I am too efficient for anarchy, I am too streamlined for chaos!

WILBERT: I'm not an actor, and never was! I want my Thaddeus back!

VITTORIO: Who is Thaddeus?

WILBERT: They kidnapped him; he has no recollection of his past, poor boy; they were going to manipulate—to corrupt—him into the broad flat pulp of mass-market vulgarization as the top T.V. romantic commodity—

VITTORIO: *(Relieved)* Good, but you must read scripts more carefully; the names you must get right. Thaddeus is the original name, but the T.V. people make him into Prince Glitz. Prince Glitz is his name. *(To both ASSISTANTS:)* These actors!

WILBERT: That's right—I heard he was renamed into that ugly, trivial name! I demand an audience with the Producer!

VITTORIO: You actors! You are an emotional caveman! *Who* are you looking for?

WILBERT: "Prince Glitz," as he's misnamed! I *must* have him back!

VITTORIO: *(Applauding)* Molto bene! You are the best character actor: The intention is right, commitment, execution, timing. But you must save it for the cameras. The time is not now. *(To WARDROBE PEOPLE:)* Hurry with the costuming!

> *(While they've been talking, the setting behind them has been gradually transformed—not yet complete—into MORTON RAY's office.)*

WILBERT: *(Wailing outcry)* Try to understand me! What do I have to do to get a little sympathy around here?!

VITTORIO: I give you very much your share of sympathy and understanding. I am no nursemaid! *Other* actors need me too. *(Attention drawn to set work: To SET MEN:)* Very good; more blue in the lights, I want more blue. *(To WILBERT:)* Prime donnas I refuse to direct unless they are stars—you are not!

WILBERT: I—

VITTORIO: *(Cutting him off. To him and WARDROBE PEOPLE:)* In costume, please. The Duke of Wilbertania must to be elegant, regal, and noble. If you see the character different, I am sorry, this is television—no-one will believe you are royalty dressed like this. You are out of character. You must let them fit you.

WILBERT: *What* Duke? Far from a Duke, I'm merely what I am: Wilbert Wills, novelist, fiction-writer, occasional essayist!

VITTORIO: What?! Script, please! *(Takes script from ASSISTANT ONE:)* See, it says "Duke" here!

WILBERT: But I write! I've seen that script before—or *some* of it, anyway.

VITTORIO: You must to have seen an early version. Please, pardon, you are right and I am wrong. Please, I am sorry. (*Screaming to* ASSISTANT TWO:) Go to get the new version of the second episode—hurry! Subitto! (ASSISTANT TWO *obediently dashes off.*)

WILBERT: (*Exasperated*) But you don't understand: I'm no actor!

VITTORIO: Absolutely no! *Prince* is the actor—you are the *uncle*, the Grand Duke! (*Looking over* WILBERT *carefully:*) You are perfect for this character!

WILBERT: You're not listening to me!—must I scream?

(*Camera crews roll in with the lights and microphones.*)

VITTORIO: No, no. We are getting you the new script. You must to look at Episode Two, Scene Thirteen. This Scene, you are convinced that the Producer has kidnapped your nephew. You will confront the evil television people at a Beverley Hills party. Then you find the precious, long-lost object of your longing soul's mortal quest.

WILBERT: (*Suddenly overjoyed at this "news"*) I will? Oh Lord! Deliverance, after long travail! (*Sighs with his first contentedness in a long time.*)

VITTORIO: Ah, at last you are happy! Finally, we have found a way to satisfy you! (*Indicating* WARDROBE PEOPLE:) Go with them now. They will get you ready to confront that evil Producer and find your dear lost one!

(WILBERT *is pulled off—but without resisting—by the* WARDROBE PEOPLE, *who, even in motion, start disrobing him of his inappropriate-for-L.A. clothes he's worn from New York; they garb him bit by bit with his new T.V.-script-scenario costume.*)

VITTORIO: Pah! These Method actors! Psycho cases! What ever happened to just pretending?

SCENE IV

(Same setting as in last Scene. An Assistant Director enters and goes to Vittorio. There's much activity—changing of lighting equipment and camera, etc.)

Assistant Director: We're almost ready with the set-up. Do you want to start with the scheduled Scene?

Vittorio: Yes, we cannot wait any longer. We shall go immediately.

Assistant Director: *(Making a general announcement)* Everybody! We're going to start with Scene Eight. Lighting and camera adjustments for Scene Eight, please.

(Lighting and Camera People go into action.)

Assistant Director: Bring in the talent!

(Morton Ray, T.V. Producer, is escorted in by a Production Assistant. Ray wears wig and jacket to make himself look bigger.)

Vittorio: *(Goes to Morton Ray)* All right, you have all your lines down this time? This is a simple scene. You must keep it light, uncomplicated.

Ray: Got it.

Vittorio: Keep your chin up—don't rush the lines.

Assistant Director: Quiet on the set. Scene Eight, Clap Boards.

Vittorio: All right, everyone, ready?—Roll 'em—and action!

(Cameras roll in and move around continually during this entire scene between Ray and Wain. Morton Ray is busy at his desk, as Vittorio and others look on.

Then BRUCE WAIN *enters, dressed the way we last saw him. He takes a quick look around, then goes to* RAY, *who, just now, startled, notices* WAIN.)

WAIN: You Morton Ray?

RAY: How did you get in here? Who are you?

WAIN: *I'm* askin' the questions. *(Pulls out his 45 automatic pistol—Bessy—and points it at* RAY.*)*

RAY: What do you want—I didn't do anything. Please, put that away—please—then we can talk.

WAIN: I want Prince Glitz.

RAY: Who?

WAIN: Clean your ears. Prince Glitz! *(Waves his gun at* RAY.*)*

RAY: Why, but, but,—if—but—and—if—

WAIN: I don't want no "ands," "ifs," or "buts!"

RAY: I mean Prince Glitz is just a *character!*

WAIN: I know that.

RAY: But *why* do you want him?—what's he to you?

WAIN: I ain't here to discuss things.

RAY: Who sent you? You're not from another network?

WAIN: What'd I tell you about questions? *(Cocks his pistol, alarming* RAY.*)*

RAY: Okay, okay! Whatever you want!

WAIN: That's better.

RAY: But you're not going to get away with this.

WAIN: You gonna stop me?

RAY: I mean, I own Prince Glitz *legally*. You can't just come in here and take one of my characters and expect to get away with it. Just a matter of time, and we'd find him and take him back—So you see, I'm trying to save you trouble and embarrassment in the first place!

WAIN: You're goin' to sign him over real legal-like, up front, fair and square—savvy? *(Waves his gun to* RAY *to signal him to write.)* Get writin'.

RAY: How can you go this!? You'd *never* get away with it! A great character like Prince Glitz—a once in a lifetime—we don't let him go that easy.

WAIN: And *I* think you will. *(Points his gun directly at* RAY, *ready to shoot.)*

RAY: *(Frightened)* No, please, control yourself—please! I'll do what you want.

WAIN: Write.

RAY: I will, but first I have to know who I'm signing him over to!

WAIN: The Grand Duke of Wilbertania.

RAY: The Grand Duke of Wilbertania!

WAIN: Yeah!

RAY: But I thought he was dead!

WAIN: Write!

RAY: I'll do it!

WAIN: Put down: He "has sole and rightful authority over Prince Glitz."

RAY: *(Writing)* But what does he want with Prince? Prince is of age: he can handle affairs for himself, he's about to become a great T.V. star—through *me*, I'm *making* him one! That's why I own him! So what could the Grand Duke possibly want with him?!

WAIN: Prince is his nephew, so he just wants what's rightfully his.

RAY: We could work out a deal. I could cut the Grand Duke in on a percentage.

WAIN: He ain't interested.

RAY: You sure? *(*WAIN *glares at him, in savage silence.)* Okay, then *you*—how about *you*? How much do you want? You want a part in the series?—you'd be great! Just name your price, you're a reasonable guy, I can trust you; you'd get a lot farther with me than some old coot like the Grand—

WAIN: *(Cutting him short)* You finished with that writin' yet?

RAY: Sorry, here it is. *(RAY gives WAIN the document, WAIN looks it over.)* Think about it, it's a great opportunity for you! You'd never have to work again. It's an offer—

WAIN: *(Interrupting)* There's some things you just can't buy, chump—or sell. Loyalty to an aesthetic ethos is one a' them.

RAY: There's got to be more to this than you're letting on.

WAIN: Okay, enough chit-chat. Where do I find him?

RAY: *(Stalling)* Who?

WAIN: Prince Glitz, dummy.

RAY: Sorry, I'd like to help you, but I just don't know—*(WAIN pistol-whips RAY a few times.)*

WAIN: Maybe that'll help to jog your memory.

RAY: Okay, please, no more. He'll be at a party in his honor. Everybody who's connected with the show will be there.

WAIN: Write down the address.

RAY: No, wait, here, here's an invitation.

(RAY hands WAIN an invitation, then suddenly reaches for WAIN's gun. They struggle, till gun goes off, blasting RAY backwards, covered with blood. WAIN looks around to make sure he hasn't been heard.)

WAIN: You shouldn't a' done that—that's how people get hurt.

(WAIN exits, with document RAY signed. RAY's body is left slumped.)

VITTORIO: Keep rolling! Zoom in for a close-up of the body! *(Camera crew do so with camera.)* That is it, get the blood. Pan up to his face ... Good! Okay! Cut! That is a keeper!

(RAY stands up, brushing the "blood" off himself.)

RAY: How'd it look?

VITTORIO: Terrific, spectacular! Very good acting. You were very real.

(Set crew eruptingly goes to work, rushing about with cameras, lights, etc., taking down walls, to prepare for and establish the next scene.)

RAY: Thanks, Vittorio. *(RAY takes off wig and jacket that made him look bigger.)* Whew! Sure feels good to get out of *this* stuff! *(To VITTORIO:)* Are you going to the party?

VITTORIO: Yes, but I will be late. There is one more scene to shoot.

RAY: *(Leaving)* See you later, then.

VITTORIO: Save me some caviar and cocaine, okay?

(RAY exits.)

VITTORIO: *(To ASSISTANT DIRECTOR)* Assistant! This scene will take place before the live audience. *(Looking at audience:)* Correct?

ASSISTANT DIRECTOR: That's right, Vittorio. Last scene of the episode.

VITTORIO: *(Looking at audience)* Good: All the audience extras are in place?

(ASSISTANT DIRECTOR is now on walkie-talkie, talking to someone unheard by audience except for walkie-talkie's metallic chords; all the while, he's looking at audience.)

ASSISTANT DIRECTOR: *(To VITTORIO)* All go.

VITTORIO: Good. We wrap this episode, so then we can go to the party.

(Blackout simultaneous with curtain fall.)

SCENE V

(T.V. monitors are in position downstage. "Applause" and "Quiet" signs appear, also an "On Air / Off Air" sign. The set is either in blackout or behind a curtain. Then ANNOUNCER enters, with microphone in hand, accompanied by a musical fanfare.)

ANNOUNCER: *(To audience)* Hello everybody and welcome to Studio Eighteen. I'm Bert Convoy and this is "Fantasy Life." *("Applause" sign flashes; an applause track echoes over the sound system.)* Thank you, thank you! As you all know, "Fantasy Life" is one of television's most popular dramatic series, and it's our pleasure to present the finest for your entertainment. *("Applause" sign flashes; a short applause over sound system.)* Thank you! For those of you who never before attended the live taping of a television program, I must explain a few ground rules. *(Looks at his notes.)* You've probably noted the signs on display here. When the "Applause" sign goes on, that of course indicates that you should applaud. And when the "Quiet" sign flashes, then everyone please be quiet. Over here *(Pointing)* we have this "On Air" sign when we're taping, and this *(Pointing)* "Off Air" sign when we're not taping. See?—it's simple. Now these *(Pointing)* two monitors will show you what the camera is seeing, and that's what will be broadcast not only throughout the country but in many other parts of the world as well. And you'll also see the commercials that will be broadcast. That's when we'd like you to cough, sneeze, shuffle your feet, and whatever else you want to do—save it for then. *(Spontaneous but moderate audience laughter.)* Okay, so does everybody got it? *(Looks approvingly at audience.)* Good! *("Applause" sign flashes; applause comes over sound system.)* Thank you, ladies and gentlemen. Thank you for coming to see "Fantasy Life." Now, sit back and enjoy the show!

(ANNOUNCER *exits. Then a commercial flashes onto the monitors. When commercial is over, the set is revealed: a patio area of* SY's *Beverly Hills home, foliage, lounge chairs, etc. Heard in distance are splashing of pool water and frolicking of friends and other guests. It's early evening just prior to sunset. Music plays in distance. Then host* SY *enters escorting* CELIA SEE, *star reporter for a personality magazine, "Peep-hole Magazine." Both are dressed casually, drinks in hand.)*

CELIA SEE: Fabulous pool, Sy.

SY: *(Oozing charm, playing the genial but commercially "operating" host)* Thanks, Celia. I just knew you'd love it. How do you like the view?

CELIA: Great! I can see all the way to Santa Monica.

SY: I tell people that from here I can see all the way across America.

CELIA: *(Professionally jotting in writing pad)* A terrific image! The whole depth and breadth of our great land, from your patio. Mind if I quote you?

SY: *(Suavely)* Mind?! I'd *love* you to!

CELIA: So tell me more about this Prince Glitz. He's the talk of the town; all Hollywood's buzzin' about him. *(Scolding:)* Sy—why are you keeping him such a big secret? Why the tease?

SY: Because he's the ultimate. It's a quantum leap; he's the beginning of something new. He'll start the rave of a wave. He'll be the biggest thing ever to hit prime time T.V.—he'll make "Dallas" look like one of the flops of ancient history.

CELIA: Oh Sy, cut the hype!

SY: Look, you're a pro; I know you've heard things like this before. But this time it's for real! I kid you not, just because it's my show; On the level: Prince represents a new way for the American image. After him, it's all been said and done, there'll be nothing else, nowhere else to go. He's *it!* Do you understand what I'm trying to say?

CELIA: You're building up my blood pressure. If I don't meet him soon, I'll *die!*

SY: *(Flattered, triumphant)* That's the spirit! *(Looking at watch:)* He's due any minute now.

CELIA: *(Suspicious)* Sy, you didn't invite any other reporters, did you?

SY: You *have* an exclusive: but only if *you* promise *me* a cover story.

CELIA: *(Admiringly)* You devil! You strike a hard bargain, as per usual!

SY: *(Nonchalant, suave)* Care for another drink, darling?

CELIA: *(Winks at SY suggestively, seductively)* I'm a working girl today, remember? *(They come closer together, betraying intimacy, familiarity.)*

> (BRUCE WAIN, *though recognizable to audience as himself, enters dressed as waiter, with fashionably servile demeanor; wearing white jacket, glasses, and moustache; and carrying a serving tray.*)

CELIA: *(Calling WAIN)* Boy—over here, please!

WAIN: *(Going over to CELIA and SY and serving them. Throughout this Scene his voice is disguised until he reveals himself)* I recommend the shrimp—it's extra tasty today.

SY: *(Eyeing WAIN with curiosity)* Don't I know you?

WAIN: No way. I'm new to town. *(Laugh track.)*

SY: In New York, possibly?

WAIN: Not me; I came here straight from Cleveland. *(Laugh track.)*

SY: You were never an extra in "Fantasy Life"?

WAIN: No, I only do principals. *(Pause.)* On principle. *(Laugh track at pun. WAIN turns politely and exits.)*

SY: *(Briefly looking after WAIN)* I know I know him. *(Perplexed, confounded:)* But where?

(VITTORIO enters. Applause sign and track.)

VITTORIO: Ah, so here is the party!

CELIA: Vittorio—darling! *(They embrace.)* It's been ages! And you haven't changed a bit!

VITTORIO: *(With Continental gallantry)* Nor have you—still as fabulously beautiful as ever! *(Kisses her hand—the Continental touch.)*

CELIA: Vittorio! Your charm is irresistible!

SY: Vittorio's been so busy at the Studio, we haven't been able to see each other since New York.

VITTORIO: *(To SY)* And you too.

SY: *(Puzzled)* Me too?

VITTORIO: *You* have not changed a bit, either! *(Kissing SY's hand, in mock-duplication-parody of his having just kissed CELIA's hand. Laugh track.)*

SY: So how's the shooting been with Prince Glitz?

VITTORIO: *(Semi-swooning)* Need you ask? It is Heaven! *Every* director should be so lucky!

CELIA: *(Professionally skeptical, suspicious of promotion ploys)* That sounds extravagant. Tell me more.

VITTORIO: *(With extravagant gesticulating)* He is a charm to work with—a dream—such a beautiful performer as never before there has been anyone like him in front of a camera. He is a blessing that God has sent us.

CELIA: Oh, my panties are getting wet! *(Laugh track.)* I haven't ever been so excited about something all my life since Santa Claus. *(Laugh track.)* In fact, maybe he *is* Santa Claus. *(Laugh track.) Adult* version, of course. *(Laugh track.)*

(MORTON RAY *and* MARCONI *enter. Applause sign and track.* RAY *is wearing same oversized jacket and wig he had on during last Scene's "shooting" scene and which, when shooting was over, he took off with relief—bloody then, but not now.*)

MARCONI: (*Making a mincingly showing-off, conspicuous self-conscious "entrance"*) Well, *hello*, darlings! I was *wondering* where all the fun people were! (*Laugh track.*)

RAY: Hi everybody!

MARCONI: High? No, not yet! Give them time. It's too early! (*Laugh track, due to pun.*)

SY: The party can't officially even *begin* to begin till you show up.

MARCONI: We've been here for an hour, haven't we, Morty?

RAY: Yes, we were sitting pool-side.

(*Both* RAY *and* MARCONI, *in unison, sniff as in comical pantomiming of cocaine-sniffing. Laugh track.*)

MARCONI: (*Phony melodramatic scene-stealing, hogging limelight, as though discovering* CELIA *there for first time*) Celia! Darling! It's been ages! (*Swooning gesticulating.*)

CELIA: We miss you here. *All* L.A. does.

MARCONI: The feeling's mutual! All this wonderful sunshine, it's so much more natural than going to those tanning spas! (*Laugh track.*)

VITTORIO: (*Greeting* MARCONI) Wonderful again to see you, sweetheart.

MARCONI: (*Sexually clowning, pulling* VITTORIO *toward himself*) "Sweetheart!" Ah, another one who's just come out of the closet! (*Laugh track.*)

VITTORIO: (*Offended; on his starchy masculine dignity*) Sorry, I not want to disappoint you. *(Laugh track.)*

MARCONI: *(Teasingly affecting disappointment)* Just kidding, macho man. We can't push our luck, can we? *(Laugh track.)*

SY: So Morton, heard it was really rough at the studio. How was the shooting? *(Laugh track, due to ambiguous pun on roughness and "shooting" by WAIN in last Scene.)*

RAY: All in a day's work. It's bloody business! I'm dead! *(Laugh track, due to puns on "bloody" and "dead".)*

VITTORIO: We knocked out several scenes.

CELIA: That's when the plot thickens—right, Morton?

RAY: Let's just say that the excitement builds to a surprise ending—but of course a happy one.

MARCONI: *(To RAY)* You don't want to tell her everything, Morty. She's Celia, the official *voyeur* for "Peep-hole Magazine." *(Laugh track, due to pun on "People Magazine," utilizing "voyeur.")*

CELIA: You're right—and I've got my *eye* on you, Marconi. *(Laugh track.)*

MARCONI: You do? Well, then, don't forget to put your "eye" at the end of my name when you try to spell it right this time. *(Laugh track.)*

CELIA: *Your* name! That's not the name that's being bandied about all around town, on everyone's tongue: you hear "Prince Glitz," "Prince Glitz." *(To RAY:)* They say he's a virtual goldmine.

RAY: Let's put it this way—and ordinarily I'm not given to exaggerate—

CELIA: *(Cynically interrupting)* No? You'd fool *me*. *(Laugh track.)*

RAY: Seriously, Celia. He's going to change the way we see television.

CELIA: *(Feigning disappointment)* That's all? *(Laugh track.)*

MARCONI: *(Feeling left out; wants to call back attention to himself: gesticulating with sexual obscenity innuendo)* He's already changed my life. *(Laugh track. Then, feigning frustration:)* Or rather, I wish he would!

(Laugh track.) I wish I could have such a hunk in my bunk! *(Laugh track.)*

CELIA: Where the hell *is* this media messiah?

RAY: My personal guarantee—you won't be disappointed.

VITTORIO: He is one of a kind.

MARCONI: Yes; and one is too few. I wish he could clone his body. *(Laugh track.)*

(WAIN re-enters as WAITER, as before, carrying tray.)

(MAGGIE enters. Applause track.)

MAGGIE: Hi, everybody!

RAY: Hi, yourself, Maggie. But where's Prince?

SY: *(To MAGGIE)* Wasn't he coming with you?

MARCONI: *(Enviously, lasciviously, erotically)* Why wasn't he coming with *me*? *(Laugh track, for punning on "coming.")*

CELIA: *(To MAGGIE)* So where is he? I'm so impatient for him, I could—

MARCONI: *(To CELIA)* Keep your panties on, dear. We're in public. *(Laugh track.)*

MAGGIE: He's in the bathroom combing his hair.

MARCONI: His *hair* needed *coming*? *(Laugh track due to risqué "combing"—"coming" pun.)*

MAGGIE: He's in the bathroom.

MARCONI: I volunteer to do everyone a favor, by going to the bathroom to get him. *(Laugh track. MARCONI making as if to go there.)* I won't be long now. *(Laugh track.)*

CELIA: No? How long will you be?

MARCONI: *(Winking, wickedly, suggestively looking down to his own crotch)* Very long—it's all *up* to *him*. *(Laugh track.)*

CELIA: *(Earnestly)* I know suspense is good publicity, but a star mustn't keep his fans waiting *too* long.

MARCONI: *(Leeringly pointing to his genitals)* I'm "too long" just waiting! *(Laugh track.)*

MAGGIE: *(Seeing THADDEUS approaching in distance, but unseen by audience)* Oh, I can see him coming!

MARCONI: Oh good!

MAGGIE: *(With proprietorship pride)* At long last! *(Laugh track, though the pun was inadvertent, unintended.)* The moment everyone's been waiting for!

> *(MAGGIE outstretches her arms to introduce THADDEUS—though he's still unseen by audience. Musical fanfare. Then stage goes dark and all the actors on stage abruptly stop their acting poses and take a "relax" break. The monitors go on, to reveal a commercial. Then the "Off Air" sign flashes—there's now a commercial break.)*

SCENE VI

> *(The "On Air" sign flashes: This immediately signals the actors to assume the exact positions and actions they each had just before commercial break. All are dramatically facing in direction of THADDEUS's long-expected entrance.)*

MAGGIE: Finally! Here he is! The moment you've all been waiting for!

> *(THADDEUS enters. He stands a moment to allow everyone to look at him. He's been transformed into a slick, "Hollywood" look, sporting ultra fashionable wardrobe. He looks tough, confident, almost defiant. All the others react strongly—they're impressed, dumbfounded,*

turned on, in awe. They freeze in long, awestruck pause. Finally:)

THADDEUS: Well, here I am. *(The others, paralyzed, remain dumbfounded and speechless.)* This is some dull party. *(Smiles with self-assurance.)*

(Following, in overlapping gushes:)

MAGGIE: Prince, you're wonderful!

THADDEUS: *(In his stride)* Why, thank you!

MARCONI: We've been waiting for you, sweetheart.

CELIA: He's been well worth the wait!

SY: He's everything he should be—and more!

VITTORIO: Finest actor I have ever been privileged to work with!

SY: You're a destined superstar.

THADDEUS: Of course.

WAIN: *(Uncertain that this star, Prince Glitz is the* THADDEUS *he's looking for)* You Prince Glitz?

MARCONI: His name is on everyone's tongue!

CELIA: *(To* SY*)* This is overwhelming. Need I even mention that you *have* that cover story?

THADDEUS: It's so nice to be here with everybody. Are you all having fun?

VARIOUSLY: *(In overlapping gushes)* Darling! / Smashing! / Fantastic / Loads of fun / Delirious! / Having a ball! / Best time in years! / Of course! / Wonderful! / etc.

THADDEUS: Good!

MAGGIE: Care for a drink, Prince?

THADDEUS: Ought I?

MAGGIE: In *this* scene—yes.

THADDEUS: Good, then I'll have one. Dry gin martini.

MAGGIE: *(To a puzzled WAIN)* You heard his order, boy. Quit your gaping and please hurry.

WAIN: *(Snapping out of it)* Huh? Oh yeah—yeah. *(Exits: shaking his head in disbelief.)*

MARCONI: *(Gushing)* Oh! I just *love* your jacket!

THADDEUS: Just something I picked up.

> *(The others disperse into their conversational groupings; however, the focus of their attention remains on THADDEUS, never straying from him.)*

> *(SY, bringing CELIA, comes over to THADDEUS.)*

MAGGIE: *(Intercepting)* Oh, hi, Celia!

CELIA: Nice to see you again, darling.

SY: Prince, I have someone special, who's been just dying to meet you. This is the well-known "Peep-hole Magazine" feature writer, Celia See.

CELIA: I'm am delighted to meet you!

THADDEUS: It's a mutual delight, Celia. *(Taking her hand with suave sophistication, and kissing it.)* Ah, I can swoon over your bouquet!

CELIA: You're too kind, too charming, Mr. Glitz. You're too much!

THADDEUS: Please . . . just call me Prince.

CELIA: Prince, your old-world charm is irresistible.

SY: You can imagine how proud of Prince we people of "Fantasy Life" are!

MAGGIE: He's Mr. Perfection itself!

SY: He's the greatest salesman of traditional American values that any advertiser could pray for!

MAGGIE: Or pay for.

THADDEUS: The charm you see in me, dear Celia See, is but the reflection of your own, as moon to sun.

CELIA: What a gorgeous compliment! What a flowery phrase! It's a line that would melt any woman in the world: make her pant for you, make her your slave.

THADDEUS: Why, Celia—

CELIA: *(With notebook and pen)* May I quote you, Prince?

THADDEUS: *(Gallantly, with old-world charm)* But Celia—of course! I'm all yours—words and all!

> *(WAIN enters with drink on tray. He wants to test to see if "Prince" identifies himself as THADDEUS, with appropriate response. WAIN has doubts, since THADDEUS defies all of WAIN's prepared description-expectations of him.)*

WAIN: Hey—Prince Glitz!

THADDEUS: *(Turns around to WAIN)* Yes? *(Takes the drink.)*

WAIN: *(Eyes THADDEUS closely, still doubting)* There—that's your drink.

MAGGIE: *(Severely, to WAIN)* Boy, don't you have better things to do than to stand with your impertinent gawking at Mr. Glitz?

WAIN: Sorry, lady.

MAGGIE: Your tray is empty. Go get the marinated caviar shrimp hors d'oeuvres and start serving them!

WAIN: The what?

MAGGIE: *(Impatient)* Go see the chef, he'll tell you what to do.

> *(WAIN exits, shaking his head doubtfully about THADDEUS really being THADDEUS, still not convinced.)*

MAGGIE: *(Muttering indignantly)* The help these days! Revolting!

CELIA: So tell me, Prince—how is Hollywood treating you?

THADDEUS: It's been wonderful, Celia. Hollywood's been heaven. Perhaps I was born to be here—perhaps it was my destiny.

CELIA: Your press packet says you derive from an ancient lineage of European royalty.

THADDEUS: Tradition has always run deep in my family, extending from the origin of language itself.

SY: Yes, Celia, Prince is the last of a long and noble line; everyone else has died off.

CELIA: *(With notebook and pen)* How quaint, Prince; but first tell me about "Fantasy Life."

THADDEUS: "Fantasy Life" is *my* life—that's how natural it comes to me. It's like I've been doing it all my life. It fits into my identity so smoothly—or rather vice versa. Were it not for "Fantasy Life," I just don't knew what I'd do with my life—I'd have no focus point, no definition.

(ROXY's voice is suddenly heard off-stage, mingled with various noises. People are trying to prevent her entrance.)

ROXY: *(Offstage)* Let me in! Let me in or I'll slug you! Leave me alone—I need to see Prince—Please—tell him I'm here—let me in!

CELIA: *(Tartly, jealously, to THADDEUS)* One of your fans.

RAY: The nerve some people have!—

(ROXY bursts into the area, frenzied, hysterical.)

SY: Hold it! Who are you, what do you want?

MAGGIE: Not *you* again!

MARCONI: *(Bitchy)* This is a private party, honey.

RAY: Crashers aren't welcome.

MARCONI: *(Bitchy)* We like to feel exclusive.

VITTORIO: *(Melodramatically, arms skyward)* Oh, Hollywood, the city of endless drama!

ROXY: *(Spotting THADDEUS)* Thaddeus! *(Passionately:)* Oh, Thaddeus!

THADDEUS: Roxy! My Roxy!

ROXY: My darling! Thaddeus!

THADDEUS: It's really you! Roxy!

MAGGIE: Stop them!

SY: *(To ROXY)* What's going on here? Who are you?!

CELIA: *(Writing in pad)* Is that Roxy with a "y" or an "i-e"?

ROXY: *(Unthinkingly, mechanically semi-posing, automatically to media)* With a "y", thank you.

THADDEUS: But Roxy! Why are you here?!

ROXY: Thaddeus—I'm here to rescue you from this den of vipers. *(Indicating all the T.V. people.)*

MAGGIE: I've had enough of this!

RAY: Somebody call the police!

SY: Why are you here?

MARCONI: You crazy intruder!

CELIA: Are you Prince's secret lover?

ROXY: I'm his *real* lover, his true-love! And anyway, he's not Prince—he's Thaddeus!

THADDEUS: Rescue me? What from?

CELIA: "Thaddeus"? Is that a pseudonym?

MAGGIE: Do something, Sy—she'll ruin us!

SY: What can I do?

RAY: Rip her away from Prince!

ROXY: *(Trying to take THADDEUS away)* Let's leave this dreadful place!

Hurry!

THADDEUS: But wait, Roxy—why?

ROXY: Don't you understand?—have they brainwashed you?

CELIA: *(Excitedly scribbling in pad)* Oh this is wonderful! A scoop sensation!

RAY: Call the police!

SY: Good idea! *(Starts rushing away to phone police.)*

MAGGIE: She wasn't invited!

MARCONI: She's trespassing!

(SY exits in hurry to phone police.)

ROXY: Let's get away, Thaddeus. You're being tampered with, manipulated, into their own degrading image. They're undermining your integrity; they're pinning the mask of a false identity on you. They're making you into Prince—

THADDEUS: *(Uncertain)* But that's who I am—? *(Weakly:)* Isn't it?

ROXY: *(Urgently)* You're Thaddeus!

THADDEUS: *(Bewildered, unsteady)* Thaddeus ... that's who I am ...

ROXY: *(Urgently, breathlessly)* Let's get out of here!

MAGGIE: You little hussy, I've just about had enough of you. *(Aggressing, laying hands on ROXY.)*

MARCONI: *(Rooting MAGGIE on)* That-a-girl!

RAY: You tell her, Maggie baby!

MARCONI: Tear her tits away!

VITTORIO: *(Ever the Director)* We have magnificent drama here!

(MAGGIE wrestles with ROXY.)

ROXY: I'll teach you to corrupt my man!

VITTORIO: Wonderful! So true to life!

RAY: Come on, Maggie!

MARCONI: Oh—sexy!

(CELIA *takes out her camera, takes flash photos.*)

ROXY: *(Struggling, puffing, out of breath)* Thaddeus—help me . . .

MAGGIE: *(Also struggling, puffing, out of breath)* Prince—don't listen to her! . . .

THADDEUS: *(Helplessly)* Roxy—haw can I help you?—I can't even help myself—*(Wailing:)* Who am I?

MARCONI: *(Obscenely rooting* MAGGIE *on)* Grab her by the crotch, Maggie!

VITTORIO: *(Ever the Director; admiring* ROXY*)* This Roxy is a sensational new actress!

CELIA: *(To* THADDEUS*)* Prince—er Thaddeus—which are you? Make up your name—I mean your mind. And who do you *really* love? Are they fighting for your love? For you? For your name? What's behind all this?

ROXY AND MAGGIE TOGETHER: *(Still struggling)* None of your business!

MARCONI: *(Amorously)* Poor Prince—I'll take care of you!

THADDEUS: I'm at a loss! I haven't the foggiest notion. Who I am—it's anyone's guess. I don't know anything except for what I'm doing now—but what *am* I doing?

VITTORIO: *(Ever the Director; admiring the wrestling)* Such a fight scene! It links the real world to art itself!

ROXY: *(Still wrestling)* Run, Thaddeus! Run for your life! They'll make a zombie out of you!

THADDEUS: Where do I go? My will is paralyzed. Like Hamlet, I'm acting the part of a man who can't take action!

CELIA: This is wonderful copy!

MARCONI: *(Ecstatic, panting sexually)* Pin her, Maggie!

RAY: Pulverize her!

VITTORIO: If this were being taped, I would get an Emmy!

> *(SY enters, rushing back.)*

SY: *(Out of breath)* The police are on their way! What's happening?

ROXY: *(Still wrestling; to SY)* You bastard!

> *(SY tries to grab hold of ROXY, but she slugs him and sends him staggering back. She and MAGGIE renew their wrestling savagery.)*

MARCONI: Good slug!

CELIA: That was a first-class sock! She's mixed media—wrestling *and* boxing! And with a romantic bottom-line: all for the love of a man!

VITTORIO: Sy, you all right?

SY: *(Still on the ground)* Stop her! She'll ruin us—we'll lose our jobs! She threatens to make this episode of "Fantasy Life" the unexpected conclusion to the whole series!

RAY: Stop that little monster—she'll destroy us, Sy! This is an emergency!

MARCONI: *(Shrieking at ROXY)* Stop already! The party's over!

VITTORIO: *(Ever the Director; looking at audience)* Will the audience find this believable? This is so astounding, I am worried about credibility!

> *(THADDEUS acts indecisive, mumbling to himself, trying to decide what to do. He makes false starts, then stops, like someone falling apart. Another false move toward*

ROXY; *then he stops, indecisively. RAY and MARCONI grab ROXY just as she's getting upper hand over MAGGIE.)*

VITTORIO: *(As if directing)* Enough! Basta! You must be civilized, refined, ladylike!

(ROXY is still kicking and struggling. RAY feels ROXY up.)

ROXY: *(Struggling)* Help me, Thaddeus! We've got to escape their clutches! Help!

THADDEUS: *(Indecisive, broken down)* I . . . you . . . I . . .

ROXY: *(Being held by RAY and MARCONI)* Who'll help us? Who'll save us?

(As if timely, dramatically answering ROXY's urgent plea-summons, WAIN enters, with full tray of hors d'oeuvres that MAGGIE had ordered.)

MAGGIE: You little bitch! You'll pay for this!

RAY: *(Still fondling, feeling up, ROXY)* We've got you now!

SY: *(To CELIA)* Celia darling, I beg you—please forget that any of this happened!

CELIA: Forget!? This is Hollywood's biggest story in years!

(WAIN throws down his full tray of hors d'oeuvres and whips out his 45 automatic "Bessy.")

WAIN: All right, everyone, I'm in charge. *(To RAY and MARCONI:)* Let that dame go, or I'll drill ya.

(MAGGIE screams; RAY and MARCONI obediently release ROXY.)

WAIN: *(To MAGGIE who's still screaming)* Shut up, lady. "Bessy" here *(Indicating gun)* is no sexist: She'd plug *you* soon as any *guy*. *(MAGGIE obediently stops screaming.)*

SY: Who are you—and what do you want?

> *(Meanwhile THADDEUS still indecisive, not too aware of what's going on around him, resumes mumbling to himself.)*

WAIN: *(To T.V. GROUP)* Everybody get over there—*(To ROXY:)* But not you, babe, you and the dizzy guy *(Indicating THADDEUS)* stay over here.

MARCONI: This is thrilling! *(Flirtatiously indicating WAIN's gun.)*

CELIA: Sy—surely this isn't for real?

SY: Celia—please!

CELIA: It *must* be! This is "Fantasy Life" to the core! Its most brilliant episode!

VITTORIO: *(Ever the Director)* This goes *beyond* television—it is a new consciousness!

MARCONI: *(Reacting erotically to WAIN)* Oh, I'd *pay* him to beat me up!

WAIN: Shut up ever there. *I'm* talkin' now.

MAGGIE: Brute!

WAIN: What'd I say, lady? *(To ROXY:)* Take care of our dizzy friend. *(Indicating THADDEUS.)*

> *(ROXY goes to THADDEUS, tenderly ministering to him; he's still mumbling, bewildered.)*

ROXY: *(Weeping)* Look what they've done to him—to my lovely Thaddeus! I hardly recognize him!

WAIN: *(To T.V. GROUP)* You scum-bags did a job on him! You nearly had *me* fooled too—and that ain't easy to do. Thought you'd get away with it, eh? Well, I'll teach yuh not to go around stealin' someone else's character and messin' around with 'em. Some people still think their character's sacred. What's the world comin' to, anyhow?

SY: *(Having been conspicuously studying WAIN's face)* You're the cleaning lady!

WAIN: Brilliant deduction, sleaze-bag. But watch out! *(Waving gun.)*

SY: *(Scared)* Sorry—I didn't mean it.

CELIA: You just *can't* be for real. I have a real nose for these things.

WAIN: Yeah? Go powder it, lady.

MAGGIE: *(Still defiant)* What do you want?

RAY: We'll make a deal.

SY: What's your price?

WAIN: *(To ROXY)* How's the kid doin'? Still dizzy?

ROXY: He's still in left field, but he's coming back to his senses.

WAIN: Think he can travel?

ROXY: Give him a minute.

WAIN: We barely got that.

RAY: Look: He's clearing his throat!

CELIA: He's trying to say something!

THADDEUS: *(Mumbling, barely coherent)* What happened? Who am I? Where am I? Who are all of you?

WAIN: *(To T.V. GROUP)* You guys really did a number on him.

ROXY: *(To T.V. GROUP)* You didn't give him a chance to find out who he really is. Knowing how vulnerable, defenseless, impressionable he was, you exploited him to your own mean ends. Indecent, cruel, inhumane!

SY: Not me—I didn't do anything!

RAY: I'm innocent!

VITTORIO: I am only under contract.

WAIN: Shut up.

MAGGIE: No-one forced him to do anything.

ROXY: He's about to speak—quiet!

WAIN: *(To THADDEUS)* Yeah, kid, you're feelin' better now?—you wanna say somethin'?

THADDEUS: *(Clearing his head and throat)* What am I? I don't know. But what do I *feel* like? A character in a television drama. Does that constitute my reality? . . . What I'm saying—is it speech? Or is it dialogue as from a script? . . . *(Falters.)*

WAIN: *(Encouraging THADDEUS)* Go on—you're doin' fine.

THADDEUS: *(Continuing)* Am I in the reality element, or the fictional element? Or have they fused together, in a weird blending?

ROXY: *(Lovingly encouraging THADDEUS)* Now you sound more like yourself, my darling!

THADDEUS: *(Continuing)* Have I been living life under false pretenses? But if so, what are the true premises, under which I may now conduct my life?

WAIN: *(Encouraging THADDEUS)* Attaboy, kid! You're pullin' through!

THADDEUS: *(Continuing)* Indeed, what *is* real? And what portion of reality can my so-called "self" claim? . . . What *defines* my "self"? By these clothes I wear, which were so much admired just now? By these words I speak? By that lumped-together compound called "feeling"?

(To audience, but also to all the other characters on stage:) By you, these people I see in front of me by looking? . . . Are we all actors in the same prime-time melodrama, strutting and reciting our lines so that they sound maximally "natural," unacted, unrehearsed? Are we all playing roles in this, our common scene? Or is this scene secretly, in actuality, the "world"? . . . What you've been saying—what connection is that to what I've been feeling? And am I feeling this privately?—or as a hired actor, in a public performance? . . . And you out there—how do I know what *you're* feeling? By the way you look? But are your looks all

posed? Are we professionals?

MARCONI: *(Marveling, and drawn amorously to* THADDEUS *as well as admiring his acted speech)* Oh, how beautiful!

VITTORIO: A brilliant actor!

RAY: *(Despairing)* There goes our whole series!

SY: *(Despairing)* We just blew it—we'll be cancelled—we'll be out on our ass, with this intellectual literary stuff.

MAGGIE: Prince—we're your friends!

RAY: We're your colleagues!

SY: We're your allies! It's a *team*, Prince!

MAGGIE: We're in a show together. Don't let us down!

ROXY: *(To counter* MAGGIE*)* Thaddeus, don't listen to them!

SY: *(To* THADDEUS*)* You just can't do this!

RAY: You're under legal contract.

MAGGIE: We can sue—

ROXY: *(Interrupting)* He'll do what he wants.

THADDEUS: My sense of self—if I ever had it, however tentatively—I've lost it. I'm directionless, lost in a maze, devoid of future, empty of past, bankrupt in will, floating free-fall in a vacuum, blind to all boundaries.

WAIN: *(Angrily accusing the T.V.* GROUP*)* Hear that? That's what you bums did to him!

THADDEUS: *(To T.V.* GROUP*)* "Him"? "I"? what "I"? ... Will someone, among you, please explain certain fundamental puzzles: What am I supposed to feel? What do I think? What am I? Who? What's my definition?

CELIA: That's *my* job.

THADDEUS: *(Exasperated; to audience)* Is there *anyone* out there, somewhere, who can possibly tell me just what or who I'm supposed to be? Someone with the authority to speak?

(In perfect, dramatic timing to that question:)

WILBERT'S VOICE OFFSTAGE: *(But from now on to end of play, in European aristocratic accent)* Yes! That is I!

(WILBERT enters, wearing goatee, dressed in cape; as the Grand Duke of Wilbertania. His entrance causes a sensation.)

WILBERT: Now—having found you—I shall inform you what, or who, you are.

THADDEUS: But first—who are *you?*

WILBERT: *(Grandly)* The Grand Duke of Wilbertania, and your uncle.

CELIA: I thought you were dead!

WAIN: Look again, lady.

WILBERT: Some would like to think I am dead and forgotten. They are wrong, as you may behold. *(To THADDEUS:)* You are my long-lost nephew, sole heir to our noble heritage. Thus have I sought you out; that you may claim your old birthright and not to allow the lapse into oblivion of our precious lineage.

MARCONI: *(Coyly)* What a cute old man!

WILBERT: Thaddeus, you will come with me. You shall assume your rightful position, which awaits you. You shall regenerate our long, illustrious dynasty; to carry our noble lineage through these wicked times, intact, for future prosperity.

THADDEUS: No.

WILBERT: *(Startled, pulled up short)* I do not comprehend your "no". You are the heir to royalty. Do you dare to doubt me?

THADDEUS: There's so much fiction going on here. How can I sort out what's true, from all this fancy electronic play-acting involving enormous advertising budgets from vast capitalistic sponsors?

WILBERT: My Thaddeus! Over many miles have I traveled, to seek you out and reclaim you, many dusty miles for a worn-out old man; and I come to you, at last, in love and duty I hold sacred. I started my journey when your absence was discovered. Now, this is my journey's end. You are here! Return with me, my nephew. You must assume the mantle of your great destiny.

THADDEUS: Sorry. Something inside me says no.

WILBERT: Your heritage is an obligation. You derive from exquisite breeding. No expense was spared in your upbringing, your education. You have a duty!

THADDEUS: Just like I reject these T.V. freaks *(Indicating the T.V. GROUP)*, so what *you* have to offer is suspect too. The family glory on which your appeal is based does seem true. But I deny any commitment to it. To me, this "noble old family" business is as much a fiction, as alien to me, as what they *(Indicating the T.V. GROUP)* represent— their T.V. fantasy. I don't want other people's reality to be imposed on me. I just want my *own* way to make.

WILBERT: Spare me, for I am venerable.

WAIN: He only means you good, kid. He came a long way for yuh.

ROXY: *(Protectively)* Please—Thaddeus must decide for himself.

THADDEUS: I will remain detached—lost—independent—remote. For all my traveling, my transformations, I belong to nothing, I'm not a part of anything. I'm not as yet a whole person—and might never be.

WILBERT: I beg you not to break my heart.

THADDEUS: *(To WILBERT)* Sir: I respect you, I venerate you—yet I must reject you. While duly appreciative how far you've come, how hard you've toiled just to find me, and how noble your intentions on my behalf, still—no. *(WILBERT weeps.)* And as for these people *(Indicating T.V. GROUP:)*, they would have lobotomized me into a T.V. robot star. They would have bleached me dry, had I remained their stultified victim. Miraculously, I was rescued by Roxy, and by this very kind man *(Indicating WAIN)*.

WAIN: Thanks, kid. But I was hired by your uncle here.

THADDEUS: Alone, I'll seek out what I'll be. A force greater than myself will direct me: I'm driven by something internal, whose force compels where yours *(Indicating WILBERT)* and yours *(Indicating T.V. GROUP)* merely provoke my resistance, my defiance.

MAGGIE: Where will you go?

THADDEUS: I shall leave: thus, to arrive.

CELIA: Arrive? But where?

WILBERT: Now, I have nothing. That is my burden to encumber my melancholy return home.

WAIN: *(Restraining WILBERT from getting to THADDEUS)* He's got to sort things out for himself. He's gotta follow his own star—where it leads him. *(To THADDEUS:)* Lots of luck, kid. Have some good adventures. Send me a post card.

CELIA: But to throw it all away—glamor and fame—it's a shame.

VITTORIO: The greatest actor I have ever had the privilege—

MARCONI: *(Interrupting, in romantic misery)* Take me with you!

THADDEUS: *(Going over to WAIN and shaking his hand)* Thanks for your help. *(Then THADDEUS goes over to the weeping WILBERT and silently embraces and kisses, European style, his old kinsman. Then, to T.V. GROUP:)* Maybe you all helped me too—more than you can realize. You inoculated me with the serum of corruption—granting me, from now on, immunity. So long, then. *(Turns and dramatically meets ROXY's stare.)*

CELIA: Oh, this is the most beautiful feature story that my byline will ever have graced!

MARCONI: He doesn't love me! *(Breaks dawn sobbing.)*

VITTORIO: *(Anguished)* The greatest actor ever—voluntary premature retirement: A cultural tragedy! Incalculable waste: of talent; of everything.

RAY: It's a disaster!

ROXY: *(She and THADDEUS still staring longingly at each other)* Thaddeus—belovèd!

THADDEUS: My Roxy of Roxys!

MAGGIE: Oh brother!

ROXY: *(Tenderly)* My Thaddeus ...

THADDEUS: *(In deep, breaking, cracking voice)* I'll carry you in my heart forever.

ROXY: No—not in your *heart*—by your *side*. Along *with* you.

THADDEUS: I can't ask you ...

ROXY: But you can! And I accept!

THADDEUS: You'll come—?

ROXY: Of course! Together, we'll find your true self—and mine. In each other! *(They embrace ferociously.)*

THADDEUS: *(With deep voice)* We'll begin our journey, into the stars, the unknown, the drama of the self, of the void, of the world. The age-old journey, but with two new travelers. *(Pause. Turns to WILBERT:)* My ancestors! Farewell. *(THADDEUS and WILBERT embrace and kiss, European style.)*

(As THADDEUS and ROXY are leaving:)

MARCONI: *(Covering his eyes)* No—I can't bear it—he's leaving us!

MAGGIE: *(To MARCONI)* You think *you've* lost something?!

VITTORIO: *(Anguished)* What a career! What a career—that shall never be!

WAIN: *(Tender-tough)* So long, pal.

(THADDEUS and ROXY exit.)

WILBERT: *(Sadly)* Goodbye, Thaddeus. *(To WAIN:)* Well, Mr. Wain, we found him. I found my character!

WAIN: Yeah—we *found* him all right.

WILBERT: And a great character he is! How right I was, to hire you, to look for him so hard. We did him good! He's saved—for something greater than we can ever know.

> *(WAIN puts his arm comradely around WILBERT. Police sirens sound in distance. Then the Applause track and sign are turned on. Sappy, sentimental violin music. Curtain almost completes falling, signifying end of play, when—belatedly—two POLICEMEN rush in, frantic, panting.)*

POLICEMAN ONE: Okay, what's the problem? .

POLICEMAN TWO: *(Looking around)* Everybody relax—we'll take care of everything!

VITTORIO: *(Holding his head in professional anguish)* Oh No! The anticlimax I have always dreaded! *(A relieved thought)* Luckily, we are on tape! We will edit it out!

(Blackout.)

A COMPLAINT AS A THEATRE GOER

I went to a play, and with the lights out the drama seemed convincing, as the stage was played over carefully by props, effects, bursting actors, lighting, to give the illusion of a strange life in a strange world, strangely real. I was taken in. I felt the truth of it.

But then the illusion was spoiled, for me, by the actors suddenly abandoning the powerful spellbinding art of their "roles," and mincing and simpering with insipid artificial smiles beseeching applause and falsely mocking gratitude of it, just as the play ended—just when I wanted most to hold on to the illusion of the magic that had been woven for me by those practiced artists in the cunning of their craft. It was as though they had just "taken back" what they had patiently and devoutly given all evening: in their avarice for applause, they had undermined the effect slowly built up by their art. They had renounced all, in the sudden corruption, sabotage, and vanity of the curtain-call. They had turned traitors, against their own labors.

That's why I always refuse to applaud: My world has burst, and I curse their undoing of what they had marvelously done. Those mere professionals!

ABOUT THE AUTHOR

Marvin Cohen (born July 6, 1931) is an American essayist, novelist, playwright, poet, humorist, and surrealist. He is the author of numerous books, two of which were published by New Directions Publishing, and several plays. His shorter writings—stories, parables, allegories, and essays—have appeared in more than 100 publications, including *The New Yorker, The New York Times, The Village Voice, The Nation, Harper's Bazaar, Vogue, Fiction, The Hudson Review, Quarterly Review of Literature, Transatlantic Review* and New Directions annuals.

His 1980 play *The Don Juan and the Non-Don Juan* was first performed at the New York Shakespeare Festival as part of the Poets at the Public Series. Staged readings of the play have featured actors Richard Dreyfuss, Keith Carradine, Wallace Shawn, Jill Eikenberry, Larry Pine, and Mimi Kennedy.

Cohen was born in Brooklyn, New York City. He has described himself as one who has "risen from lower-class background to lower-class foreground." He studied art at Cooper Union but left college to focus on writing. He supported himself with a series of odd jobs including mink farmer and merchant seaman. Although not typically associated with the Beat Generation, his first published piece appeared in *The Beat Scene* (Corinth Books, 1960) alongside works by Jack Kerouac, Allen Ginsberg, Gregory Corso, and Lawrence Ferlinghetti.

Cohen also taught creative writing at The New School, the City College of New York, C.W. Post of Long Island University, and Adelphi University. He is married and currently lives with his wife in New York City.

ACKNOWLEDGMENTS

Profound thanks are extended to the following for their generous financial support which helped to defray some of this book's production costs:

Theo Alpert, Adrian Astur Alvarez, E.R. Auld, Ross Barkan, Thomas Young Barmore Jr, Tom Bleecker, Brian R. Boisvert, Luke Bolle, Chris Call, Mike Cassella, Scott Chiddister, C. Colla, Sheri Costa, Randy Cox, Robert Dallas, Curtis B. Edmundson, Isaac Ehrlich, Rodney David Falberg, John Feins, GMarkC, Natalie Grand, Beverly Jean Harris, Kyle P. Havenhill, Erik Hemming, Aric Herzog, Ania Honess, Peter and Deborah Jackson, Erik T. Johnson, Justin Johnson, Steven T. Johnson, Haya .K., Gautham Kalva, Alvin Krinst, Ray Kutch, Don and Trish LaRocca, J.J. Larrea, Katie and Walter Lee, Gardner Linn, Theodore Marks, Jim McElroy, Conall McGarrigle, Jack Mearns, Tim Mentuis, Dr. Melvin "Steve" Mesophagus, Mark Mitchell, Doug Milam, Spencer F. Montgomery, Geoffrey Moses, Gregory Moses, Matt "Devilboy" Murray, Michael O'Shaughnessy, Marshall Parks, Zac Petrillo, Stephen Press, Patrick M. Regner, Gavin Russell, Christopher Sartisohn, Spike Schwab, K.L. Stokes, Dan Theodore, Matthew Tobias, Cato Vandrare, Ernest Weaver, Paulie Wenger, Rachel Wells, Christopher Wheeling, Isaiah Whisner, Karl Wieser, Charles Wilkins, Matt Williams, T.R. Wolfe, Andrew Philip Wright, Gilbert Zenner, and Anonymous